Al McCann
2001

WE HOLD
THESE TRUTHS

WE HOLD THESE TRUTHS

The Liberators
with
Al McCann

For additional copies of this book, contact:

Liberty Books
Post Office Box 595051
Dallas, TX 75359

Cover design: Jeremiah Pent, Lincoln-Jackson, (888) 922-8450

ISBN 9635272-3-1

Printed in the United States of America

DEDICATION

To my wife, Glenda Pearson McCann

whose enduring patience made the preparation and publication
of this book possible.

*To our son, Michael, and our daughter, Gwendolyn, and to
Jamie, Jeremy, Michelle and Angela.*

May they and yours inherit a land as good and as free as the America
handed down to their grandparents.

APPRECIATION

We express special appreciation for the librarians at the Library of
Congress, Manuscripts Division, the Fort Worth Public Library, and
Regent University. Bless the librarians, those unheralded custodians of
our accumulated knowledge. Without them books of historical signifi-
cance would not be generally available.

We are especially indebted to David Barton and staff of Wallbuilder
Press for blazing the research trail before us. It was largely Mr. Barton's
works that motivated the writing of this book and furnished invaluable
resource materials for portions of it.

Special thanks goes to our editor, Val Cindric, for making this book
more "reader friendly."

CONTENTS

Part Two: No Other Gods

Appendix

INTRODUCTION

A 1996 opinion poll revealed that a full 60 percent of Americans believe our country is going in the wrong direction. Even more disturbing, the average American feels helpless to do anything about our societal and political circumstances. Such universal disillusionment with our society and government is a recent development.

During our first 170 years as a nation, most Americans – while aware of the government's faults – were proud of their country and convinced that she would (as George Washington stated it) be "right at last."

What has caused us to become disillusioned with our government? When and how did the gap between the people and their government begin to widen? Such difficult questions require a journey back in time.

In preparation for this book, we felt compelled to a historical research tour of the 13 original states – formerly the 13 British colonies – where we studied the most original documents available from the colonial and founding era. Our search led us to bookstores and libraries at the University of Virginia, Harvard University, and the U. S. Government printing office, where the writings of the founders are still being printed from original handwritten documents.

In these historical and geographical settings our nation's founders stand out as real people. This intimate, personal environment allows us to understand the foundations upon which they established our nation and the direction in which they set her course. This book is our attempt to share that understanding with our readers.

In Their Own Words

Certain philosophers and some theologians have expended great effort to discredit or re-define the religion and political philosophy of our nation's founders.

Patricia Bonomi states in the preface to her book, *Under the Cope of Heaven:*

> Professor Richard Hofstadter . . . suggested . . . that if there was a single determinant of the colonists' political responses more important than any other, it might have been religion.

"Once this notion was implanted in my mind," Bonomi said, "it continued to grow, in part because so much of what I read thereafter seemed to bear it out."

Anchored in the momentous founding years (1776-1789), *We Hold These Truths* gives the reader a unique opportunity to visit personally with our founding fathers. Questions are posed, and our forefathers answer in their own words. The reader can then judge for himself where America's founders stood on important religious, political, and governmental issues.

Since the goal of *We Hold These Truths* is to give America's founders an opportunity to speak for themselves, they are quoted without regard to chronological order. Our purpose is to extract statements of the founders that express their views on many subjects and in their own writings. We feel we have been successful in this regard.

Beginning with America's liberation from the despotic British monarchy, we explore the founders' religious and philosophical principles that established the nation and directed her first 170 years. Then, moving through the tragic Civil War period to the twentieth century, we trace America's departure from the founders' worldview and reveal how these deviations have resulted in our present political and societal decline.

This thoughtful walk through our nation's history enables us to answer such questions as:

- What was our guiding worldview when America was great?
- When and how did our nation get onto the wrong track?
- Who is responsible for sidetracking us and why did they do it?
- Why does America continue in the wrong direction against the better judgment of the majority?

Right For Today

This book and its companion book, *A New Birth of Freedom*, deal with many issues of present concern in our national life, each issue requiring a book or volumes to cover it thoroughly. Space and time limitations, however, require that we only touch upon the substantial points of each issue.

Along with the authors' personal contributions and analyses, this book, in a sense, provides a condensation of many good books more narrowly focused as to subject matter. We trust that the reader will find in this one small volume a clear overview of what we as Americans were, what we are now, what we will become if we continue in the wrong direction, and what we the people might do to rescue our country before it is damaged beyond repair.

Early in our research, we discovered that we were retracing the steps of many authors who had gone on a similar search before us. Their works, heavily footnoted, saved us countless hours of research by putting us quickly on the trail of more primary source documents.

While reviewing many primary source documents we realized that these documents would never be seen by most of our readers. Therefore, we have referred our readers to reprints which are currently in circulation or readily available in most libraries. These reprints will refer our more studious readers to the original source documents. We also encourage our readers to further study from the recommended reading list at the end of each chapter and the bibliography at the back of the book.

We have intensely researched the worldview of our nation's founders and foundations. We – like all Americans – have been the benefactors of the most free and most prosperous system of government ever devised by mortal man.

Although Christian in worldview, this book is not written to a Christians-only audience. It is directed to all Americans – friends and foes alike of our nation's founders and foundations. The purpose of this book is not to convert anyone to Christianity; although, admittedly, this writer would be pleased with such a beneficial secondary affect.

The authors make no claim to literary accomplishment. We simply write as people who hold the traditional American worldview.

This book is written by the layman for the layman. It was born – not merely of intensive research – but also from many years of observation, study, and experiencing the American religious, social, and political scenes. It is our message to the people of America.

We believe it is also the good people's message to those entrusted with our government and other institutions. Let the reader judge us in this assumption.

In Part One of this book– One Nation under God – our nation's founders clearly define their foundational worldview and principles of government for our readers. In Part Two – No Other Gods – the founders' present-day detractors clearly present their worldview which declares their hostility to the faith of our fathers and the system of government which they established upon that faith. This opposing worldview exposes its religious doctrines and self-declared *program* and *purpose* for our nation and the world.

If we have faithfully turned the light on these two opposing worldviews vying for the heart and soul of America – their comparative value systems, and their agendas and tactics – we trust the people to rightly decide who is friend and who is foe of our free, self-governing republic.

We Americans are an innovative people. We love new things. Our technology will continue to advance. The principles upon which we originally built our national character, however, are timeless – and these principles are derived from our traditional religion.

For our part, we are fully persuaded that our founders' worldview and principles of government are right for all time. We, therefore, call upon the good people of America to re-establish our original foundations and set our country back on her original course.

In the companion book, *A New Birth of Freedom*, we hold forth for your consideration some ideas for significant restoration and renewal, which we believe will lead to a happier, safer, more virtuous, more peaceful, and more universally prosperous America.

First we present – we trust in the best interest of our people –*We Hold These Truths.*

The Liberators with Al McCann

★ PART I ★

ONE NATION
UNDER GOD

"... one nation, under God,
indivisible, with liberty
and justice for all."

1

WITH PATRIOT BLOOD

"Fire, fellow soldiers, for God's sake, fire!"
Major John Buttrick of Concord, April 19, 1775.

That fateful day of deadly conflict was cast in the destiny of the American people. For decades our colonial ancestors had been on a collision course with a distant, oppressive and unrepresentative government.

Petition after petition had been respectfully submitted to the British king. Petition after petition had been ignored or treated with pompous contempt. Redress had been promised and then denied. Then, while a final attempt at reconciliation was being prepared, the tyrant declared our colonial ancestors to be in a state of rebellion and marched his troops against Concord.

On April 19, 1775, the colonists' smoldering discontent erupted into open conflict. Under cover of darkness the night before, 800 British grenadiers and light infantry had crossed in boats from Boston Neck to East Cambridge and begun their march for Concord. The warning signal was first beamed from two lanterns in the tower of Boston's Old North Church, then relayed by church bells in neighboring towns. Seeing the signal from Old North Church, Paul Revere took the northern route for Lexington and Concord to warn the militia there. William Dawes was dispatched on the southern route to the same destination.

Progress along the messengers' routes could be marked by the toll of church bells as they arrived in Charlestown, Medford, Roxbury, Brookline, Arlington, and Lexington. Arriving at Lexington, Revere and Dawes notified Samuel Adams and John Hancock of the British approach; then, with Dr. Samuel Prescott they rode on for Concord. Between Lexington and Concord, the three couriers were halted by the British, but Prescott escaped and rode on to warn the militia at Concord. At about two in the morning, the church bells tolled in Concord, "The British are coming!"

There was no "wall of separation between Church and State" when America was being liberated with patriot blood.

The First Casualties

Around seven o'clock on the morning of April 19, the British marched into Concord and started their plunder of the town. By midmorning the American minutemen started to assemble in ranks on a small hill overlooking North Bridge across the Concord River – and opposite the British regulars. Smoke from their burning village ascended heavenward in the clear morning air.

The minutemen from Acton arrived with their captain, Isaac Davis. Others soon assembled from Bedford, from Westford, from Littleton, from Carlile, from Chelmsford. Farmers, tradesmen, craftsmen – and, yes, patriot parsons with musket in hand and powder horn slung over the shoulder. These "sons of the Pilgrims" had "so hallowed the enthusiasm of [their flocks] that they held the defense of their liberties a part of their covenant with God."

Of this worthy company the noted historian, George Bancroft, would later write, "The whole was a gathering not so much of officers and soldiers, as of brothers and equals; of whom every one was a man well known in his village, observed in the meeting-house on Sundays, familiar at town meetings, and respected as a freeholder or a freeholder's son."

As these novice citizen-soldiers faced His Majesty's redcoats at North Bridge, the British troops opened fire. Americans Isaac Davis and Abner Hosmer fell dead.

Who were these first casualties? Hosmer was the son of the deacon of Acton church. Isaac Davis, "just thirty years old, the father of four little ones, stately in his person, a man of few words, earnest even to solemnity, had parted from his wife, saying, 'Take good care of the children,' as though he had foreseen that his own death was near; and while she gazed after him with resignation, he led off his company to the scene of danger."

Three and a half hours later, "he was carried home and laid in her bedroom. His countenance was little altered and pleasant in death." He had given "the last full measure of devotion."

Fulfilling Right and Duty

Not until patriot blood stained American soil did Major Buttrick shout his urgent command, "Fire, fellow soldiers, for God's sake, fire!"

Would these minutemen – loyal subjects of the King – obey the command? In that fleeting moment of decision they held your liberty in their hands.

By what authority would they draw the blood of their King's men? By authority of their company commander alone? Or would they recognize a sovereign higher than the King?

For 500 years their mentors in religion, law, and government had proclaimed a higher law – "the law of nature and of God." This intuitive knowledge, placed in every human soul by the Creator – "self-evident truths," as Thomas Jefferson and his forebears stated it – was deep-rooted in the American patriots at Concord.

"With seriousness and acknowledgment of God," the governed asserted their collective supremacy over despotic government; and, the order passed down the patriot line: "Fire! Fire! Fire!"

Then rang out the shots "heard 'round the world."

Petitions had ceased; and The War for American Independence had begun.

Fourteen months later, by the pen of Thomas Jefferson, the Continental Congress vindicated the action of the Minutemen at Concord:

> When a long Train of Offenses and Usurpations, pursuing invariably the same Object, evinces a Design to reduce them under absolute Despotism, it is their Right, it is their Duty, to throw off such Government, and to provide new Guards for their future Security. *Thomas Jefferson, The Declaration of Independence.*

"From the nineteenth of April, 1775," said Clark of Lexington, "will be dated the liberty of the American world." And so it was when historian George Bancroft was writing our history as our history ought to be written.

Today, some two hundred years after the first liberation of America, the people in growing numbers sense something fundamentally wrong with government's role in our society. Why is it that an increasing number of Americans today do not have the same devotion to their country as did their colonial ancestors?

While the "law of nature and nature's God" is working in the human breast, a conflicting law – a despotic worldview – is capturing the reins of our government and all other institutions of power and influence. This clash of worldviews creates an irreconcilable conflict between the good people of America and those in control of their institutions. This conflict has resulted in the almost indefinable frustration and disillusionment we feel toward our government today.

Is a new birth of freedom possible in this country? Yes, but we must understand that our problems do not arise from differing opinions within a commonly held worldview. We are experiencing a life or death struggle between two diametrically opposed worldviews that cannot be reconciled.

In later chapters the despotic worldview will clearly identify itself and its agenda for America, but for now we return to the founding era for a look at our nation's founders and their founding documents.

Thirteen Momentous Years

The thirteen years between 1776 and 1789 are undeniably the most momentous years in the history of the American continent – if not, indeed, in the history of the world. In this mere tick of time, for the first time in the history of the world, a bold new experiment was launched – a new nation, under God, in which the people could govern themselves, reserving to themselves all personal liberties consistent with living peaceably in decent society.

This American experiment, however, was not without risk. Would the people be basically moral and self-disciplined in spite of man's tendency to corruption? The founders' faith in the people's ability to govern themselves evidently came from their confidence in their commonly-held worldview.

What was the source of the people's commonly-held worldview? From centuries of the Hebrew-Christian experience, America's founders – according to their own testimony – derived the concept of the primordial and universal "law of nature and nature's God." The founders will speak to us about these matters in later chapters.

All our founding documents were written during these momentous 13 years and portray the cumulative and condensed product of at least 500 years of theological and legal philosophy. During thousands of hours of debate by at least 200 of the people's most able representatives, these documents were hammered into the foundation stones of America's government.

Their work was accomplished while serving in:

- The Continental Congress;
- Colonial (later State) Legislatures;
- The Constitutional Convention of 1787; and
- State ratifying conventions (1787-1789).

Whatever our race, religion or national origin, America's colonial patriots and founding fathers are the adopted ancestors of all Americans who love liberty. We, their posterity, whether by naturalization or natural descent, are the direct beneficiaries of their arduous struggle for liberty.

From these founding documents – signed in your ancestors' blood – we can learn why our nation was formed, on what foundations, and how it is to be governed. You hold two of these documents in your hands.

As Americans we should revere these documents second only to our Holy Bible, from whose pages their principles were derived. We have been taught to defend them against enemies within and without who would destroy them. We should be just as faithful to defend them against all who aspire to rule over us while ignoring or perverting them.

Our colonial ancestors justified their resistance to Great Britain's despotic government by the religious and legal teaching of their predecessors – Aquinas, Calvin, Hooker, Rutherford, Locke, Blackstone, and others. They called the vindication of their resistance *The Unanimous Declaration of the Thirteen United States of America*, dated July 4, 1776. We call it *The Declaration of Independence*.

In the Declaration, more than any other founding document, we discover the foundational principles upon which our nation is built.

Recommended Reading:

Bancroft, George, *History of the United States*, (New York: Little Brown and Co., 1858) Volume VII, pp. 288-310.

> The historical overview of this chapter is adapted from this old history book which catches both the spirit and the truth of early American history. To restore America's greatness it ought to be reprinted and taught in all our nation's schools. Because it favorably mentions our ancestors' God, Christianity, and our European/American culture, it is judged politically incorrect and is officially unwelcome in government classrooms today.

Amos, Gary T., *Defending the Declaration*, (Brentwood, TN: Wolgemuth and Hyatt Publishers, Inc., 1989).

> This fine book is required reading for all who wish to understand *The Declaration of Independence*. Please get this book. Its content is censored in government classrooms today.

2

COUNTDOWN TO THE DECLARATION

"We hereby declare ourselves free and independent people; are, and of right ought to be, a sovereign and self-governing association, under control of no power other than that of our God and the general government of Congress; to the maintenance of which we solemnly pledge to each other our mutual cooperation and our lives, our fortunes and our most sacred honor." *The Mecklenburg Declaration, May 20, 1775.*

From Concord and Lexington the patriots, in hot pursuit, harassed the British troops all the way back to Boston. "Darkness closed upon the country and upon the town, but it was no night for sleep."

Heralds on swift relays of horses transmitted the war message from hand to hand, "till village repeated it to village; the sea to the backwoods; the plains to the highlands; and it was never suffered to droop, till it had been borne north, and south, and east, and west, throughout the land."

Hunters in the Kentucky wilderness, hearing the message, named their encampment Lexington. "With one impulse the colonies sprung to arms: with one spirit they pledged themselves to each other 'to be ready for the extreme event.' With one heart, the continent cried, 'Liberty or Death.'"

With the dawning of April 20, 1775, the Massachusetts Committee of Safety distributed a circular letter to the towns in Massachusetts:

> We conjure you by all that is dear, by all that is sacred; we beg and entreat, as you will answer it to your country, to your consciences, and above all to God himself, that you will hasten and encourage by all possible means the enlistment of men to form the army; and send them forward to head-quarters at Cambridge with that expedition which the vast importance and instant urgency of the affair demands.

The people of Massachusetts, however, had not waited for the call. "The country people, as soon as they heard the cry of innocent blood from the ground, snatched their firelocks from the walls; and wives, and mothers, and sisters took part in preparing the men of their households to go forth to war." Not from Massachusetts alone they came, but from all across New England – Massachusetts, New Hampshire, Connecticut, and Rhode Island.

Who were these colonial patriots?

> The New England volunteers were men of substantial worth, of whom almost every one represented a household. . . . They were sure to be remembered weekly in the exercises of the congregations; and morning and evening in the usual family devotions, they were commended with fervent piety to the protection of Heaven. . . . The camp of liberty was a gathering in arms of schoolmasters, neighbors, and friends; and Boston was beleaguered round from Roxbury to Chelsea by an unorganized, fluctuating mass of men, each with his own musket and little store of cartridges, and such provisions as he brought with him, or as were sent to him, or were contributed by the people round about.

This patriot army – or rather this "unorganized", fluctuating mass of men" – had been besieging General Gage's British occupying forces for three weeks when the second Continental Congress met on May 10, 1775.

Men of the Second Continental Congress

With war already raging between the Massachusetts colony and Great Britain, the men of the second Continental Congress, like the constituents they represented, were torn. It is difficult to determine whether "they were more swayed by regard for the country from which the majority of them sprung, or by the sense of oppression." The parent land they loved was an "ideal England" of which "they cherished the language, the laws, and the people."

Even the truest patriots were unconvinced that independence from England was "the only security for the preservation of their own inherited rights." This left many colonists in a "divided state of their affections." Add to that "the unpreparedness of the country for war, and the feeble and narrow powers with which they were intrusted" and divided allegiances were inevitable. The colonists' devotion "to the old relations" were "weighed against the call of freedom to the new." Still, the conservative movement "maintained its energy, and forbade any change, except where change was demanded by instant necessity."

The men of the second Continental Congress came together undecided, and "they long remained undecided. They struggled against every forward movement, and made none but by compulsion. Not by foresight, nor by the preconceived purpose of themselves or their constituents, but by the natural succession of inevitable events, it became their office to cement a union and constitute a nation."

The delegates from Massachusetts brought with them letters from the Massachusetts assembly, beseeching the aid of Congress against "the rapid progress of a tyrannical Ministry" and "the inhuman Ravages of mercenary Troops."

On grounds that the militia in Boston was defending the rights of all Americans, Congress took over the supervision and regulation of the continental army and appointed Colonel George Washington, delegate from Virginia, as their Commander-in-Chief.

A state of undeclared war existed for eight months between the colonies and Great Britain until December 23, 1775. On that day the British Parliament passed the American Prohibitory Bill, providing that all trade and commerce with the colonies be cut off, and that American ships in harbors and on the high seas be forfeited to the British navy.

The Continental Congress saw this act as a formal abdication, an "Act of Independency," and a declaration of war by the British government.

Three months later, Richard Henry Lee wrote from Philadelphia to Landon Carter, "whilst people here are disputing and hesitating about independency, the Court by one bold Act of Parliament, and by a conduct the most extensively hostile, have already put the two Countries asunder."

As the calendar turned from 1775 to that fateful year, 1776, our colonial ancestors had a dreadful war on their hands and only the beginning concept of a central government to conduct it.

A Free and Independent People

On May 20, 1775, one month after the battle of Concord and Lexington, a group of Scotch-Irish Presbyterians met in Charlotte, North Carolina and drafted the Mecklenburg Declaration. This document, prepared by Ephraim Brevard, a Presbyterian elder, seems to be the first official act of independence by the colonists. It was sent to the Continental Congress and was almost certainly in the possession of Richard Henry Lee and Thomas Jefferson. Phrases from it appear verbatim in Lee's resolution for independence and in the last paragraph of the Declaration of Independence. Compare these phrases from the Mecklenburg Declaration:

> We do hereby dissolve the political bands which have connected us with the mother-country, and hereby absolve ourselves from all allegiance to the British crown. – We hereby declare ourselves free and independent people; are, and of right ought to be, a sovereign and self-governing association, under control of no power other than that of our God and the general government of Congress; to the maintenance of which we solemnly pledge to each other our mutual cooperation and our lives, our fortunes and our most sacred honor.

By May, 1776, at the recommendation of Congress, some colonies had already set up revolutionary governments; and on May 4, Rhode Island formally declared her independence.

On May 15, Congress passed a resolution, presented by John Adams, that those colonies, which had not already done so, be encouraged to adopt a provincial government "as shall, in the opinion of the representatives of the people, best conduce to the happiness and safety of their constituents in particular, and America in general."

Attached to the resolve was a preamble recommending that "the exercise of every kind of authority under the [British] crown should be totally suppressed, and all powers of government exerted, under authority of the people of the colonies, for the preservation of internal peace, virtue, and good order, as well as for the defense of their lives, liberties, and properties, against the hostile invasions and cruel depredations of their enemies."

Soon after Congress' May 15 resolution, Virginia, by far the largest of the colonies, declared her independence from Great Britain; and, the move for independence for all colonies was underway. Virginia instructed her delegates in Congress to resolve that the United Colonies are "free and independent States, absolved from all allegiance to, and dependence upon, the Crown or Parliament of Great Britain."

Following these instructions, Richard Henry Lee rose in Congress on June 7, 1776, and introduced the following resolution:

> That these United Colonies are, and of right ought to be, free and independent States, that they are absolved from all allegiance to the British Crown, and that all political connections between them and the State of Great Britain is, and ought to be, totally dissolved. That it is expedient forthwith to take the most effectual measures for forming foreign Alliances. That a plan of confederation be prepared and transmitted to the respective Colonies for their consideration and approbation.

The resolution was adopted, and out of it came the Declaration of Independence and the Articles of Confederation, creating the central government of the United States. A portion of Lee's resolution, adapted from the Mecklenburg Declaration appears verbatim in the last paragraph of the Declaration of Independence.

Writing the Declaration

Acting upon Lee's resolution, the Continental Congress appointed John Adams, Benjamin Franklin, Roger Sherman, Robert Livingston, and Thomas Jefferson to form a committee and draft a document declaring independence from Great Britain. With instructions as to the form of the document, the committee appointed Thomas Jefferson to write the first draft.

Jefferson understood that he was not commissioned to create a new concept of government, but to put into legal form the people's justification for dissolving their government whenever it becomes tyrannical, and replacing it with another. This justification was already known to the colonists and to the people in Europe, since the legal concepts involved had been developed and defended in Europe over a period of at least 500 years.

During these five centuries preceding the Declaration, political theorists, law scholars, and theologians had developed all the legal concepts and most of the terminology contained in the Declaration. Most notable among these scholars are:

- St. Thomas Aquinas (1225-1274)
- Henry De Bracton (12??-1268), Catholic Archdeacon and "Father of the Common Law"
- John Calvin (1509-1564), French theologian and reformer
- Thomas Hooker (1586-1647)
- Sir Edward Coke (1552-1634), Chief Justice of King's Bench and author of *Petition of Rights*
- Samuel Rutherford, Scottish theologian and author of *Lex Rex, The Law and the Prince* (1644)
- John Locke (1632-1704)
- Sir William Blackstone (1723-1780), English jurist and writer of law books.

Blackstone was a contemporary of America's founders and their chief mentor in law. His *Commentaries on the Laws of England* in four volumes was required reading in all the universities of the colonies. As a result, America's founders were no strangers to the concepts of liberty and self-government. Developed by theologians and law scholars, these concepts had been claimed and defended by the people – from Magna Carta (1215) – to the Petition of Rights (1628), defining the "rights of Englishmen" – to the Puritan Revolution of 1640, leading to the English Bill of Rights (1689) – to the American Declaration of Independence (1776).

All writers can relate to the words of Montaigne, "I have gathered a posie of other men's flowers, and nothing but the thread that binds them is mine own."

Thomas Jefferson lays claim to authorship of the Declaration of Independence and that credit is given him. The Declaration is made up largely of grievances which had already been petitioned before King George III, over a period of time.

In addition to Richard Henry Lee's resolution, the Continental Congress added three more phrases to Jefferson's original draft. Nevertheless, Jefferson, recognized by his colleagues as a writer of excellence, is rightly honored as primary writer of the Declaration, furnishing "the thread that binds them." The document is a literary and legal masterpiece.

From Professor Gary Amos of Regent University, we borrow words better than our own:

> Jefferson's Declaration was a masterpiece of law, government, and rights. He tied together with a few words hundreds of years of English political theory. The long shadows of Magna Carta, the common law, Catholic and Calvinist resistance theories, the English Bill of Rights, and the Petition of Rights are cast within its lines. The ideas were not Jefferson's, but the writing was. And it is magnificent. With the king's English, Jefferson parted the king from his colonies. Through the Declaration, America became the direct heir of the best of the British liberal tradition.

Unlike the French and the Russian revolutions, the Declaration of Independence does not seek to liquidate the existing order. It does not repudiate the people's religion, their European/American culture, nor the British form of government. It is better understood as a continuation of the Englishman's centuries-long struggle against despotic government.

The colonists were simply demanding the same rights as other Englishmen. The continued denial of these rights finally goaded them into a bid for independence. For this reason, the war, thus provoked, is more properly called the War for American Independence rather than the Revolutionary War or the American Revolution.

There was little revolutionary about the war. The independent Americans retained their European/American culture, English language, common law, religion, and – in essence – the British form of government, absent a monarch. Great Britain remains to this day the mother country of a rather independent-minded daughter.

The real American revolution was a revolutionary idea – the conviction that a moral and religious people are thoroughly capable of governing themselves without a ruling master.

Foundations of Government from the Declaration

The Declaration of Independence is best understood as our most fundamental founding document, the charter for the nation's legal existence.

The Declaration contains, in condensed form, the organic political theory and the legal concepts and values upon which the nation exists. In its statements are the foundation principles of the government of the United States.

1. The United States is a Nation under God.

The people of the United States are entitled to their own independent nation only by authority of "the laws of nature and nature's God." These laws pronounce all peoples and all nations of all times under the sovereignty of Almighty God.

The roots of our Pledge of Allegiance – "one nation under God" – can be traced back through the Declaration of Independence to the Mecklenburg Declaration ("under control of no power other than that of our God and the general government of Congress").

All actions forbidding or restricting prayer and the worship of the God of our Fathers in any place in this country are direct assaults on this bedrock principle. Such actions are a grave threat to our continued existence as a free, self-governing people.

Government without God is tyranny.

2. Citizens of the United States are equal under law.

This equality under law comes from God, the Creator, Who is no respecter of persons; but, "all men are created equal."

The government will not bestow titles of nobility, create a system of social castes, nor grant special rights and privileges to any individual, group of individuals, or class of individuals.

"Gay rights," women's rights," "affirmative action," "hate crime laws," "ethnic preferences," and all such "laws" that prefer one citizen over another are stark violations of the principle of "equality under law."

Government without God, the Great Equalizer, is tyranny.

3. Certain human rights are inalienable.

"Among these rights are life, liberty, and the pursuit of happiness." These rights are "endowed by their Creator," and come automatically with conception of human life.

Government does not own these rights; therefore, government cannot bestow them nor justly take them away.

Government infringement upon these inalienable rights is tyranny.

4. The government of the United States exists to secure the rights of the people.

"To secure these rights governments are instituted among men."

Any government which fails to secure these rights has abdicated its rulership, and has lost its just right to govern.

Continued governance after such abdication is tyranny.

5. The government of the United States is a "government of the people, by the people, for the people."

"Deriving their just powers from the consent of the governed."

This nation is to be ruled by the will of the majority, while securing the just rights of all citizens. To secure the rights of the peaceful and self-governing, government must of necessity be given the power to suspend or alter the rights of those who endanger the rights of others.

Thus our government derives its powers to administer justice from the consent of the people collectively, and from the "laws of nature and nature's God."

Government without the consent of the governed is tyranny.

6. The people of the United States collectively have the right and the responsibility to maintain, alter, or even abolish and re-institute their government.

Our founding fathers are forever to be praised for instituting a form of government that can be altered without abolishing it. Within the Constitution itself, they provided the means of periodic alteration by the people.

This probably explains why we have lived peaceably under one constitution longer than any other republic in history. The people's right to periodic alteration is made effective when we, with knowledge, participate in the elective process – when we elect members to Congress:

- who are committed to repealing bad laws;
- who are dedicated to enacting laws compatible with the Declaration and the Constitution;
- who will call the President and the Supreme Court to task (by impeachment if necessary) when they profane our foundational principles, and violate or ignore the clear statements of our Constitution;
- who will institute proceedings for Constitutional amendment when such is needed.

Armed overthrow of the government is justified only after "a long Train of Abuses and usurpations, pursuing invariably the same object, evinces a Design to reduce [the people] under absolute Despotism."

To be justified, such last-resort overthrow would be – as it was with the colonists – by the great majority of the people, acting under bona fide provisional government, by consent of the governed. Never would armed overthrow of government be justified, if by acts of terrorism or rebellion by small bands of self-appointed militia.

Armed overthrow of government in the United States is not likely ever to happen. If the people become too apathetic or dissipated to alter their government by Constitutional process, they are not likely to rally en masse and alter it by any other means. The great danger is that the people will allow our form of government to be altered by Executive Order, Court Decree, or Act of Congress in violation of the Constitutional process.

Any Executive order, act of Congress, or Supreme Court decree that tends to alter our constitution of government, before our Constitution has been altered by Constitutional Amendment, by consent of the people, is tyranny.

7. The government of the United States is based on a covenant between each individual citizen and the whole body politic and the whole body politic and each individual citizen, sworn in the presence of the Supreme Judge of the World, by the duly elected representatives of the people of the United States.

"And for the support of this Declaration, with firm Reliance on the Protection of divine Providence, we mutually pledge to each other our Lives, our Fortunes, and our sacred Honor."

The body politic violates this covenant when it denies commonly enjoyed liberties to any individual, group of individuals, or class of individuals, except as punishment for crimes against the body politic.

Such denial of liberty is tyranny.

The individual violates this covenant when he commits acts against the commonly held rights of others. Such acts are criminal, not only against another individual, but against the whole body politic. Such acts call for the just action of the whole body politic against the individual criminal.

Failing to act effectively against criminals is tyranny against the law-abiding.

So, let us, each and all, be faithful to our covenant with one another. And, of infinitely more importance, let us not, as a people, break our sacred covenant with our Creator by becoming derelict in our duties to God.

And let all good people be ever on guard against any who would deceive us into breaking that sacred covenant – against any who aspire to represent us, or rule over us, without an understanding of, and a commitment to, that sacred covenant.

Recommended Reading:

Amos, Gary T., *Defending the Declaration*, (Brentwood, TN: Wolgemuth and Hyatt Publishers, Inc., 1989).

The serious student of these matters is again urged to get a copy of this book for a clear insight into the Christian background and Biblical concepts of the Declaration of Independence.

Jefferson, Thomas, *The Declaration of Independence*, July 4, 1776.

This founding document is the Birth Certificate and Charter of the United States of America. If the Supreme Court were to follow through on its infamous interpretation of the First Amendment in our Bill of Rights, the Declaration would not be allowed in government classrooms today, because of its four acknowledgments of God. The full text of the Declaration follows. It belongs to you. Please read it carefully before proceeding to the next chapter of this book.

In Congress, July 4, 1776

The Unanimous Declaration
of the thirteen
UNITED STATES OF AMERICA

When in the Course of human Events, it becomes necessary for one People to dissolve the Political Bands which have connected them with another, and to assume among the Powers of the Earth, the separate and equal Station to which the Laws of Nature and of Nature's God entitle them, a decent Respect to the Opinions of Mankind requires that they should declare the causes which impel them to the Separation.

We hold these Truths to be self-evident, that all Men are created equal, that they are endowed by their Creator with certain unalienable Rights, that among these are Life, Liberty, and the Pursuit of Happiness-That to secure these Rights, Governments are instituted among Men, deriving their just Powers from the Consent of the Governed, that whenever any Form of Government becomes destructive of these Ends, it is the Right of the People to alter or abolish it, and to institute new Government, laying its Foundation on such Principles, and organizing its Powers in such Form, as to them shall seem most likely to effect their Safety and Happiness. Prudence, indeed, will dictate that Governments long established shall not be changed for light and transient Causes; and accordingly all Experience hath shewn, that Mankind are more disposed to suffer, while Evils are sufferable, than to right themselves by abolishing the Forms to which they are accustomed. But when a long Train of Abuses and Usurpations, pursuing invariably the same Object, evinces a Design to reduce them under absolute Despotism, it is their Right, it is their Duty, to throw off such Government, and to provide new guards for their future Security. Such has been the patient Sufferance of these Colonies; and such is now the necessity which constrains them to alter their former Systems of Government. The History of the present King of Great Britain is a History of repeated Injuries and Usurpations, all having in direct Object the Establishment of an absolute Tyranny over these States. To prove this, let Facts be submitted to a candid World.

He has refused his Assent to Laws, the most wholesome and necessary for the public Good.

He has forbidden his Governors to pass Laws of immediate and pressing Importance, unless suspended in their Operation till his Assent should be obtained; and when so suspended, he has utterly neglected to tend to them.

He has refused to pass other Laws for the Accommodation of large Districts of People, unless those People would relinquish the Right of Representation in the Legislature, a Right inestimable to them, and formidable to Tyrants only.

He has called together Legislative Bodies at Places unusual, uncomfortable, and distant from the Depository of their public Records, for the sole Purpose of fatiguing them into Compliance with his Measures.

He has dissolved Representative Houses repeatedly, for opposing with manly Firmness his Invasions on the Rights of People.

He has refused for a long Time, after such Dissolutions, to cause others to be elected; whereby the Legislative Powers, incapable of Annihilation, have returned to the people at large for their exercise; the State remaining in the mean time exposed to all the Dangers of Invasion from without, and Convulsions within.

He has endeavoured to prevent the Population of these States; for that Purpose obstructing the Laws for Naturalization of Foreigners; refusing to pass others to encourage their Migrations hither, and raising the Conditions of new Appropriations of Lands.

He has obstructed the Administration of Justice, by refusing his Assent to Laws for establishing Judiciary Powers.

He has made Judges dependent on his Will alone, for the Tenure of their offices, and the Amount and Payment of their Salaries.

He has erected a Multitude of new Offices, and sent hither Swarms of Officers to harass our People, and eat out their Substance.

He has kept among us, in Times of Peace, Standing Armies, without the consent of our Legislatures.

He has affected to render the Military independent of and superior to the Civil Power.

He has combined with others to subject us to a Jurisdiction foreign to our Constitution, and unacknowledged by our Laws; giving his Assent to their Acts of pretended Legislation:

For quartering large Bodies of Armed Troops among us:

For protecting them, by a mock Trial, from Punishment for any Murders which they should commit on the Inhabitants of these States:

For cutting off our Trade with all Parts of the World:

For imposing Taxes on us without our Consent:

For depriving us, in many Cases, of the Benefits of Trial by Jury:

For transporting us beyond Seas to be tried for pretended Offenses:

For abolishing the free System of English Laws in a neighbouring Province, establishing therein an arbitrary Government, and enlarging its Boundaries, so as to render it at once an Example and fit Instrument for introducing the same absolute Rule into these Colonies:

For taking away our Charters, abolishing our most valuable Laws, and altering fundamentally the Forms of our Governments:

For suspending our own Legislatures, and declaring themselves invested with Power to legislate for us in all Cases whatsoever.

He has abdicated Government here, by declaring us out of his Protection and waging War against us.

He has plundered our Seas, ravaged our Coasts, burnt our Towns, and destroyed the Lives of our people.

He is, at this Time, transporting large Armies of foreign Mercenaries to compleat the Works of Death, Desolation, and Tyranny, already begun with circumstances of Cruelty and Perfidy, scarcely paralleled in the most barbarous Ages, and totally unworthy the Head of a civilized Nation.

He has constrained our fellow Citizens taken Captive on the high Seas to bear Arms against their Country, to become the Executioners of their Friends and Brethren, or to fall themselves by their Hands.

He has excited domestic Insurrections amongst us, and has endeavoured to bring on the Inhabitants of our Frontiers, the merciless Indian Savages, whose known Rule of Warfare, is an undistinguished Destruction, of all Ages, Sexes, and Conditions.

In every stage of these Oppressions we have Petitioned for Redress in the most humble Terms: Our repeated Petitions have been answered only by repeated Injury. A Prince, whose Character is thus marked by every act which may define a Tyrant, is unfit to be a Ruler of a free People.

Nor have we been wanting in Attentions to our British Brethren. We have warned them from Time to Time of Attempts by their Legislature to extend an unwarrantable Jurisdiction over us. We have reminded them of the Circumstances of our Emigration and Settlement here. We have appealed to their native Justice and Magnanimity, and we have conjured them by the Ties of our common Kindred to disavow these Usurpations, which, would inevitably interrupt our Connections and Correspondence. They too have been deaf to the Voice of Justice and of Consanguinity. We must, therefore, acquiesce in the Necessity, which denounces our Separation, and hold them, as we hold the rest of Mankind, Enemies in War, in Peace, Friends.

We, therefore, the Representatives of the UNITED STATES OF AMERICA, in General Congress, Assembled, appealing to the Supreme Judge of the World for the Rectitude of our Intentions, do, in the Name, and by Authority of the good People of these Colonies, solemnly Publish and Declare, That these United Colonies are, and of Right ought to be, Free and Independent States; that they are absolved from all Allegiance to the British Crown, and that all political Connection between them and the state of Great-Britain, is and ought to be totally dissolved; and that as Free and Independent States, they have full Power to levy War, conclude Peace, contract Alliances, establish Commerce, and do all other Acts and Things which Independent States may of right do. And for the support of this Declaration, with a firm Reliance on the Protection of divine Providence, we mutually pledge to each other our Lives, our Fortunes, and our sacred Honor.

3

THE ABSOLUTE OWNERS
AND MOVERS

"The people alone are the absolute owners and uncontrollable movers of such sovereignty as human beings can claim to exercise; subject to the eternal and unchangeable rules of justice, truth, and good Faith."
G. M. Dallas, Vice President of the United States, 1847

The United States Code Annotated lists the four documents fundamental to the establishment of the American Republic. In chronological order of their enactment they are:

- The Declaration of Independence, 1776
- The Articles of Confederation, 1781
- The Northwest Ordinance, 1787
- The United States Constitution, 1789.

While the Declaration lays the foundations of our federal government, the Constitution defines, organizes, and limits its powers. The

Declaration is the nation's charter and birth certificate. The Constitution is the *modus operandi* – the rules for the operation of our federal government. Equally important, the Constitution defines the people's rights and the limitations of the just powers of our federal government.

Understanding the Constitution of the United States requires a study of the original 13 state constitutions. This is necessary because the Articles of Confederation (forerunner of the Constitution) and the state constitutions were written simultaneously and by the same men, rotating their services between state governments and the Continental Congress. A study of state constitutions, therefore, gives us a clear understanding of these men and the people they represented – their philosophy of law and government, and their religious beliefs as they relate to law and government.

The original 13 state constitutions are the rich seedbed from which grew the Articles of Confederation, the United States Constitution, and the Bill of Rights.

The organization and operation of the federal government is essentially the same as that written in the original state constitutions. All articles of the Bill of Rights are contained in most of the state constitutions, except Articles IX and X, which pertain strictly to the federal government, limiting its powers.

Today, we have degenerated to such a sorry state of affairs that our federal government routinely issues "mandates" to the states, encountering little resistance. In such a political climate, it is easy to forget that in the beginning it was not so. On the contrary, the states created the federal government, granting it limited powers.

How did our present condition come to pass? We shall deal with that question generally in a later chapter. Also, in our companion book, *A New Birth of Freedom,* we explore the question in greater detail.

Originating from "The People"

The preamble to the New Hampshire constitution illustrates what the founders understood to be the true source of all just government – the people.

All men are born equally free and independent; therefore all government originates from the people, is founded in consent, and instituted for the general good.

A more complete statement of the founders' basic theory of government is the preamble to the Massachusetts constitution. Note how many times the authors mention "the people" and "individuals."

> The end of the institution, maintenance, and administration of government, is to secure the existence of the body politic, to protect it, and to furnish the individuals who compose it, with the power of enjoying, in safety and tranquillity, their natural rights, and the blessings of life: and whenever these great objects are not obtained, the people have a right to alter the government, and to take measures, necessary for their safety, prosperity, and happiness. The body politic is formed by a voluntary association of individuals. It is a social compact, by which the whole people covenants with each citizen, and each citizen with the whole people, that all shall be governed by certain laws for the common good. It is the duty of the people, therefore, in framing a constitution of government, to provide for an equitable mode of making laws, as well as for an impartial interpretation, and a faithful execution of them; that every man may, at all times, find his security in them.
>
> We, therefore, the people of Massachusetts, acknowledging, with grateful hearts, the goodness of the Great Legislator of the Universe, in affording us, in the course of his providence, an opportunity, deliberately, and peaceably, without fraud, or surprise, of entering into an original, explicit, and solemn compact with each other, and of forming a new Constitution of civil government, for ourselves and posterity; and devoutly imploring his direction in so interesting a design, do agree upon, ordain, and establish, the following declaration of rights, and frame of government, as the Constitution of the Commonwealth of Massachusetts.

From the beginning of our nation, "government of the people, by the people, for the people" was thoroughly established as the first principle of American government. The "consent of the governed" is always paramount to the authority of the rulers.

The States' Position on Religion

All states guaranteed freedom of religion to everyone "provided he doth not disturb the public peace of others in their religious worship." Their understanding of "establishment of religion" is most clearly stated in the North Carolina constitution:

> That there shall be no establishment of any one religious church or denomination in this State, in preference to any other.

Article III of the Massachusetts constitution gives us an insight into the founders' views on "legislating morality" and on Bible instruction in public schools:

> And the happiness of a people, and the good order and preservation of civil government, essentially depend upon piety, religion, and morality; and as these cannot be generally diffused through a community, but by the institution of the public worship of God, and of public instruction in piety, religion, and morality: – Therefore, to promote their happiness, and to secure the good order and preservation of their government, the people of this Commonwealth have a right to invest their Legislature with the power to authorize and require, and the Legislature shall, from time to time, authorize and require, the several towns, parishes, precincts, and other bodies politic, or religious societies, to make suitable provision, at their own expense, for the institution of the public worship of God, and for the support and maintenance of public Protestant teachers of piety, religion, and morality, in all cases, where such provision shall not be made voluntarily.
>
> And the people of this Commonwealth have also a right to, and do, invest their Legislature with authority, to enjoin, upon all the subjects, an attendance upon the instructions of the public teachers, as aforesaid, at stated times and seasons, if there be any, on whose instructions they can conscientiously and conveniently attend:
>
> Provided, notwithstanding, that the several towns, parishes, precincts, and other bodies, or religious societies, shall, at all times, have the exclusive right of electing their public teachers, and of contracting with them, for their support and maintenance.

Most of the state constitutions had a religious test for holding office in state government.

Pennsylvania required an acknowledgment of "Almighty God." Rhode Island required belief in a "Supreme Being." These two states allowed all but Atheists to hold public office.

Religious tests, in the other states that had them, required adherence to the Christian religion. Three states – New Hampshire, New Jersey, and North Carolina – allowed only Protestant Christians to hold public office.

While the Protestants and Catholics had serious doctrinal differences, all Christian denomination have their roots in the Catholic Church. We may logically conclude that the prejudice against Roman Catholics was as much political as religious.

The colonists were two centuries closer than we are today to the bitter struggles between Protestants and Roman Catholics for political ascendancy in medieval Europe. Perhaps they were still keenly sensitive to those conflicts. Their frequent reference to "popery" may indicate that they felt a threat to their civil and religious liberties because of the Roman Catholics' allegiance to the Bishop of Rome.

In any case, the election of a Roman Catholic to the Presidency in 1960 seems to have laid these prejudices to rest. Whatever caused these prejudices in the colonials is apparently not a critical issue today.

The authors are not advocating a religious test for public office. On the other hand, we emphatically support the people's right to know whatever they desire about their representatives – including their religious beliefs.

We also find it necessary to study original state constitutions in regard to church/state relationships. Neglecting such a study leaves a serious gap in our understanding of the founders' view of religion as it pertains to law and government in a free society.

Our nation's founders not only helped to write and ratify the state constitutions in their home states but took the religious oaths required by them. Then these same men were sent as delegates to the Continental Congress to write and ratify the Constitution of the United States. In fact, less than 10 years passed between the writing of the state constitutions and the U. S. Constitution.

Is it reasonable to conclude that the founders en masse, within such a short period of time, somewhere on the road to Philadelphia, renounced their Christian faith and their Christian oaths of office? Is it possible they arrived at Congress as atheists and deists, and established our federal government on a non-Christian worldview?

Such a ridiculous conclusion is unthinkable to any logical mind; yet many today would have us believe such an illogical and historically false myth.

Limiting Federal Control

Ever since William Penn first proposed a colonial union in 1698, there was no question that certain matters should be under authority of a central government. These matters included: commerce between the colonies, the extradition of fugitives from justice, and defense against common enemies.

Later, the need for central government in standardizing weights and measures, coinage of money, and operation of post offices, was generally understood and accepted. These provisions were written into the Articles of Confederation and passed down to us through the Constitution fairly intact and with little controversy.

The resolution of Congress, dated June 7, 1776, ordered "that a plan of confederation be prepared and transmitted to the respective Colonies for their consideration and approbation." The resulting plan, the Articles of Confederation, was written in 1776 and 1777, approved by Congress on November 15, 1777, and ratified by all 13 States by March 1, 1781. Since it was superseded by the United States Constitution just eight years later, we are not including its full text here.

Keep in mind that at this time, the States were locked in mortal combat with the all-powerful and despotic central government of Great Britain. Article II of the Articles of Confederation reflects the apprehension of the founding fathers about forming another central government that would, itself, have all the potentiality of a home-grown tyrant.

Each state retains its sovereignty, freedom and independence, and every power, jurisdiction, and right, which is not by this confederation expressly delegated to the United States, in Congress assembled.

Article II of the Articles of Confederation was transferred in essence to the Tenth Amendment to the United States Constitution, which reads:

The powers not delegated to the United States by the Constitution, nor prohibited by it to the States, are reserved to the States respectively, or to the people.

The twentieth-century usurpation of coercive powers by the federal government is ample proof of the founders' wisdom in constitutionally limiting its powers. Perhaps what plagues America most today is that our federal government is so busily engaged in operating outside the bounds of the Tenth Amendment that it cannot do well those things for which the people created it, and to which they limited its powers.

Article V also merits our attention today. It provides for term limits for, and recall of Congressmen and for payment of their salaries by the State they represent. Unfortunately, these three good ideas did not find their way into the U. S. Constitution.

The intention of both Articles II and V was to keep government as close to the people as possible and always under their watchful eye.

The Tenth Amendment to the Constitution is for the same purpose. It is useless against tyrants, however, if the people cease to be watchful against those who aspire to rule and permit them to pervert our founding documents.

The Northwest Ordinance

At the time of the nation's founding, 1776-1789, the "Northwest Territory" extended no further west than the Mississippi River and lay to the north and west of the Ohio River. The present States of Ohio, Illinois, Indiana, Michigan, Wisconsin, and part of Minnesota comprise the old Northwest Territory.

Most of this land had been claimed by the Virginia colony, which ceded it to the newly established federal government, believing her land holdings too expansive for democratic government. The town of Virginia, Minnesota – far to the north and west of Jamestown – is situated on land which was once part of the Virginia colony.

During the early years of expansion, thousands of settlers were moving into the Northwest Territory. As a result, some form of law and government was required until the territories could be formed into states and admitted into the union. The Northwest Ordinance was enacted specifically to meet this special need. The Articles of Confederation, the nation's constitution at the time, made no provision for such matters.

While most of the Northwest Ordinance served a temporary purpose, a study of this document is necessary for a clear understanding of
our nation's founding and foundations. The "Ordinance," as it came to
be called, remains significant to us today for several reasons. First of all,
it was the first national law prohibiting slavery. Slavery was forbidden
in the states to be formed out of the Northwest Territory.

For decades after the nation was founded, the Northwest Ordinance remained the authority and the provision by which new states
were admitted to the union. The enabling acts of Congress, admitting
new states, required that the people of the territory form a state government and write its constitution "not repugnant to the Ordinance."

In addition to the states that were formed out of the Northwest
Territory, a number of states outside the Territory were admitted to the
union by enabling acts requiring that their constitutions be "not repugnant to the Ordinance."

Since most public libraries have copies of the Northwest Ordinance, we are not including a copy in this book.

"Religion, Morality, and Knowledge"

Nebraska was admitted to the union in 1875, and included Article
III of the Northwest Ordinance, in essence, in her state constitution:

> Religion, morality, and knowledge, however, being essential to
> good government, it shall be the duty of the legislature to pass
> suitable laws . . . to encourage schools and the means of in-
> struction.

Leading up to and into the twentieth century it was common understanding in America that:

- Morality and knowledge were essential to good government;
- Both morality and knowledge were linked to religion;
- Religion, morality, and knowledge were the responsibility of the
  school system.

As late as the 1940's there was no federal government restraint on
prayer, God, and the Bible in America's public schools or any other place.

Article III of the Northwest Ordinance states:

Religion, morality, and knowledge, being necessary to good government and the happiness of mankind, schools and the means of education shall forever be encouraged.

This 1787 "forever" law has never been repealed by an act of Congress – and certainly not by an act of the people. The present tyranny against God and the Bible in public schools and other public places is not only destructive of liberty and good government, it is patently illegal.

Please note carefully that state government is to "encourage" education, not necessarily to supply it. Encouraging education was defined strictly as the responsibility of state government. Today, the federal government is outside the bounds of the Tenth Amendment to the Constitution when it involves itself in education.

The wisdom behind this restraint on the federal government is obvious. It was never intended that the government should indoctrinate children, so that the people would become subservient to the government. That is the method of every despotic system. It perpetuates a ruling elite.

It was rather intended that children should be educated in the Christian religion, morality, and common knowledge, so that the people would be well-informed and morally upright. The government would then be subservient to a well-informed people, and the people subservient to God. This, until recent decades, was the American system. This system perpetuates liberty.

Goals 2000, Educate America Act is a direct assault by the federal government on our time-tested American way in education and a sinister threat to our God-given liberties. It is an open road to tyranny. We will deal with this subject to some extent in the companion book, *A New Birth of Freedom.*

The Best Book in the World

Contrary to popular belief, the words did not originate with Abraham Lincoln. Possibly Lincoln or his speech writer had read a copy of John Wycliff's translation of the Bible. There, in the prologue, they would have seen the words written by Wycliffe in 1384, 479 years before Lincoln repeated them at Gettysburg – "The Bible is for the Government of the People, by the People, and for the People." [1]

The Bible is so visible in colonial America, and in the works of the nation's founders, that its role in establishing the United States should be plainly visible to every honest observer. There can be little doubt that all the Founding Fathers possessed Bibles and studied them. With a few possible exceptions, all were affiliated with a Christian church of one of the denominations then existing.

Whatever their doctrinal preferences, the founders were all believers in the God revealed in the Bible. From its pages they derived concepts for the foundation pillars of the nation: "the Laws of Nature and Nature's God," "unalienable rights," "endowed by their Creator," "Supreme Judge of the World," and "the Protection of Divine Providence."

So evident is the Bible's role in shaping the minds of the founders and the people of the founding era that we are strongly inclined to recognize it as the primary source of the founding documents.

The Wisdom of the Ages

Numerous utterances of the founders – and other American leaders who followed them – affirm this position. These quotations illustrate the point:

Patrick Henry: (*Patriot of "Give me Liberty, or Give me Death" fame*) The Bible is worth all other books which have ever been printed.[2]

John Adams: I have examined all [philosophies], as well as my narrow Sphere, my streightened means and my busy Life would allow me; and the result is, that the Bible is the best book in the World. It contains more of my little Philosophy than all the Libraries I have seen.[3]

The Bible is rightly understood, among other considerations, as a record of the wisdom of the ages. To reject this wisdom because it is recorded in a Book that Christians and Jews devoutly believe to be God's Word is unconscionable folly. To forbid others to receive that wisdom in any place in this free nation is intolerable tyranny.

The Presidents and the Bible

The Bible is the most ancient Book of fundamental principles of human society still in common use in the Western world today. Both Old and New Testaments are God's gift to the Hebrews, and the Hebrews' gift to the world.

President John Adams: (1797-1801)
The Hebrews have done more to civilize men than any other nation. . . . [God] ordered the Jews to preserve and propagate to all mankind the doctrine of a supreme, intelligent, wise, almighty sovereign of the universe. . . . [this doctrine] to be the great essential principle of morality, and consequently all civilization.[4]

So far as the record shows, all Presidents of the United States have believed the Bible. Possibly Bill Clinton's and Al Gore's attack on Christian conservatives during the 1996 Presidential campaign came close to an attack on the Bible. The values of the "radical religious right" – as these two candidates and their political party called them – are compatible with the Bible, with the founders, and with Christian America.

Most Presidents have publicly venerated the Bible. Many more than those quoted above have recognized the Bible's place in the foundations of this nation and have publicly expressed that understanding:

President Andrew Jackson: *(1829-1837)*
Go to the Scriptures . . . the joyful promises it contains will be a balsam to all your troubles . . . that book . . . is the rock on which our republic rests.[5]

President Abraham Lincoln: *(1861-1865)*
In regard to this great book, I have but to say, it is the best gift God has given to man. All the good the Saviour of the world gave to the world was communicated through this Book. But for it we could not know right from wrong. All things most desirable for man's welfare, here and hereafter, are to found portrayed in it.[6]

President Ulysses S. Grant: *(1869-1877)*
Hold fast the Bible as the . . anchor of liberties. Write its precepts on your hearts and practice them in your lives. To the influence of this Book we are indebted for the progress made in civilization, and to this we must look as our guide in the future.[7]

President Woodrow Wilson: *(1913-1921)*
The Bible . . is the one supreme source of revelation of the

meaning of life, the nature of God and spiritual nature and need of man. It is the only guide of life which really leads the spirit in the way of peace and salvation. America was born a Christian nation.[8]

President Calvin Coolidge: *(1921-1929)*
The foundations of our society and our government rest so much on the teachings of the Bible that it would be difficult to support them if faith in these teachings would cease to be practically universal in our country.[9]

President Franklin D. Roosevelt: *(1933-1945)*
We cannot read the history of our rise and development as a nation, without reckoning with the place the Bible has occupied in shaping the advances of the Republic.... Where we have been truest and most consistent in obeying its precepts, we have attained the greatest measure of contentment and prosperity.[10]

President Harry S. Truman: *(1945-1953)*
The fundamental basis of this nation's law was given to Moses on the Mount. The fundamental basis of our Bill of Rights comes from the teachings we get from Exodus and St. Matthew, from Isaiah and St. Paul. I don't think we emphasize that enough these days. If we don't have the proper fundamental moral background, we will finally wind up with a totalitarian government which does not believe in rights for anybody but the state.[11]

President Dwight D. Eisenhower: *(1953-1961)*
The Bible is endorsed by the ages. Our civilization is built upon its words. In no other book is there such a collection of inspired wisdom, reality and hope.[12]

President Gerald R. Ford: *(1974-1977)*
Without God there could be no American form of government, Recognition of the Supreme Being is the first . . . most basic . . . expression of Americanism. Thus the founding fathers of America saw it, and thus with God's help, it will continue to be.[13]

President Ronald W. Reagan: *(1981-1989)*
Renewing the knowledge of and faith in God through Holy
Scripture can strengthen us as a nation and a people. . . . The
Bible, the Word of God, has made a unique contribution in
shaping the United States as a distinctive and blessed nation. .
. . Deeply held religious convictions springing from the Holy
Scriptures led to the early settlement of our Nation. . . . Bibli-
cal teaching inspired concepts of civil government that are con-
tained in our Declaration of Independence and the Constitu-
tion of the United States.[14]

Only Tyrants Need Fear It

This, my fellow citizens, is the Book your federal judges have banned
from American public education; and, at this very moment, they are
trying to ban it from our courts of law. Shall we stand by and allow
these black-robed untouchables to rip the foundations from under our
free self-governing republic?

When tyrants abuse or misuse the Bible, it always turns on them.
The Bible: Only tyrants need fear it.

Forming a More Perfect Union

While the Declaration of Independence and the Articles of Confederation were being written by the Continental Congress, the War
for American Independence raged on. The armed conflict ended at
Yorktown in 1781 when General Cornwallis surrendered his British
forces to General George Washington.

Your patriot ancestors had declared their independence from despotic government and had backed their declaration with their "lives,
their fortunes, and their most sacred honor." Having birthed a new
nation and having laid her foundations, they now faced the task of
forming a more perfect union.

Since the Articles of Confederation was not adequate to conduct
the business of the new central government, the founders replaced it
after only eight years with our present Constitution of the United States.

Recommended Reading:

The Bible.

May be purchased in any Christian bookstore and most other bookstores. Children should be given Bibles as soon as they are able to read. From it they will receive the best part of their education and preparation for adult life. The Bible is likewise the best source of continuing education for every adult.

- *The King James Version* (KJV) was in general use at the time of the nation's founders. Its literary style and language is the most compatible with theirs.
- *The New International Version* (NIV), a translation in modern English, is sometimes quoted in this book.
- *The New American Bible* is a Catholic version in modern English.

Federer, William J., *America's God and Country*, (Coppell, TX: Fame Publishing, Inc., 1994).

Eidsmoe, John, *Christianity and the Constitution*, (Grand Rapids, Michigan: Baker Book House, 1987) pp. 51-73.

DeMar, Gary, *The Untold Story*, (Atlanta, GA: American Vision Publishers, Inc., 1993).

The Constitutions of the Sixteen States which compose the Confederated Republic of America, (Boston: Manning and Loring, 1797).

Quotes from original State constitutions were taken from this old book, which is no longer generally available. Books containing the original constitutions of the original thirteen states are available in most large libraries.

Jensen, Merrill, *The Articles of Confederation*, (Madison, WI: The University of Wisconsin Press, 1940).

Readers who desire a greater insight into the political and legal developments leading from the Declaration to the first Constitution of the United States will find a valuable guide in professor Jensen's book.

4

A MORE PERFECT UNION

"A constitution of government is addressed to the common sense of
the people, and never was designed for trials of logical skill, or
visionary speculation" *Joseph Story, Justice, U. S. Supreme Court,* 1833

E very corporate entity – religious, charitable, commercial, or
civil – requires a charter – a document authorizing its legal
existence. The charter of the civil entity – the United States of
America – is the Declaration of Independence.

The Declaration did not establish a new government over the colonies. It merely severed their connection with their central government
in Great Britain and gave the new nation-to-be legal status among the
nations of the world. As the nation's charter, the Declaration is sometimes
referred to as the Birth Certificate of the United States.

The Declaration spells out the fundamental principles upon which
the new nation would be built – and to which its constitution of government would conform. The Declaration defines the foundation of the
United States government. The Constitution defines its structure.

The founders bound the Constitution forever to the Declaration and its principles of government when they added the Bill of Rights to the Constitution. As their European forefathers had for centuries forced the rights of the people upon the monarchy, our American forefathers forced the Bill of Rights upon the federal government of the United States.

It was the tyrannical denial of the people's rights that goaded them into their Declaration of Independence. It was the fear of home-grown American tyrants that forced the Bill of Rights into the Constitution. The Bill of Rights, therefore, binds these two great documents together into virtually one document. Government that ignores the principles of the Declaration is tyranny, even though rulers may pretend to follow the Constitution.

The Constitution is best understood when studied side by side with the Declaration of Independence. We could hardly have had one without the other. Without the Declaration, the Constitution would illy define the fundamental principles of our federal government. Without the Constitution, the Declaration would have left that government without form and order of operation.

The Declaration did not specify the form of government for the new nation. It left that choice to the people – the "organizing [of] its Powers in such Form, as to them shall seem most likely to effect their Safety and Happiness."

The People's Choice

The people chose for themselves a republican form of government – government by representatives, duly elected by the people. Except for the overruling British monarchy, the people were long accustomed to this form of government in their town halls and colonial assemblies – all derived from their Congregational and Presbyterian forms of church government.

In short order, after signing the Declaration, elected representatives of the people wrote the state constitutions specifying the republican form of government. As noted in an earlier chapter, a composite of these state constitutions, with their bills of rights, formed the pattern and most of the substance of the Constitution of the United States. Procuring a federal constitution of government was no simple undertaking.

George Washington and the Continental army were left to defend the Declaration, which at the time was backed by a federal government poorly organized and with powers insufficient to the task.

Under the Articles of Confederation, the federal government was a weak union of 13 essentially sovereign nations, rife with sectional differences and jealousies. Perhaps the only bond that held them together at the beginning was their common struggle for survival against the British monarchy.

The old adage, "If we don't hang together, we shall surely hang separately," created a strong argument for unity. Even so, the union would almost surely have crumbled except for the impeccable character, the undaunted courage, and the selfless devotion of "the gentleman from Virginia" – Colonel George Washington.

The powers surrendered by the states to the Continental Congress, under the Articles of Confederation, were so limited as to make it ineffective as a federal government. The deplorable condition of finances and credit of the central government, along with its inability to raise a revenue, to regulate trade and commerce, and to provide for the common safety of the country led to a call for a convention in Philadelphia to review and amend the Articles of Confederation.

Writing the Constitution

"Gridlock" in Congress is no new thing.

The Constitution, without its 26 amendments, is not a lengthy document; and, there was enough experience among the framers to write it quickly. Yet the 55 delegates to the Constitutional Convention of 1787 labored from May 14 to September 17 to hammer the document into existence.

These were four months of intense, sometimes heated, debate, hundreds of written pages stating the positions of the Federalists and Antifederalists, merchants and planters, North and South, East and West, slave holders and abolitionists. Except for the promise that Congress would add a Bill of Rights the next year, the Constitution doubtless would have been rejected by both the Congress and the States.

Again, it is likely that because of divergent interests, the delegates would have given up on writing and ratifying the Constitution, except for the presence of two highly respected men, George Washington and Benjamin Franklin.

George Washington was elected president of the Convention. His strength of character, the power of his unassuming presence, and his stamp of approval calmed the doubts and fears of the delegates. Even George Washington at times must have despaired of the proceedings.

By the end of June the delegates were embroiled in bitter debate over equitable representation of the larger and smaller states. Some delegates had already left the convention.

Benjamin Franklin's Call to Prayer

On June 28, delegate Benjamin Franklin, Governor of Pennsylvania, wisened by 81 years of age stood and addressed the convention:

Mr. President:

The small progress we have made after 4 or five weeks close attendance & continual reasonings with each other – our different sentiments on almost every question, several of the last producing as many noes as ayes, is methinks a melancholy proof of the imperfections of the Human Understanding.

We indeed seem to feel our own want of political wisdom, since we have been running about in search of it. We have gone back to ancient history for models of government, and examined the different forms of those Republics which, having been formed with the seeds of their own dissolution, now no longer exist. And we have viewed Modern States all round Europe, but find none of their Constitutions suitable to our circumstances.

In this situation of this Assembly, groping as it were in the dark to find political truth, and scarce able to distinguish it when presented to us, how has it happened, Sir, that we have not hitherto once thought of humbly applying the Father of lights to illuminate our understanding?

In the beginning of the Contest with G. Britain, when we were sensible of danger, we had daily prayer in this room for Divine Protection. Our prayers, Sir, were heard, & they were graciously answered. All of us who were engaged in the struggle must have observed frequent instances of a superintending Providence in our favor.

To that kind Providence we owe this happy opportunity of consulting in peace on the means of establishing our future national felicity. And have we now forgotten that powerful Friend? or do we imagine we no longer need His assistance?

I have lived, Sir, a long time, and the longer I live, the more convincing proofs I see of this truth – that God Governs in the affairs of men. And if a sparrow cannot fall to the ground without His notice, is it possible that an empire can rise without His aid?

We have been assured, Sir, in the Sacred Writings, that "except the Lord build a House, they labor in vain that build it." I firmly believe this; and I also believe that without his concurring aid we shall succeed in this political building no better than the Builders of Babel: We shall be divided by our partial local interests, our projects will be confounded, and we ourselves shall become a reproach and bye word down to future ages.

And what is worse, mankind may hereafter from this unfortunate instance, despair of establishing Governments by Human wisdom and leave it to chance, war or conquest.

I therefore beg leave to move – that henceforth prayers imploring the assistance of Heaven, and its blessing on our deliberations, be held in this Assembly every morning before we proceed to business, and that one or more of the clergy of this city be requested to officiate in that service.[1]

To Pray or Not to Pray?

Jonathan Dayton, delegate from New Jersey wrote in his records:

The Doctor (Franklin) sat down; and never did I behold a countenance at once so dignified and delighted as was that of Washington at the close of the address; nor were the members of the convention generally less affected. The words of the venerable Franklin fell upon our ears with a weight and authority, even greater than we may suppose an oracle to have had in a Roman senate! We assembled again; and . . every unfriendly feeling had been expelled, and a spirit of conciliation had been cultivated.[2]

Roger Sherman of Connecticut seconded Dr. Franklin's motion. Alexander Hamilton and several others expressed their apprehensions that however proper such a resolution might have been at the beginning of the convention, it might at this late day . . . lead the public to believe that the embarrassments and dissentions within the convention, had suggested this measure.

Franklin, Sherman, and others answered that the past omission of duty could not justify a further omission. Hugh Williamson of North Carolina observed that the true cause of the omission could not be mistaken – the convention had no funds [to pay a clergyman]. [3]

Edmond Randolph of Virginia proposed in order to give a favorable aspect to the measure,

> That a sermon be preached at the request of the convention on the 4th of July, the anniversary of Independence; & thenceforward prayers be used in ye Convention every morning. [4]

A few days later, the delegates assembled at the Reformed Calvinist Lutheran Church to hear a sermon by James Campbell, trusting in the wisdom of the delegates to establish a "free and vigorous government."

On April 9, 1789, the first Constitutional Congress appointed two Chaplains, one to the House of Representatives and one to the Senate. Dr. Franklin would be pleased to know his motion finally carried; and to this day, both houses of Congress are opened daily with prayer.

In later chapters, the founders will affirm that both our Declaration and our Constitution were written in an atmosphere of conciliation on "the general principles of Christianity."

There was no "wall of separation between Church and State" when our Constitution was written.

The Longest-Lived Republic

In the spirit of Christian conciliation, the writing of the Constitution was finished and approved by Congress on September 17, 1787.

The requisite number of States had signed by June 21, 1788, when New Hampshire ratified the Constitution.

By March 4, 1789, the several States had chosen their electors and had cast their ballots for President and Vice President, according to

Article II of the Constitution; and, on that date their ballots were presented to the Senate.

On April 6, 1789, the first electoral ballots were opened and counted. George Washington had been unanimously elected President, and John Adams duly elected Vice President.

John Adams appeared on April 21, and assumed the chair as President of the Senate.

On April 30, 1789, George Washington was attended to the gallery in front of the Senate Chamber by the Vice President, the Senators and Representatives, and other public officials. There the Oath of Office as required by the Constitution was administered by the Chancellor of the State of New York, who then proclaimed, "Long live George Washington, President of the United States."

After taking the oath, President George Washington returned to the Senate chamber and delivered his first inaugural address. Thus commenced what has become the republic to live longer under the same constitution than any other republic in the history of the world – The United States of America.

The Preamble to the Constitution

We the people of the United States, in order to form a more perfect union, establish justice, insure domestic tranquility, provide for the common defense, promote the general welfare, and to secure the blessings of liberty to ourselves and our posterity, do ordain and establish this Constitution for the United States of America.

What does, "We the people" mean? "The people alone are the absolute owners and movers. . . ."

The Constitution belongs to the people, one and all. It is not the property of the President, the Congress, nor the Supreme Court. It is the duty of each and all of us, therefore, to understand, to interpret, and to defend the Constitution, just as much as it is the duty of any elected official.

From the Supreme Court, itself, in a better day, comes this admonition to the people:

It must perish, if there be not that vital spirit in the people, which alone can nourish, sustain, and direct all its movements.

It is in vain that statesmen shall form plans for government, in which the beauty and harmony of a republic shall be embodied in visible order, shall be built upon solid substructions, and adorned by every useful ornament, if the inhabitants suffer the silent power of time to dilapidate its walls, or crumble its massy supporters into dust; if the assaults from without are never resisted, and the rottenness and mining from within are never guarded against.

Who can preserve the rights and liberties of the people, when they shall be abandoned by themselves? Who shall keep watch in the temple, when the watchmen sleep at their posts? Who shall call upon the people to redeem their possessions, and revive the republic, when their own hands have deliberately and corruptly surrendered them to the oppressor, and have built the prisons or dug the graves of their own friends?

This dark picture, it is to be hoped, will never be applicable to the Republic of America. And yet it affords a warning, which, like all the lessons of past experience, we are not permitted to disregard. America, free, happy, and enlightened as she is, must rest the preservation of her rights and liberties upon the virtue, independence, justice, and sagacity of the people. If either fail, the republic is gone. its shadow may remain with all the pomp, and circumstances, and trickery of government, but its vital power will have departed.[5] *Joseph Story, Justice of the U. S. Supreme Court*, 1833

Where are we today? Is our republic in reality already gone – with only its shadow and all the pomp, circumstances, and trickery of government remaining?

The Purpose of the Preamble

The preamble to the Constitution is a statement of the high ideals of the United States. It is beautiful; but it is not – and never was intended to be part of the supreme law of the land.

The Preamble explains the purpose of the Constitution:

- To form a more perfect union.

(The Articles of Confederation was inadequate.)
- To establish justice.
("All men are created equal . . . they are endowed by their Creator with certain unalienable rights.")
- To insure domestic tranquility.
(To keep the peace between the states and to quell violence within a state, if requested by the Governor.– see Article IV, Section 4.)
- To provide for the common defense.
(Against enemies without.)
- To promote the general welfare.
(The well being of the whole population as opposed to special rights or "entitlements" for special individuals or special-interest groups.)
- To secure the blessings of liberty to ourselves and our posterity.
("To secure these rights, governments are instituted among men.")

A political newspaper columnist recently observed that the body of the Constitution is as boring as Roberts Rules of Order. The federal government, she feels, is at its best when ruling from the preamble. Nothing could be further from the truth; nothing a more certain road to federal tyranny.

If the framers had intended that the President, the Congress, or the Supreme Court, rule from the preamble, they could have shortened the Constitutional Convention to one week or less, avoided all the political debate, written the preamble, and turned the federal government over to King George of America. (George Washington, however, would have declined).

Ruling from the preamble has justified (in their own minds) every kind of tyrannical and socialistic action of the federal government, outside the bounds of its Constitutional powers.

Our ruinous Welfare State, with its loads of "entitlements" and invitation to indolence and dissipation was created by the federal government "to promote the general welfare."

Thomas Jefferson – the misapprehended idol of liberal Democrats – would be appalled.

"If we can prevent the government from wasting the labor of the people under pretense of taking care of them," said Jefferson, "they must become happy." [6]

The main body of the Constitution along with its 26 amendments – not the preamble – defines the federal government's role in promoting the general welfare. All other powers, rights, and responsibilities are specifically reserved to the states respectively or to the people by the Tenth Amendment.

Federal laws, policies, programs, and court actions based on the preamble and unrestrained by the Tenth Amendment are largely the source of our federal government's current problems – and the people's problems with their federal government. This is part of the "rottenness and mining within" that we have not guarded against. And have not all tyrants ruled under pretense of promoting the general welfare of their people?

With a firm conviction that all adult citizens should possess a copy of the United States Constitution, we have included a copy with all amendments at the back of this book. For the rest of this chapter, we extract only those portions relevant to the focus of this writing.

The Bill of Rights

The first 10 amendments (The Bill of Rights) were added to the Constitution in 1791 to guarantee that the federal government would not infringe the powers of the States nor violate the God-given rights of the people.

In the twentieth century, the Congress to some extent – and the Supreme Court in particular – have seriously perverted the Bill of Rights. On the one hand, they infringe the religious liberty of Christians while at the same time driving other rights to ridiculous and irresponsible extremes. By exaggerating "minority rights" they have created government by judicial decree, whereby the minority often rules the majority.

Certain jurisdiction is specifically given to the Supreme Court by the Constitution. And, as the third branch of the federal government, the Court's true role is to furnish interpretive restraint on the President and the Congress. The Court has largely abandoned that latter role in favor of re-directing society by judicial decree.

When "Rights" Become "Wrongs"

Freedom of religion was rightly distinguished as the most basic of all liberties, and placed as the first order in the Bill of Rights. The

Constitution simply forbids the federal government to interfere with the people's religion. A violation of this linchpin liberty will place all other liberties in serious jeopardy, either by their denial or by their ridiculous overindulgence.

> **Article I.** Congress shall make no law respecting an establish-
> ment of religion, or prohibiting the free exercise thereof; or
> abridging the freedom of speech, or of the press, or the right of
> the people to peaceably assemble, and to petition the govern-
> ment for redress of grievances.

Today freedom of the Christian religion is being seriously restricted by the federal courts, while freedom of speech – which is second in priority of liberties – is being sanctioned in the extreme. Freedom of speech has been stretched by the courts to cover the most vile forms of speech, music, art, publications, and actions, while all expressions of the Christian religion are being vigorously removed from all public places.

Federal agencies have even presumed to muzzle Christian minis-ters, whose sermons were considered to be politically incorrect. Con-gress, in complicity with the Court, has made no effort to restrain this runaway of raw judicial power and the usurpation of the legislative process.

> **Article IX.** The enumeration in the Constitution, of certain
> rights, shall not be construed to deny or disparage others re-
> tained by the people.

This article was obviously intended to put the federal government on notice that there could be further restrictions of its power in case some of the people's God-given rights had been overlooked in writing the Bill of Rights.

The Supreme Court, however, under the delusion that "the Con-stitution is what the judges say it is," has seized upon the Ninth Amend-ment to invent "rights" of the most peculiar nature, and often destruc-tive of decent society and good government.

Each year in America, one and a half million human lives are killed in their mothers' wombs, sanctioned by a Court-invented Ninth-Amendment "right to privacy." The Court is so dedicated to this invented "right" that it strikes down any State law attempting to regulate this slaughter of the innocents.

Article X. The powers not delegated to the United States by the Constitution, nor prohibited by it to the States, are reserved to the States respectively, or to the people.

Article X is closely related to Article IX. It was added to the Bill of Rights to exclude the federal government from all aspects of State and local governments, except those clearly authorized by the Constitution. The federal government, in the beginning, had almost no contact with the people's private affairs.

The other seven Articles of the Bill of Rights are generally outside the scope of this writing. They are included with the main body of the Constitution at the back of the book. Some of these rights are also being perverted by the Supreme Court, as we have documented in the companion book, *A New Birth of Freedom.*

The Bill of Rights was added to the Constitution to keep the federal nose out of the people's business, except as specifically authorized by the Constitution.

Governing from the preamble, along with violation of the Tenth Amendment and perversion of the other nine Articles of the Bill of Rights has created our dilemma with federal tyranny today.

How did this come about?

Breaching the Wall of Separation

Imagine, if you will, the following conversation.

G. M. Dallas: (Vice President of the United States, 1847)

The Constitution in its words is plain and intelligible, and it is meant for the homebred, unsophisticated understandings of our fellow citizens. The people alone are the absolute owners and uncontrollable movers of such sovereignty as human beings can claim to exercise; subject to the eternal and unchangeable rules of justice, truth, and of good Faith. . . .[7]

Such a fundamental and paramount law, in the picture of its origin and in the purity of its text, should be placed within the reach of every freeman. It should be found wherever there is a capacity to read: not alone in legislative halls, judicial councils, libraries, and colleges, but also in the cabins and steerages of our mariners, at every common school, log hut, factory or fireside. It should form the rudimental basis of American thought, by being made a perpetually recurring object of memory.

Restless and innovating as we are in most things, we have not invaded, and I do not think we shall invade for centuries to come, the sacred stability of the Constitution.[8]

The Liberators: Gladly we join you, Mr. Dallas, in venerating our Constitution. But even as you spoke, sir, Civil War clouds loomed ominously in America's Southern skies. Our supreme law would soon be put to the supreme test.

That fundamental and paramount law survived, but not without severe damage – damage that remains, to our day, in most urgent need of repair. For the War between the States breached the "wall of separation" that had held would-be federal tyrants away from the powers reserved to the States respectively or to the people.

Today, it is our painful duty to inform you, sir, that scarcely had another half century passed, before "visionary speculators" on the Supreme Court marched through that Civil War breach, and began their unlawful assault on the States and the sacred liberties of the people.

The Constitution has become a "thing of wax" in the despotic hands of federal judges; and, the "sacred stability of the Constitution" is no more.

The Civil War Amendments (1865-1870)

From 1791, the Constitution had served very well for the next 75 years, with only two more amendments, until the end of the Civil War. During this period there was no federal income tax, except a small and temporary tax to finance the Civil War; and federal government interference in the private lives of individual citizens was unheard of.

That evil institution, slavery – which the nation's founders could not muster the strength to abolish – continued to plague the people and divide the nation.

Slavery, along with the smoldering resentment between two opposing political factions left over from the founding era, finally led to the secession of the Southern states. The Northern states, under the leadership of President Abraham Lincoln, refused to accept the right of secession from the Union; and the nation was soon embroiled in the devastating Civil War.

Three amendments were added to the Constitution shortly after the Civil War. The Thirteenth Amendment abolished slavery.

> **Article XIII.** (1865) Section 1. Neither slavery nor involuntary servitude, except as a punishment for crime whereof the party shall have been duly convicted, shall exist within the United States, or any place subject to their jurisdiction.

The Fourteenth Amendment granted citizenship to the emancipated slaves; and, the Fifteenth gave them the right to vote.

> **Article XIV.** (1868) Section 1. All persons born or naturalized in the United States, and subject to the jurisdiction thereof, are citizens of the United States and of the state wherein they reside. No state shall make or enforce any law which shall abridge the privileges or immunities of citizens of the United States: nor shall any state deprive any person of life, liberty, or property, without due process of law: nor deny to any person within its jurisdiction the equal protection of the laws.

The Union defeat of the seceding states has had far-reaching and long-lasting results in the social and political structure of the United States – some good and some threatening to our liberties. The Union was saved, slavery abolished, and the former slaves granted citizenship. This was the justice of the Civil War – correcting conditions that should have been set aright in the founding of the nation.

Liberating the slaves and granting them all rights of citizenship seems to have been the only intent of the Civil War Amendments. Such was the interpretation of the Supreme Court until the middle of the twentieth century when the Court placed a despotic spin on the Fourteenth Amendment.

When Liberty Was Lost

While slavery was the catalyst of the Civil War, it was not the only cause. In a very real sense, the war was also the result of smoldering resentment between the Federalists and Antifederalists, which had been a reality since the founding era. In 1860, their disagreements erupted into armed conflict.

The Federalists had wanted an overpowering federal government. Indeed, some of them wanted State governments abolished altogether. The Antifederalists wanted to retain the sovereignty of the States under a federal government with limited powers. The Civil War was a crushing defeat for the Antifederalists.

The defeated Antifederalists, North and South, could bring no influence to bear during the "reconstruction" years following the Civil War. Lincoln, the great conciliator, was dead.

A vindictive Congress declared the Southern States to be "conquered provinces" of the federal government. Real Southern representation was nullified; and, a vengeful Congress, in full control of the government, set about with a vengeance to "reconstruct" the Southern States.

After the passage of so much time, perhaps it is not possible to know whether the victorious Federalists intended to destroy the coveted rights reserved to the States respectively or to the people, or whether they merely meant to do justice to the emancipated slaves.

Whatever the case may be, Section I of Article XIV – although beneficial in its time and for its original purpose – has opened the door for the federal government to invade the private lives of individual citizens and to issue mandates to the States. Originally good, it has become a useful tool in the hands of federal tyrants. Thus, as Thomas Jefferson foresaw, the evil that came with slavery has brought its bondage, not upon the African only, but upon all Americans.

The loss of liberty springing from abuse of the Fourteenth Amendment is possible because of the twisted logic of the Supreme Court, seeking to extend its powers beyond the obvious intent of the Constitution. The Court has seized this despotic power by declaring that the Bill of Rights has been absorbed into the Fourteenth Amendment, thus giving the federal government arbitrary power over all liberties. This insidious betrayal has come, however, under pretense of protecting our civil rights. As a result, Americans today are more in need of protection from the federal courts than from one another.

How should the Fourteenth Amendment be revised to protect our liberties? First of all, automatic citizenship for persons born in the United States to non-citizen parents should be ended.

Liberating our Bill of Rights from federal tyrants will take a Constitutional Amendment, revising the Fourteenth.

The Federal Income Tax Amendment

Wounds of the Civil War healed in time, although never completely. Federal judges, long accustomed to judicial restraint, as well as the Congress, did not infringe the people's rights until the middle of the twentieth century.

Not until that late date did the Supreme Court decide that the Fourteenth Amendment of 1868 had given the federal government the right to swallow up our Bill of Rights. This strange twist in Supreme Court logic supplied the supposed justification for the federal invasion into every corner of our public and private life. The Federal Income Tax Amendment of 1913 supplied the means.

> **Article XVI.** (1913) The Congress shall have power to lay and collect taxes on incomes, from whatever source derived, without apportionment among the several states, and without regard to any census or enumeration.

The Federal Income Tax, along with state and local taxes, licenses, fees, and federal mandates and regulations, currently takes 53 percent of the people's income.

Now we know why the Constitution's framers, by Article I, Section 9, forbade the federal government's direct taxing of the incomes of individual citizens. How foolish of State Legislatures to ratify the Sixteenth Amendment, thus placing this federal noose around the people's neck.

Having the wink of the Supreme Court, the inclination, and the means, federal tyrants now harass the people far beyond anything ever envisioned by the nation's founders or authorized by the Constitution. We live in an America today where the Constitution is ignored, unless it can be bent to agree with our rulers' concept of social and political correctness.

To breathe the fresh air of freedom again, it will be necessary to repeal the Sixteenth Amendment and find a better way to finance the federal government in the performance of its necessary, but limited, Constitutional duties. This also will require another Constitutional Amendment.

We offer some suggestions regarding constitutional amendments in the companion book, *A New Birth of Freedom.*

Let us now take a trip back in time to the founding era to better acquaint ourselves with the men who wrote the great documents creating the United States of America.

We will hear them speak on a wide range of issues crucial to our lives and liberties today. We can then decide whether we will identify with our noble ancestors – their religion, their values, and their love of liberty – or whether we will identify with their present-day enemies who are tearing the foundations from under the great country they gave us.

Recommended Reading:

Hickey, W., *The Constitution,* (Philadelphia: T. K. & P. G. Collins, 1853).

This is the official printing of the Constitution ordered by the U. S. Senate in 1853. From it comes the copy of the Constitution at the back of this book and the statements of Joseph Storey and G. M. Dallas.

Madison, James, *Notes of Debates in the Federal Convention of 1787,* (New York: W. W. Norton & Co., 1987).

Benjamin Franklin's address to the Constitutional Convention was taken from Madison's notes.

Hall, Verna M. *The Christian History of the Constitution of the United States.* (San Francisco: The Foundation for American Christian Education, 1966).

Eidsmoe, John, *Christianity and the Constitution,* (Grand Rapids, Michigan: Baker Book House, 1987). Especially Part 3.

Bradford, M. E., *Original Intentions,* (Athens, GA: The University of Georgia Press, 1993).

This book exposes the error of the Supreme Court's present interpretation of the Constitution as compared to what it meant to its framers.

5

WHO WERE THE
FOUNDING FATHERS?

"There never was an assembly of men, charged with a great and arduous trust, who were more pure in their motives, or more exclusively or anxiously devoted to the object committed to them, than were the members of the Federal Convention of 1787..."
James Madison, Chief Architect of the Constitution.

Americans have a tendency to give all the credit for a team effort to one person. The President is often credited or blamed for the condition of the economy. Whatever the role played by the President, in the final analysis, it is the production and consumption of the people that determines the economy's strength or weakness.

Sports fans often praise the quarterback or the pitcher for winning the game, diminishing the role of the other players – without whom there would have been no game.

Likewise there is a tendency today to limit the list of founding fathers to the framers of the Constitution only. The men who wrote the Constitution, however, considered the signers of the Declaration to be our nation's founders.

Without the Declaration, there would have been no Constitution. Furthermore, if the individual states had not ratified the Constitution, it would have become a meaningless scrap of paper. This is why, in our study of the founding fathers, we must include all the men who signed the Declaration and the Constitution and all who served in the State Ratifying Conventions.

In a still broader sense, all of the colonials who supported "the glorious cause" with their "lives, their fortunes, and their most sacred honor" are our nation's founders. The "founding fathers" could do no more than act as the representatives of the people – "the absolute owners and uncontrollable movers of such sovereignty as human beings can claim to exercise."

Nevertheless, we give special honor to those special men who led the people in their bid for independence and in establishing the United States as a separate and independent nation. These special men, we believe, are truly representative of the people of the founding era – in concepts of government and in religious faith.

The Faith of our Fathers

Our purpose for examining the founders' religion is to come to an honest conclusion concerning our nation's foundations. The founders' worldview, we believe, is the worldview upon which they laid the nation's foundations, organized it powers, and ordered its operation.

What determines a person's worldview? His religious beliefs. Even if a person is an atheist, his religiously held atheistic beliefs affect the way he thinks and views the world. The same is true of men of faith who believe and order their lives by the Bible.

1. Signers of the Declaration of Independence

The Declaration of Independence was enacted by 56 men in Continental Congress. Like all men, they possessed religious convictions that affected their concept of right and wrong, justice and injustice, life and death. These 56 men represented the people of the 13 colonies, which had recently been declared the Thirteen United States of America.

Philadelphia at that time was America's largest city and the capitol of the nation-to-be. The church records of Old Christ Church in Philadelphia furnish the following lists of church affiliations of the signers of the Declaration:

Episcopalian

Carter Braxton	Samuel Chase	George Clymer
Benjamin Franklin	Elbridge Gerry	Button Gwinnett
Benjamin Harrison	Joseph Hewes	Thomas Haywood, Jr.
William Hooper	Francis Hopkinson	Thomas Jefferson
Francis Lightfoot Lee	Richard Henry Lee	Francis Lewis
Philip Livingston	Thomas Lynch, Jr.	Arthur Middleton
Lewis Morris	Robert Morris	John Morton
Thomas Nelson, Jr.	William Paca	John Penn
George Read	George Ross	Caesar Rodney
Benjamin Rush	Edward Rutledge	Thomas Stone
George Taylor	George Walton	James Wilson
Oliver Wolcott	George Wythe	

Congregational

John Adams	Samuel Adams	Josiah Bartlett
William Ellery	Lyman Hall	John Hancock
Samuel Huntington	Robert Treat Paine	Roger Sherman
Matthew Thornton	William Whipple	William Williams

Quaker

Stephen Hopkins   Richard Stockton

Baptist

John Hart

Roman Catholic

Charles Carroll

Presbyterian

Abraham Clark	William Floyd	Thomas McKean
James Smith	John Witherspoon	

2. Framers of the United States Constitution.

Professor M. E. Bradford, in his book, *A Worthy Company: Brief Lives of the Framers of the United States Constitution*, supplies the church affiliation of the framers of the Constitution:

New Hampshire

John Langdon, Congregationalist
Nicholas Gilman, Congregationalist

Massachusetts

Elbridge Gerry, Episcopalian
Rufus King, Episcopalian
Caleb Strong, Congregationalist
Nathaniel Gorham, Congregationalist

Connecticut

Roger Sherman, Congregationalist
William Samuel Johnson, Episcopalian
Oliver Ellsworth, Congregationalist

New York

Alexander Hamilton, Episcopalian
John Lansing, Dutch Reformed (?)
Robert Yates, Dutch Reformed

New Jersey

William Patterson, Presbyterian
William Livingston, Presbyterian

Jonathan Dayton, Episcopalian
David Brearly, Episcopalian
William Churchill Houston, Presbyterian

Pennsylvania

Benjamin Franklin, Deist
Robert Morris, Episcopalian
James Wilson, Episcopalian/Deist
Gouverneur Morris, Episcopalian
Thomas Mifflin, Quaker/Lutheran
George Clymer, Quaker/Episcopalian
Thomas Fitzsimmons, Roman Catholic
Jared Ingersoll, Presbyterian

Delaware

John Dickinson, Quaker/Episcopalian
George Read, Episcopalian
Richard Bassett, Methodist
Gunning Bedford, Presbyterian
Jacob Broom, Lutheran

Maryland

Luther Martin, Episcopalian
Daniel Carroll, Roman Catholic
John Francis Mercer, Episcopalian
James McHenry, Presbyterian
Daniel of St. Thomas Jennifer, Episcopalian

Virginia

George Washington, Episcopalian
James Madison, Episcopalian
George Mason, Episcopalian
Edmund Jenning Randolph, Episcopalian
James Blair, Jr., Episcopalian
James McClung, (?)
George Wythe, Episcopalian

North Carolina

William Richardson Davie, Presbyterian
Hugh Williamson, Presbyterian/Deist (?)
William Blount, Presbyterian
Alexander Martin, Presbyterian/Episcopalian
Richard Dobbs Spaight, Jr., Episcopalian

South Carolina

John Rutledge, Episcopalian
Charles Cotesworth Pinckney, Episcopalian
Pierce Butler, Episcopalian
Charles Pinckney III, Episcopalian

Georgia

Abraham Baldwin, Congregationalist
William Leigh Pierce, Episcopalian
William Houstoun, Episcopalian
William Few, Methodist

Representing the People

Eight men signed both the Declaration of Independence and the Constitution: Elbridge Gerry of Massachusetts; Roger Sherman of Connecticut; Benjamin Franklin, George Clymer, James Wilson, and Robert Morris of Pennsylvania; George Read of Delaware; and George Wythe of Virginia.

The signers of the Declaration and the Constitution were a fair representation of all Christian denominations existing at the time in America. At the time the people were:

97.8% Protestant
2% Roman Catholic
2% all other persuasions

Later migrations from Europe, and the annexation of territory settled earlier by Spaniards increased the Roman Catholic percentage considerably.

Although many of today's denominations were in their infancy or not yet organized at the time, all current Christian denominations have their roots in those represented at the nation's founding. This overwhelming predominance of Christianity among the earliest American people – and the nation's founders – explains why the United States has been called a Christian nation for most of her history.

At one point, Benjamin Franklin wrote that an atheist or infidel scarcely could be found in America. Traveling the length and breadth of the land, a visitor scarcely could have found a copy of any holy writ other than the Bible, which was a cherished possession in every household. In this Christian environment America was born; and, on the Hebrew-Christian worldview her foundations were laid.

Deists or Christians?

In a concerted effort to de-Christianize America, much debate has arisen in recent years regarding the religion of the founders. Some secularist historians have sought to prove that these godly men were not Christians but Deists.

Who were the Deists and what did they believe? The Deists were a relatively small group of European philosophers in the seventeenth and eighteenth centuries. They believed a Supreme Being had created the universe then abandoned its operation to natural laws, requiring no further intervention from any Deity. They saw the world as operating much as a clock, wound up and set in perpetual motion. They did not deny the Creator but merely His presence in our world and in man's affairs. It was not until Charles Darwin (1809-1892) advanced his theory of evolution that the Deists could outrightly deny the existence of God.

If the founders were all Deists – or predominantly so as some would have us believe – it would logically follow that the colonial church in America had abandoned her cardinal doctrines and converted to Deism. It would mean that the American people, who sent these men as representatives to the Continental Congress, were also Deists. Nothing in our American history – nothing in the founding documents, state or federal – presents such a scenario.

Some misguided theologians of the late nineteenth and twentieth centuries, micro-analyzing the founders' religion, have also attempted to discredit the founders' Christianity. In so doing, they have (some wittingly, some unwittingly) joined with the secularists in trashing the

Declaration of Independence and perverting the Constitution.

Splitting theological hairs, as some theologians are inclined to do, they failed to distinguish between Biblical principles of God and State, and Biblical principles of God and Church. This kind of teaching and preaching caused countless genuine Christians, throughout the twentieth century, to abandon the public arena and government service. These theologians, therefore, are as much to blame as the secularists for setting the stage for the present secularization of America.

What Did the Founders Believe?

Much evidence – rather than reason or speculation – exists regarding the religion of our colonial ancestors and the nation's founders. What is that evidence? The written sermons and prayers and copious religious confessions of America's founders – in their own handwriting!

The few founders who wrestled with the Deistic schism were still solidly within the Hebrew-Christian worldview. Two such notables were Benjamin Franklin and Thomas Jefferson, both claimed as members by the Episcopal Church.

At one point in his life, Franklin called himself a Deist; but, his religious acts and statements, taken in total, by no means portray a true Deist. His Christian orthodoxy is difficult to confirm; but, we cannot place him in the Deist camp as Bradford does. His speech in the Constitutional Convention reveals a faith very contradictory to Deism. We shall hear directly from Mr. Franklin on this topic a little later.

Thomas Jefferson, on the other hand – while indicating some Deistic tendencies and disdain for the clergy of his day – contended to the end of his life that he was, indeed, a true Christian. We shall also hear from Mr. Jefferson on this subject.

Perhaps the few founders whose Christianity has been called into question are more accurately understood as being Christian in worldview while wrestling with some contradictory philosophies. They should not, therefore, be called Deists as we define that eighteenth century religion today.

Where the Founders Worshipped

Old Christ Church, established in 1695, is located in Philadelphia near the State House, where the Continental Congress assembled. Seven signers of the Declaration were members of Old Christ Church. Eight other signers also worshipped there. Most notable of these was Benjamin Franklin, a member for sixty years.

The Franklin pew, Number 57, bears this inscription:

> Here worshipped Benjamin Franklin, philosopher and patriot. . . . Member of the Committee which erected the Spire of the Church. Interred according to the terms of his will in this churchyard.

Franklin's self-composed epitaph, cast in bronze and most fitting for a writer, hangs on the churchyard wall near his grave:

> The Body of
> B. Franklin, Printer
> Like the Cover of an Old Book,
> And stript of its Lettering & Gilding,
> Lies here, Food for Worms.
> But the Work shall not be lost;
> For it will, as he believ'd,
> appear once more
> In a new and more elegant Edition
> Corrected and Improved
> By the Author.

Clearly, Benjamin Franklin believed in the resurrection of the dead.

Members of the Continental Congress regularly joined local parishioners in worship at Old Christ Church.

In 1775, while agonizing over the grave circumstances of the War for American Independence, the founding fathers heard Reverend Jacob Duche's famous sermon, "The Duty of Standing Fast in our Spiritual and Temporal Liberties." (There was no "wall of separation between Church and State" in those "times that try men's souls.")

George and Martha Washington's pew marker is on Pew Number 58. They were members of Old Christ Church during the eight years of Washington's presidency.

President John Adams and wife, Abigail, occupied the same pew until their relocation to the White House on November 2, 1800. John Adams, first President to occupy the White House, had this prayer engraved on the mantel in the state dining room:

I pray Heaven to bestow THE BEST OF BLESSINGS
ON THIS HOUSE and All that shall hereafter inhabit
it. May none but Honest, and Wise Men ever rule under
this Roof.

Visitors to – and occupants of – the White House may read this
engraved prayer today, 200 years later.

The Missing Windows

In 1861, two stained glass windows were installed in Old Christ
Church. The "Patriots' Window" portrayed the founding fathers in their
family pews, with open Bibles, worshipping God. The "Liberty Window" depicted the first prayer meeting in Congress.

You can tour Old Christ Church today, but you cannot see the two
stained glass windows. They were removed in 1986 "for cleaning" and
placed in permanent storage. Old Christ Church, "The Nation's
Church," had been designated a national shrine in 1950 and placed
under the custody of the National Park Service, U. S. Department of
the Interior.

Why, after so many years, have the windows not been replaced?
Could it be that a department of the United States government has
decided to carry out the Supreme Court's despotic decree, "The first
Amendment has erected a wall of separation between church and state.
That wall must be kept high and impregnable. We could not approve
the slightest breach?" Maybe impostors in high places do not want
America's school children and other visitors to Old Christ Church to
see our founding fathers portrayed as they were in reality: Bible-read-
ing, praying Christians.

How do we know the stained glass windows of Old Christ Church
portray an accurate picture of our founding fathers and their beliefs?
We need no other evidence than the rich legacy left by these courageous and God-fearing men.

Let us now journey back in time and allow the founders to speak
for themselves.

Recommended Reading:

Archives of Old Christ Church, Old Christ Church, Philadelphia.

Bradford, M.E., Founding Fathers, (Lawrence, KS: University of Kansas Press, 1982).

Explores the religious beliefs of the framers of the Constitution.

Bradford, M.E., Original Intentions, (Athens, GA: University of Georgia Press, 1993).

Explores the religious beliefs of many of the founders, some prominent and some not so well known, and relates their religious beliefs to their understanding of the Constitution.

Millard, Catherine, Rewriting America's History, (Camp Hill, PA: Horizon House Publishers, 1991)

6

IN THEIR OWN WORDS

*"We have this day restored the Sovereign to Whom all men
ought to be obedient. He reigns in Heaven, and from the
rising to the setting of the sun, let his kingdom come."*
Samuel Adams, "Father of the Revolution,"
Signer of the Declaration of Independence

I n this chapter, you and I will be obliged to put ourselves in the
place of the well-informed and articulate "Humble Inquirer," who
– if we employ our imaginations – has been permitted to interview
an assembly of America's founding fathers.

The responses of our nation's founders, however, require no
imagination or speculation on our part. They are, in fact, word for
word quotations taken directly from the writings of such well-known
statesmen as Benjamin Franklin, Thomas Jefferson, John Adams,
and many others.

Keep in mind that these quotations are recorded as they were written – in their original wording, spelling, and grammar – and at times

vary from modern English usage. To assist our understanding, additional paragraph breaks have been made at some points. In no way, however, have any alterations been made to the founders' original texts.

Let us now join the Humble Inquirer and his guests.

The Humble Inquirer: Gentlemen – founders of our nation – I am supremely privileged to be present with you, and to address this assembly of our honorable ancestors.

Upon the advise of wise Dr. Benjamin Franklin, I introduce myself simply as an humble inquirer from the dawn of the twenty-first century. If I sometimes slip from this role, please understand that I am agitated over the social and political condition of my generation.

You accomplished a great feat, gentlemen, such as no other people have accomplished before or since your time: You wrested your government from a powerful tyrant, and established a new nation. But you did not raise a new empire for yet another strongman. You created a free, self-governing republic, laying its foundations on "the laws of nature and nature's God." You organized its powers in liberty and justice, by the consent of the governed. You guaranteed this system of government to your posterity, if they are able to sustain it against enemies without and tyrants within.

It is not flattery when I say that, compared to your stature among great men, your twentieth-century detractors are but pitiable dwarfs. The same may be said of those in authority who ignore or pervert your principles of government. Of all people who ever lived, you surely must understand best those burning issues that every generation of Americans must resolve if they are to survive as a free, self-governing society.

The purpose of my visit, gentlemen, is three-fold.

First, I should like to avail myself of your wisdom concerning those timeless principles that undergird every successful society and every good government.

Secondly, I hope to get a better acquaintance with George Washington. I would like to understand why you named this man the "Father of our Country."

Third and finally, having heard your wisdom in these matters, I hope to persuade my generation that our American heritage is worth saving for our posterity.

For you see, sirs, treacherous professors have long since occupied our colleges and universities. From their privileged tenured positions, vainly imagining themselves to be masters of social and political correctness, they trash our nation's history, defame our nation's founders, and ridicule the Faith of our Fathers. Their disciples, thus indoctrinated, are destroying our foundations and leading our people blindly down a path to tyranny more odious than that of the British Crown.

Above All Religions

H. Inquirer: Gentlemen, I have read the Declaration of Independence over and over; and, I have been impressed by your frequent appeals to the Almighty in the founding of the United States of America – Creator, Nature's God, Supreme Judge of the World, Divine Providence. I have studied the Constitution and the Bill of Rights.

I particularly noticed that you addressed the matter of religion as the first order of liberty. In fact, I have read many of your religious expressions in your own writing. My observations conclude that you are more honest and open in your discussion of religion than twentieth-century public officials. Reassured by these facts, and feeling the necessity to understand the affect of your religious beliefs upon the founding of the republic, I open the sometimes sensitive subject of religion.

Some philosophers and theologians of the nineteenth and twentieth centuries have left no stone unturned in their effort to discredit the Christianity of our nation's founders. Their fervor in this pursuit adds to the suspicion that their intention is to conceal the truth. Their contention seems to be that you were not true Christians, but Deists. They strive to convince their followers that you established this republic upon the foundations of ancient Greek and Roman humanism and upon eighteenth century rationalism, as espoused by Thomas Paine after he fell from grace.

Mr. Adams, you seem a bit agitated.

John Adams: (*Signer of the Declaration of Independence, Second President of the United States*)
The Christian religion is, above all the Religions that ever prevailed or existed in ancient or modern times, the religion of Wisdom, Virtue, Equity, and Humanity. Let the Blackguard Paine say what he will; it is Resignation to God, it is Goodness itself to man.[1]

Common Sense or Rationalism?

H. Inquirer: Two centuries of historical evidence indicate that you gentlemen wove these Christian virtues into the fabric of American government as the people wove them into the fabric of American culture.

But the same spirit that turned Thomas Paine from *Common Sense* to *The Age of Reason* remains, and, I fear, will prevail unless the Christian community can be awakened and quickly infused with a massive dose of public spirit.

I understand that Mr. Paine, in his zeal for liberty, mistakenly saw the French Revolution as being on equal ground with the American Revolution. Unlike George Washington, he did not understand that the anti-Christian French Revolution was far different from the American Christian resistance, and would end, as it did, in bloody tyranny.

Dr. Franklin, you had some sage advice for Mr. Paine upon reviewing his manuscript –*The Age of Reason.* Will you please read for this audience the gist of your letter sent to him on that occasion?

Benjamin Franklin: (*Signer of both the Declaration and the Constitution) to Thomas Paine* – I have read your Manuscript [*The Age of Reason*] with some Attention. By the Arguments it contains against the Doctrines of a particular Providence, tho' you allow a general Providence, you strike at the Foundation of all Religion. For without the belief of a Providence, that takes Cognizance of, guards, and guides, and may favour particular Persons, there is no Motive to Worship a Deity, to fear its Displeasure, or to pray for its Protection.... At present I shall only give you my Opinion, that, though your Reasonings are subtile, and may prevail with some Readers, you will not succeed so as to change the general Sentiments of Mankind on that Subject, and the Consequences of printing this Piece will be, a great deal of Odium drawn upon yourself, Mischief to you, and no Benefit to others. He who spits against the Wind, spits in his own Face.

But, were you to succeed, do you imagine any Good would be done by it? You yourself may find it easy to live a virtuous Life, without the Assistance afforded by Religion; you having a clear Perception of the Advantages of Virtue, and the Disadvantages of Vice, and possessing a Strength of Resolution sufficient to enable you to resist common Temptations. But think how great a Proportion of Mankind consists of weak and ignorant Men and Women, and of inexperienc'd, and inconsiderate Youth of both Sexes, who have need of the Motives of Religion to restrain them from Vice, to support their Virtue, and retain them in the Practice of it till it becomes habitual, which is the great Point for its Security. *And perhaps you are indebted to her originally, that is, to your Religious Education, for the Habits of Virtue upon which you now justly value yourself.*[2]

H. Inquirer: A wise insight indeed, Dr. Franklin – Rationalists who succeed in resisting common temptations to do evil have actually gained their sense of right and wrong from religious education – Bible teaching passed down by generations of Christian forebears.

Breaking that generational Christian heritage would, after two or three generations, I believe, produce a generation of people void of that sense of right and wrong. Sir, at the end of the twentieth century, I live with such a generation.

Twentieth-century Rationalists are more commonly known as Humanists; and, they recognize Thomas Paine as one of their mentors. Cynics of their persuasion routinely bash Christianity, revile our nation's Christian founders, and ridicule virtue – which was highly respected by your generation and many generations that followed. Oh, that Mr. Paine had heeded your sage advice!

Benjamin Franklin: *(to Thomas Paine)* I would advise you, therefore, not to attempt unchaining the Tyger, but to burn this Piece [*The Age of Reason*] before it is seen by any other Person; whereby you will save yourself a great deal of Mortification from the Enemies it may raise against you, and perhaps a good deal of Regret and Repentance.[3]

H. Inquirer: Thomas Paine did indeed come to bitter regrets for not heeding your sage advice, Dr. Franklin. After publishing *The Age of Reason* against your advice, this once popular revolutionary writer so fell from favor with the people that he was hard pressed to earn a living. Only the intervention of George Washington landed him a minor staff job in Congress.

I think Thomas Paine's falling from favor with the people because of his attack on God and the Bible is strong evidence of the overwhelming predominance of Christianity in the founding of our nation.

Thomas Paine came to a tragic end. He was heard to groan toward the end of his life, "I would give worlds, if I had them, if *The Age of Reason* had never been published. O Lord, help! Stay with me! It is hell to be left alone!"[4]

Could it be that Mr. Paine's tragic end forebodes the end of a nation which comes to despise its Christian foundations, and chooses to rebuild on foundations of man's godless rationalism?

Benjamin Franklin: If men are so wicked as we now see them *with religion*, what would they be *if without it*? [5]

H. Inquirer: In late twentieth-century America, sir, we need not speculate on the answer to that question. We need only open our eyes and behold.

Dr. Franklin, in reading your *Autobiography*, I learned that you were brought up a Presbyterian. Yet some twentieth-century scholars have studied your religious professions and classified you as a deist.

Benjamin Franklin: Some books against deism fell into my hands... It happened that they wrought an effect on me quite contrary to what was intended by them. . . . I soon became a thorough deist. My arguments perverted some others. . . and recollecting Keith's conduct toward me (who was another freethinker) and my own toward Vernon and Miss Read, which at times gave me great trouble, I began to suspect that this doctrine, though it might be true, was not very useful. [6]

H. Inquirer: You were "scarce fifteen" at the time. Looking back upon your own "inexperienc'd, and inconsiderate Youth," what do you think of those days?

Benjamin Franklin: The kind hand of Providence, or some guardian angel, or accidental favorable circumstances and situations, or all together, preserved me, through this dangerous time of youth and the hazardous situations I was sometimes in among strangers, remote from the eye and advice of my father, free from any willful gross immorality or injustice that might have been expected from my want of religion. [7]

H. Inquirer: May I ask, Did you continue to follow the deist doctrines?

Benjamin Franklin: The great uncertainty I found in metaphysical reasonings disgusted me, and I quitted that kind of reading and study for others more satisfactory. [8]

H. Inquirer: Mr. Adams, I believe I can say without stooping to flattery, that you, of all the founders, are the most knowledgeable of the founding era. You experienced it all from the Boston Massacre to the Boston Tea Party, to Concord and Lexington, to the signing of the Declaration of Independence, through the long and arduous War for Independence.

You, Mr. Adams, never left the service of your country until the United States Constitution was written and ratified and you had served as Vice President under George Washington and as the second President of the United States. I dare say you were personally acquainted with most of the signers of the Declaration and the Constitution, and a great many of the delegates to the State Ratifying Conventions. In short, sir, you knew the Americans of your day; and, I am compelled to place great weight upon your insight and evaluation of these matters.

"Very Few of These Species"

H. Inquirer: Please tell us, Mr. Adams, what was the religious persuasion of that "Army of fine young Fellows" who won our independence and founded these United States of America?

John Adams: There were among them, Roman Catholicks, English Episcopalians, Scotch and American Presbyterians, Methodists, Moravians, Anabaptists, German Lutherans, German Calvinists, Universalists, Arians, Priestleyans, Socinians, Independents, Congregationalists, Horse Protestants and House Protestants, Deists and Atheists; and "Protestans qui ne croyent rien ['Protestants who believe nothing']". [9]

H. Inquirer: Add a few Mohammedans, Buddhists, and Hindus and it sounds pretty much like the religion of America at the end of the twentieth century, with one noticeable difference – staunch Christians are not so well represented in government as we approach the twenty-first century.

Were Deists and Atheists well represented in the founding of the nation?

John Adams: [There were] very few . . . of several of these species. [10]

H. Inquirer: Which species were very few in number?

Benjamin Franklin: Atheism is unknown [here], Infidelity rare and secret, so that persons may live to a great age in [this] country without having their piety shocked by meeting with either an Atheist or infidel.[11]

John Adams: All [were] educated in the general principles of Christianity.[12]

H. Inquirer: Mr. Jefferson, your Christianity has been questioned more than most others. What is your response?

Thomas Jefferson:(*Author of the Declaration, Third President of the United States*) My views . . . are the result of a life of inquiry and reflection, and very different from that anti-Christian system imputed to me by those who know nothing of my opinions. To the corruptions of Christianity I am indeed opposed, but not to the genuine precepts of Jesus himself. I am a Christian in the only sense in which he wished anyone to be, sincerely attached to his doctrines in preference to all others.[13]

"Let His Kingdom Come"

H. Inquirer: This is the great question, gentlemen: Was your faith in Jesus Christ and your understanding of the general principles of Christianity instrumental in laying the foundations of the United States and writing her Constitution?
     Mr. Samuel Adams, what was it you said on the day you signed the Declaration of Independence?

Samuel Adams: *(Signer of the Declaration, "Father of the Revolution")* We have this day restored the Sovereign to Whom all men ought to be obedient. He reigns in Heaven, and from the rising to the setting of the sun, let his kingdom come.[14]

H. Inquirer: That is quite a statement of faith! Human experience has shown that, while men ought to be obedient to Jesus Christ, it takes a Power greater than our own to write the precepts of God upon the human heart.

Samuel Adams: I conceive we cannot better express ourselves than by humbly supplicating the Supreme Ruler of the world . . . that the confusions that are and have been among the nations may be overruled by the promoting and speedily bringing in the holy and happy period when the kingdom of our Lord and Saviour Jesus Christ may be everywhere established, and the people willingly bow the sceptre to Him who is the Prince of Peace. [15]

H. Inquirer: Your statement reminds me of the Lord's Prayer, Mr. Adams, "Thy kingdom come, thy will be done in earth as it is in Heaven."

It seems to me, Mr. Adams, that you and many other founders of this nation longed for the liberty, security, and peace of Christ's kingdom on earth. Is it possible that you, in a feeble way, attempted to establish the government of the United States upon the principles of that blessed hope?

None "More Pure"

H. Inquirer: Mr. Madison, your record of the Constitutional Convention of 1787 is by far the most complete. Please tell us why you felt compelled to write such a complete record?

James Madison: (*"Chief Architect of the Constitution," Fourth President of the United States*) The curiosity I had felt during my researches into the history of the most distinguished confederacies, particularly those of antiquity, and the deficiency I found in the means of satisfying it more especially in what related to the process, the principles, the reasons, & the anticipations, which prevailed in the formation of them, determined me to preserve as far as I could an exact account of what might pass in the convention . . . the objects, the opinions, & the reasonings from which the new System of Gov't was to receive its peculiar structure and organization . . . a Constitution on which would be staked the happiness of a people great even in infancy, and possibly the cause of Liberty throughout the world. [16]

H. Inquirer: In your opinion, Mr. Madison, were our nation's founders, representing such a mixed bag of Christian communions, capable of opinions and reasonings necessary to lay a sound foundation and organize the structure of the government of the United States?

James Madison: I feel it a duty to express my profound & solemn conviction,. . . that there never was an assembly of men, charged with a great & arduous trust, who were more pure in their motives, or more exclusively or anxiously devoted to the object committed to them, than were the members of the Federal Convention of 1787, to the object of devising and proposing a constitutional system which would best . . . secure the permanent liberty and happiness of their country. [17]

United By Christian Conviction

H. Inquirer: One is made to wonder, what common conviction held these men together in such devotion to the birthing of this nation.

John Adams: The general principles, on which the Fathers achieved independence, were the only Principles in which that beautiful assembly of young Gentlemen could Unite. [18]

H. Inquirer: And what were these general principles, Mr. Adams?

John Adams: I answer, the general Principles of Christianity, in which all these Sects were United and the general Principles of English and American Liberty, in which all those young Men United, and which had United all Parties in America, in Majorities sufficient to assert and maintain her Independence. [19]

H. Inquirer: Your words, Mr. Adams, confirm the conclusion reached by the learned Professor Hofstadter in late twentieth century that, "If there was a single determinant of the colonists' political responses more important than any other, it might have been religion."

"The Finger of God"

H. Inquirer: Gentlemen, in our Declaration of Independence I have seen the term, "laws of nature and nature's God." What does this mean?

George Mason: (*Signer of the Constitution, author of the Bill of Rights and the Virginia Bill of Rights*) The laws of nature are the laws of God, whose authority can be superceded by no power on earth. [20]

H. Inquirer: Mr. Pinckney?

Charles Cotesworth Pinckney: (*Signer of the Constitution, Aide-de-camp to General George Washington*) And consequently, as man depends absolutely upon his Maker for everything, it is necessary that he should, in all points, conform to his Maker's will. This will of his Maker, is called the law of nature. [21]

Samuel Adams. In the supposed state of nature, all men are equally bound by the laws of nature, or to speak more properly, the laws of the Creator. . . . They are imprinted by the finger of God on the heart of man. Thou shalt do no injury to thy neighbor, is the voice of nature and reason, and it is confirmed in written revelation. [22]

H. Inquirer: By "written revelation," I understand that you mean the Bible – the Apostle Paul's writing in Romans, chapters 1 and 2, as one example.

It seems that the intuitive knowledge of right and wrong is imparted by our Maker to every human being. Violating that intuitive knowledge brings upon mankind all the painful consequences of sin, including the tyranny that you all have recently overthrown.

May the free, self-governing republic that you all have established, endure 'til we bring forth the Royal Diadem and crown Him whose right it is to reign.

No Religion; No Freedom

James Madison. Before any man can be considered as a member of Civil Society, he must be considered as a subject of the Governour of the Universe. . . . Religion . . . [is] the basis and Foundation of Government. [23]

H. Inquirer: This agrees with my own conviction, Mr. Madison, that all enduring governments must be undergirded by the predominant religion of the governed.

How can a government which suppresses the religion of the people, derive its just powers from the consent of the governed?

John Adams: Statesmen, my dear Sir, may plan and speculate for liberty, but it is religion and Morality alone, which can establish the Principles upon which Freedom can securely stand. [24]

Benjamin Rush. (*Signer of the Declaration*) The only foundation for . . . a republic is to be laid in Religion. Without this there can be no virtue, and without virtue there can be no liberty, and liberty is the object and life of all republican governments. [25]

H. Inquirer: So, the people's religion, whatever it may be, cannot be separate from their government. It is the very foundation of their government. To fundamentally change a people's government, tyrants must subdue them, scoundrels must deceive them, or teachers of another religion must convert them. In twentieth-century America, all three of these forces are at work to create "a wall of separation between Church and State," thereby cutting off our government from what George Washington recognized as its "indispensable support."

Incidentally, Mr. Rush, how do you classify yourself politically?

Benjamin Rush. I have alternately been called an Aristocrat and a Democrat. I am neither. [26]

H. Inquirer: So then, what are you, sir, a Republican?

Benjamin Rush. I am a Christocrat. [27]

H. Inquirer: (musing silently) Would all these men today sneeringly be called the "Radical Religious Right" by the media, anti-Christian educators, politicians, and the willfully ignorant?

The Only Lasting Foundation

H. Inquirer: Doctor Franklin, you signed both the Declaration and the Constitution. Inventor, author, publisher, statesman, you heard all the deliberations, and nothing in the founding era escaped your notice.

Can you tell me, sir, upon what foundation is the American republic established?

Benjamin Franklin: We have gone back to ancient history for models of government, and examined the different forms of these Republics which, having been formed with the seeds of their own dissolution, now no longer exist. And we have viewed Modern States all round Europe, but find none of their Constitutions suitable to our circumstances. I have lived, Sir, a long time, and the longer I live, the more convincing proofs I see of this truth . . . that God governs in the affairs of men. [28]

H. Inquirer: (musing silently) Hmm, these are not the words of a Deist.

If, as you all seem to agree, religion is the basis and foundation of government, what must I logically conclude? Christianity is the basis and foundation of the government of the United States, since Christianity was the only significant religion of the people of the founding era. I understand that you do not refer in this instance to sectarian doctrines, but to what Mr. Adams calls "the general principles of Christianity."

John Adams. I will avow that I then believed, and now believe, that the general Principles of Christianity, are as eternal and immutable, as the Existence and Attributes of God; and those Principles of Liberty, are as unalterable as human Nature. [29]

H. Inquirer: To sum up this part of our discussion, gentlemen, this is what I understand:

- You studied the forms and foundations of ancient Greek and Roman republics and found no satisfactory pattern for the republic you anticipated for your posterity.
- You searched the European systems of your day and were likewise disappointed in them.
- Then you discovered the basis and foundation of the new republic where it had been all along – in the Christian faith of the American people, therefore:
- The general principles of Christianity are the basis and foundation of the United States of America.
- These Christian principles are eternal and, therefore, the only lasting foundation for liberty, both religious and civil.

I believe a search of world history, ancient and modern, regarding the relationship between religion and government will support this latter understanding. Other religions have supported long-standing governments. None of these governments, however, has secured the people's life, liberty, and pursuit of happiness as has the United States, supported by Christianity.

Enough for today. Let us continue our enlightening conversations tomorrow. Until we meet again, may God be with you.

7

A NATION THOROUGHLY CORRUPTED?

*"Our Constitution was made for a moral and religious people.
It is wholly inadequate to the government of any other." John Adams*

Humble Inquirer: Good morning, gentlemen. I pray you are well rested and prepared to continue my inquiry into the fundamental principles upon which you founded the government of these United States.

Since we last met, I have spent much time reflecting on the topics we have discussed. I must now confess my anguish, gentlemen, over the decline of Christian virtue in my generation.

Permit me to list just some of the problems faced by the people of the United States as we near the twenty-first century.

- Big money (both foreign and domestic) buys our national elections and our elected officials; and Congress will not act to reform campaign laws.
- The President of the United States – a draft dodger – accused of unabashed adultery – an alleged perjurer – is making our nation the laughingstock of the world.
- Our Christian foundations are routinely assaulted by university professors, powerful legal organizations, appointed judges, and public administrators, under pretense of freedom of religion.
- Our society is fed a constant diet of incivility and immorality through the theater, magazines, and other media, under guise of freedom of speech.
- Half of our marriages end in divorce, leaving millions of children to be traumatized by poverty, neglect, and abuse.
- Fifty percent of our children are born out of wedlock.

The depth of our depravity, however, may be the annual two and a half million irresponsible conceptions of human life abandoned by the so-called men who procreate them. Over 35 million babies have been put to death in their mothers' wombs. Most of the other abandoned children and their mothers are cast upon the taxpayers for support. The slaughter of the innocents and the tragedy of single-mother homes continues with government approval and encouraged by government policy.

What shall be our end as a nation?

John Adams: Have you ever found in history one single example of a Nation thoroughly Corrupted, that was afterward restored to Virtue, and without Virtue, there can be no political Liberty? [1]

H. Inquirer: I can think of none, sir. And I earnestly beseech our Merciful Father that we are not so thoroughly corrupted that we, as a nation, cannot turn back to Him for pardon and restoration.

Some pass it off as mere coincidence; others believe there is a direct cause/affect relationship; but, the honest will tell you this: Since the middle of the twentieth century, America has witnessed a steady and dramatic decline in both morality and quality education. The official assault on our Christian foundations began in earnest at mid-twentieth century.

The State of American Education

H. Inquirer: Gentlemen, I recall these words from the Northwest Ordinance:

> Religion, morality, and knowledge, being necessary to good government and the happiness of mankind, schools and the means of education shall forever be encouraged.

Many of you gentlemen helped to enact the Northwest Ordinance into law. Some of you received new states into the Union under the provisions of the Ordinance.

Perhaps you were correct when you perceived a link between religion, morality, education, and good government. In any case, we know that American education – once the best in the world – began a steady decline at mid-twentieth century after the Supreme Court removed all trace of Christianity from government classrooms. The steady societal and educational decline has been accompanied by a steady growth of intrusion and coercion by the federal government.

Strange as it may seem to you, the Supreme Court cited the First Amendment in its assault on Christianity. It seems that in the name of liberty, this Court will destroy real liberty and sanction licentiousness.

Congressman Fisher Ames, you suggested the wording for the First Amendment in our Bill of Rights. Do you have a statement on this issue?

Fisher Ames: Should not the Bible regain the place it once held as a schoolbook? Its morals are pure, its examples captivating and noble. . . . In no Book is there so good English, so pure and elegant, and by teaching all the same they will speak alike, and the Bible will justly remain the standard of language as well of faith. [2]

H. Inquirer: It is my unpleasant duty to report to you gentlemen the sad state of American education at the beginning of the twenty-first century.

Not only is the Bible banned from government classrooms (the majority of all schools in the United States), but English is being challenged as our official language. Multiculturalism – promoted vigorously in public schools and touted as a great unifier of the people, may level all the people – but certainly not on the principles of the Bible.

On the contrary, Mr. Ames, multiculturalism, I firmly believe, will take the unique American culture and break it back into the cultural fragments of which it is composed.

Do any of you other gentlemen wish to comment on this topic?

Mixing Religion, Morality, and Education

Gouverneur Morris: (*Writer of the final draft of the Constitution*) Religion is the only solid basis of good morals; therefore education should teach the precepts of religion, and the duties of man toward God. [3]

Benjamin Rush: (*Signer of the Declaration of Independence, Surgeon General under George Washington, principal promoter of the American Sunday School Union, "Father of Public Schools"*) I know there is an objection among many people to teaching children doctrines of any kind, because they are liable to be controverted [argued against]. But let us not be wiser than our Maker. If moral precepts alone could have reformed mankind, the mission of the Son of God into all the world would have been unnecessary. The perfect morality of the Gospel rests upon the doctrine which, though often controverted, has never been refuted: I mean the vicarious life and death of the Son of God. [4]

H. Inquirer: (musing silently) Over 200 years have passed; and, we have learned less than nothing.

- Five decades of public education in a moral vacuum, without God and the Bible.
- Broken families: Absentee fathers; single mothers striving to be provider, father and mother; pain and sorrow in families; babies aborted or abandoned on the taxpayers' doorsteps.
- Children on mind-altering drugs.
- Metal detectors at schoolhouse doors to locate guns and knives on school children.
- Teen on teen murder, number one killer of teenagers.
- Suicide: Number two killer of teenagers – without roots, without purpose, without hope.
- Teenage gangs terrorizing our streets and neighborhoods.
- Teenage violence increasing on every hand.

- High school graduates who cannot read their diplomas.
- Teenage pregnancy and abortion commonplace.
- Public education: more and more money to buy more and more ignorance.

The bureaucrats' touted solution: More humanist fixes for humanist-created problems.

Americans must re-establish our government and our culture on our original foundations, or we shall surely sink deeper and deeper into this dark abyss.

The Secret to Peace and Order

H. Inquirer: I beg your pardon, gentlemen, my mind had wandered to late twentieth-century America. I was contemplating how far our Ship of State has drifted from her original moorings, dragging our American society along with her into dangerous and uncharted waters. Please continue.

James McHenry: (*Signer of the Declaration of Independence, Secretary of War*) Neither, in considering this subject, let it be overlooked, that public utility pleads most forcibly for the general distribution of the Holy Scripture.

The doctrines they preach, the obligations they impose, the punishment they threaten, the rewards they promise, the stamp and image of divinity they bear, which produces a conviction of their truths, can alone secure to society, order and peace, and to the courts of justice and constitutions of government, purity, stability and usefulness.

In vain, without the Bible, we increase penal laws and draw entrenchments around our institutions. Bibles are strong entrenchments. Where they abound, men cannot pursue wicked courses, and at the same time enjoy quiet conscience. [5]

H. Inquirer: (musing silently) Supreme Court, U. S. Congress, State Legislatures, are you listening; or perchance, are you removing Bibles so that you also can pursue wicked courses?

H. Inquirer: So, gentlemen, I am to infer that you created the judiciary and wrote the Constitution on the precepts of the Bible.

John Adams: We have no government armed with power capable of contending with human passions unbridled by morality and religion. Avarice, ambition, revenge, or gallantry, would break the strongest cords of our Constitution as a whale goes through a net. Our Constitution was made for a moral and religious people. It is wholly inadequate to the government of any other. [6]

Christianity and Common Law

H. Inquirer: At the end of the twentieth century, the Supreme Court has decreed itself into a strange contradiction – a contradiction, I think, embarrassing to any but tyrants who wrap themselves in long, black robes.

While the Ten Commandments are engraved in stone above the chair of the Chief Justice, the Court forbids the Ten Commandments to be displayed in public schools. The Supreme Court is opened daily with "God save the United States and the Honorable Court;" but, the Court forbids that prayer be offered to God in public schools. Yet, these black-robed untouchables refuse to reverse themselves out of this awkward corner.

You, gentlemen, have offered ample testimony to the crucial role of Christianity in the founding of this nation; yet, at the end of the twentieth century, the faith of our fathers is under severe attack by the very Court they created. I ask you, Is it not a strange thing?

James Wilson: (*Signer of both the Declaration and the Constitution, George Washington appointee to the first Supreme Court*)
Christianity is part of the common law. [7]

Samuel Chase: (*Signer of the Declaration, George Washington appointee to the first Supreme Court*) Religion is of general and public concern, and on its support depend, in great measure, the peace and good order of government, the safety and happiness of the people.

By our form of government, the Christian religion is the established religion; and all sects and denominations of Christians are placed upon the same equal footing, and are equally entitled to protection in their religious liberty. [8]

Are We a Christian Nation or Not?

H. Inquirer: The things that you have spoken, gentlemen, along with records reaching back to the first European exploration of this continent, led our Supreme Court, 100 years after your time, to declare:

> This is a religious people. This is historically true. From the discovery of this continent to the present hour, there is a single voice making this affirmation. These and many other matters which might be noticed, add a volume of unofficial declarations to the mass of organic utterances that this is a Christian nation. [9]

Before another half-century had passed, however, a handful of Atheists petitioned the Supreme Court to suppress the free exercise of Christianity, the very religion which had created this free, self-governing republic. Incredibly, against 150 years of precedent and in violation of the First Amendment, the Supreme Court at mid-twentieth century, by despotic decree, obliged them.

What shall I conclude, then? By the testimony of our nation's founders, by a great mass of both unofficial and organic utterances, and by the affirmation of the Supreme Court for over a century and a half, Christianity is the "indispensable support" for our free, self-governing republic. Then, at mid-twentieth century, five Supreme Court justices in one edict – the most ignominious in all American jurisprudence – commenced the replacement of that solid foundation with their own religious humanism, based on the shifting sand of the fallible and corruptible nature of man.

So, what is the question before the American people at the dawning of the twenty-first century? It is simply this: Shall we mend and defend our Christian foundations and save our free, self-governing republic; or, shall we surrender our government to an atheistic religion which denies the Creator and Sovereign of the Universe – the only possible source of "unalienable rights" that cannot be taken away at the whim of any despot?

Judges – The Ultimate Arbiters?

Thomas Jefferson. (*"Author of the Declaration of Independence," Third President of the United States*) You seem ... to consider the judges as the ultimate arbiters of all constitutional questions; a very dangerous doctrine, indeed, and one which would place us under the despotism of an oligarchy. [10]

H. Inquirer: Your evaluation of twentieth-century mentality is correct, Mr. Jefferson. In the twentieth century, we have been indoctrinated with the idea that the judges are the ultimate arbiters of constitutional questions.

One despot of their number brazenly declared, "We are under a Constitution, but the Constitution is what the judges say it is." [11]

The President and the Congress seem to be in slavish agreement. This mentality, along with enforcement powers of the courts, has indeed placed us largely under judicial despotism.

James Madison: This makes the Judiciary dept. paramount in fact to the Legislature, which was never intended, and can never be proper. [12]

Thomas Jefferson. Our judges are as honest as other men, but not more so . . . and their power the more dangerous, as they are in office for life and not responsible, as the other functionaries are, to the elective control. The Constitution has erected no such single tribunal, knowing that, to whatever hands confided, with corruptions of time and party, its members would become despots. [13]

H. Inquirer: Please allow me to say, Mr. Jefferson, you have a keen insight into the nature of man and his inherent bent to the corruption of power.

Very true, the Constitution has erected no single tribunal, unrestrained by the consent of the governed. It has failed, however, to place any restraint upon the Supreme Court – except the now-forgotten counterbalancing powers vested in the Executive and the Legislative branches, and its provision for the very difficult Constitutional amendment. Even the Constitutional amendment is not available to the people, if neither the Congress nor the State Legislatures will initiate it.

I understand you to say, sir, that not just one, but all three branches of the federal government are charged with the interpretation and defense of the Constitution.

Thomas Jefferson: Nothing in the Constitution has given them [the federal judges] a right to decide for the Executive, more than to the Executive to decide for them. . . . But the opinion which gives to the judges the right to decide what laws are constitutional, and what not, not only for themselves in their own sphere of action, but for the legislature and the executive also, in their spheres, would make the judiciary a despotic branch. [14]

The "Most Dangerous Branch"

H. Inquirer: In late twentieth century, the President is quite content to be the head of his political party, to rule over his vast bureaucracy, to extend it if he can, and to get himself re-elected. Our legislators likewise have built themselves cozy, lifetime nests in the Congress. They seem disinclined to disturb their special-interest constituents, or their self-endowed perks and privileges by challenging that "most dangerous branch." Or perhaps they no longer understand their duty to prevent abuse of power by the federal courts.

To be sure, the Constitution is not at fault here. The fault is, I believe as you stated, in the corruption of time and party, and (I might add) the power of deception and the apathy of the people.

If I may quote Dr. Franklin, you gentlemen examined the forms of republics, both ancient and modern, and found in all of them the seeds of their own dissolution. Is it possible that our American republic also contains the seed of its own dissolution?

Thomas Jefferson. The germ of dissolution of our federal government is in . . . the federal judiciary; an irresponsible body [for impeachment is scarcely a scarecrow] working like gravity by night and by day, gaining a little today and a little tomorrow, and advancing its noiseless step like a thief, over the field of jurisdiction, until all shall be usurped from the States. [15]

H. Inquirer: That, sir, is the unhappy state of our affairs at the end of the twentieth century.

Thomas Jefferson: I see . . . with the deepest affliction the rapid strides with which the federal branch of our government is advancing towards . . . the consolidation in itself of all powers, foreign and domestic. . . . The great object of my fear is the federal judiciary. That body, like gravity, ever acting with noiseless foot and unalarming advance, gaining ground step by step, and holding what it gains, is engulfing insidiously the special governments into the jaws of that which feeds them. [16]

H. Inquirer: Your insight and foresight is amazing, Mr. Jefferson. Sir, over 100 years before it happened, you have described the process exactly. Early in the twentieth century, the Supreme Court cast aside all judicial restraint, and started the creeping advance into judicial despotism, which you have just described.

Stealthily, the Court makes a small advance outside its Constitutional bounds, then, stops and holds steady. People who are not affected do not react at all, often totally unaware of any change in their government. People who are affected become agitated for a while, then settle once again into their easy chairs, thinking things really are not so bad after all, or feeling helpless to oppose the federal tyrants.

The despotic Court has gained ground and held what it has gained. And so it goes, step by step, until finally "government of the people, by the people, for the people" shall have "perished from the earth."

The Christian Response

H. Inquirer: The Christian response to the Court's assault on Christianity has been no different.

First, sectarian wrangling divided and conquered any concerted resistance by the Church. Christians who were aware of the threat to religious liberty were agitated for a while, but, with little leadership from the clergy, in time settled back into the supposed sanctuary of their church houses. Deceived, confused, and frustrated, multitudes refuse to get involved in their government at all.

While Christians sit cloistered in the supposed security of their church houses, outside, the sacking of their government by anti-Christian forces creeps steadily forward. And these forces are knocking at the church-house door. Religious liberty has been severely damaged by a despotic Court; and, the Court has held its ground.

To counterbalance powers and prevent judicial despotism, it seems to me that the President, by Executive order, and the Congress by Resolution, could, and should, declare the unconstitutional edicts of the Supreme Court to be null and void, and unenforceable against the people. It seems to me that the Constitution gives that power and duty to the Executive and the Legislative branches; but, I am unaware of any such action being taken in the twentieth century.

Thomas Jefferson: Both magistracies are equally independent in the sphere of action assigned to them. The judges, believing the law constitutional had a right to pass a sentence ... because that power was placed in their hands by the Constitution. But the Executive, believing the law to be unconstitutional, was bound to remit the execution of it, because that power has been confided in him by the Constitution. [17]

H. Inquirer: Could it be that the Presidents and the Congress are in collusion with the Court to concentrate all power in the federal government?

No Wall of Separation

H. Inquirer: The rapid strides with which the federal government advanced, consolidating all powers into itself, did not stop at the church house door. Judicial despots presume to dictate to the people where they may pray, erect a manger scene or menorah, sing Christmas carols at Christmas time, and many other acts of petty tyranny too numerous to name.
Holding the threat of taxation and legal action over churches, the tyrants presume to keep the clergy socially and politically correct. Petty tyrants – anti-Christian administrators and legal organizations – dutifully carry out the unconstitutional edicts of the judicial despots.

Thomas Jefferson: Believing with you that religion is a matter which lies solely between man and his God, that he owes account to none other for faith or his worship, that the legislative powers of government reach actions only, and not opinions, I contemplate with solemn reverence that act of the whole American people which declared that their legislature should "make no law respecting an establishment of religion, or prohibiting the free exercise thereof," thus building a wall of separation between Church and State. [68]

H. Inquirer: It is my sad duty to inform you, sir: Just 40 years after your departure from this earthly life, a horrible civil war, and the resulting amendments to the Constitution, breached that wall of separation between Church and State.

Another half century passed. Then, the Supreme Court – "like gravity, ever acting with noiseless foot and unalarming advance, gaining ground step by step, and holding what it gains" – discovered that breach and, in one despotic grab for power, engulfed the first ten amendments into the fourteenth.

The Bill of Rights, once the sacred possession of the people, has since been held in the despotic clutch of the nine justices on the Supreme Court – none willing to admit their error and reverse the wrongs of their predecessors.

Incredibly, Mr. Jefferson, to suppress the Christian religion, by some twisted logic, the Court stood upon your letter to the Danbury Baptists, regarding a "wall of separation between Church and State." and upon the First Amendment:

> Congress shall make no law respecting an establishment of religion, or prohibiting the free exercise thereof.

Please correct me if my reasoning is faulty. It seems evident to me that, when the Court presumes to interpret and enforce a law, after the people have expressly forbidden the Legislature to make a law, the Court usurps the power of the Legislature, and despotically rules without the consent of the governed.

Thomas Jefferson: I consider the government of the U. S. as interdicted [prohibited] by the Constitution from intermeddling with religious institutions, their doctrines, discipline, or exercises. This results not only from the provision that no law shall be made respecting the establishment, or free exercise, of religion [First Amendment], but from that also which reserves to the states the powers not delegated to the U. S. [Tenth Amendment].

Certainly no power to prescribe any religious discipline has been delegated to the general government. It must then rest with the states as far as it can be in any human authority. [18]

H. Inquirer: Searching the records of your Presidency, Mr. Jefferson, we have found no occasion of your attempting any separation of Church and State that remotely resembles the demands of twentieth-century courts.

Thomas Jefferson: In matters of religion I have considered that its free exercise is placed by the Constitution independent of the powers of the General government. I have therefore undertaken, on no occasion, to prescribe the religious exercise suited to it; but have left them, as the Constitution found them, under the direction and discipline of state and church authorities by the several religious societies. [19]

H. Inquirer: It naturally follows, then, that the Supreme Court acted outside its Constitutional bounds when it ruled on the exercise of religion. The Court should have, as the First Amendment requires, declared the issue outside its jurisdiction and refused to hear the case. But the judges' lust for despotic power could not be restrained; and, they (as Mr. Adams has stated it) broke through the Constitution as a whale goes through a net. In so doing, these honored guardians of the law became, themselves, the lawless ones.

Why the Silence?

H. Inquirer: I understand you to say, Mr. Jefferson, that the President and the Congress have equal power and responsibility with the Supreme Court to interpret and protect the sanctity of the Constitution.

That being the case, the President by executive order, and the Congress by resolution should have declared the Court out of Constitutional order, and their despotic edict null and void. But the silence of these two branches has been deafening.

If ever there was an act of tyranny begging for civil disobedience, it is the federal courts' actions against Christianity in America. But where were the Christians? Cloistered within their religious comfort zones?

Were there not enough Christians to pack every school house with a prayer meeting – enough to overflow every jail house? Where was Churchman Simon Peter ("We ought to obey God rather than man")? Where was Statesman Thomas Jefferson ("Rebellion to tyrants is obedience to God")?

Actually, some theologians have played into the secularists' hands by analyzing and comparing your Christianity with theirs. Striving to promote, or sometimes to alter, their own denominations, these theologians are prone to forget the Apostle Paul's admonition that Christians, comparing themselves among themselves, are not wise.

They are prone to forget that the roots of all Christians extend back through older denominations to the Catholic Church, thence back to the primitive Christianity of converted Jews; that many of their denominations did not exist or were in their infancy at the time of the nation's founding.

Perhaps these theologians simply overlook the fact that you gentlemen were Christian statesmen, not churchmen – that you spoke and wrote principally of God and State, not God and Church.

In any case, in their theological hair-splitting, they divide and conquer Christianity. They cast doubts upon the genuineness of your Christianity. They discourage Christian participation in the political process. Thus they aid the secularists in damaging our Christian foundations, upon which our free, self-governing republic stands.

The Duty of the Clergy

H. Inquirer: What do you gentlemen consider to be the role of the clergy in the realm of God and State?

John Adams: It is the duty of the clergy to accommodate their discourses to the times, to preach against such sins as are most prevalent, and recommend such virtues as are most wanted. For example, if exorbitant ambition and venality are predominant, ought they not to warn their hearers against those vices? [20]

H. Inquirer: It seems so to me, Mr. Adams.

Exorbitant ambition rode into the White House in 1992 with the President elected that year. And all indications are that corruption accompanied ambition. I say this because so many of the man's associates who accompanied him in his rise to political power were later dead, disgraced, or dismissed from office.

Yet this master politician survives, even as two investigations proceed: one concerning his integrity while Governor of Arkansas and the other, in Congress, concerning millions of campaign dollars, which his political party accepted from foreign governments (selling the White House as some have stated it). In addition, a private lawsuit is being brought against him concerning his sexual immorality and marital infidelity.

This politician survives, I believe, because of the corruptions of time and party, the power of deceit, and the apathy of the people. And objections from the clergy have been less than a whisper.

John Adams: If public spirit is much wanted, should [the clergy] not inculcate this great virtue? If the rights and duties of Christian magistrates and subjects are disputed, should they not explain them, show their nature, ends, limitations, and restrictions, how much soever it may move the gall of Massachusetts? [21]

H. Inquirer: I believe so, sir; and, Heaven knows public spirit has been woefully wanting in the better part of American Christendom throughout the twentieth century.

"When the righteous are in authority," the Scripture states, "the people rejoice." And where are the upright to be found if not in the churches where such virtues are inculcated? Would God, who is Sovereign over the State as well as the Church, put the righteous in charge of His Church and scoundrels in charge of His State?

Perhaps our seminaries should educate the clergy in Constitutional law and early American history as well as theology. Then they might be less likely to comply with whatever the judge or public administrator may misconstrue the law to be. They might be more able to discern tyranny and resist it. I understand that the clergy of your day were thus educated and so inspired and motivated their congregations.

It seems to me that, with a few notable exceptions, the best of the clergy of my day are largely withdrawn from public affairs. Thus they fail to speak out against evil politics and corrupt politicians and fail to challenge staunch Christians to participate in the process and seek public office.

The specter of the judge, the Internal Revenue Service, or party spirit in the churches may cause them to falter and shun their duty to promote righteous government.

"A Wolf by the Ears"

H. Inquirer: Before we continue, gentlemen, please allow me to say incidentally to Mr. Jefferson that I had the good pleasure of visiting Monticello recently. The great house has been restored as a tourist attraction; and it is in good repair. The clock in the foyer still keeps good time; and the cannonball weight on its power chain indicated that our visit was on a Thursday.

I think you will be pleased to know, Mr. Jefferson, that the slave shanties on Mulberry row have long since crumbled into dust; and their foundations have been buried by the sands of time. Slavery, that "peculiar institution," likewise is no more in America; although, I understand the evil practice still persists within Africa itself.

I understand, Mr. Jefferson, that, in writing the Declaration of Independence, you attempted to free the African slave, as well as the colonists, from oppression.

Thomas Jefferson: The clause [in the original draft of the Declaration] . . . reprobating the enslaving of the inhabitants of Africa was struck out in complaisance to South Carolina and Georgia, who had never attempted to restrain the importation of slaves, and who, on the contrary, still wished to continue it. Our Northern brethren also, I believe, felt a little tender under those censures; for though their people had very few slaves themselves, yet they had been pretty considerable carriers of them to others. [22]

What a stupendous, what an incomprehensible machine man is! who can endure, toil, famine, stripes, imprisonment, and death itself in vindication of his own liberty, and the next moment be deaf to all those motives whose power supported him through his trial and inflict on his fellow men a bondage one hour of which is fraught with more misery than ages of that which he rose in rebellion to oppose. [23]

H. Inquirer: A most compelling reason why we must ever keep our nation founded upon, and guided by the eternal principles of Christianity, and not upon the corruptible and fallible nature of man.

What do you think will become of slavery in America, Mr. Jefferson? Surely, nothing can be more inconsistent with the concepts of liberty.

Thomas Jefferson: Nothing is more certainly written in the book of fate than that these people are to be free. The whole commerce between master and slave is a perpetual exercise . . . of the most unremitting despotism on the one part, and degrading submission on the other. The Almighty has no attribute which can take side with us in such a contest. . . .

But it is impossible to be temperate and to pursue this subject through the various considerations of policy, of morals, of history natural and civil. We must be contented to hope they will force their way into everyone's mind. I think a change is already perceptible . . . the spirit of the master is abating, that of the slave rising from the dust, his condition mollifying, the way I hope preparing, under the auspices of heaven, for a total emancipation, and that this is disposed in the order of events to be with the consent of the masters rather than by their extirpation. As it is, we have a wolf by the ears, and we can neither hold him, nor safely let him go. [24]

H. Inquirer: Total emancipation did come, sir, just 40 short years after you departed this earthly life. But, sadly I must inform you, it did not come with the consent of the masters, but with a bloody civil war, and whether under the auspices of heaven, I cannot tell.

When you were born, Mr. Jefferson, the population of these colonies was about one million. In the War between the States, one half of that number, north and south, died in battle because of slavery and the smoldering political war between the Federalists and Antifederalists.

Most tragically, all Americans of all races, north and south, a century and a half later, are still suffering loss of original liberties because of transcendent power confiscated in war and reconstruction by the federal government.

Thomas Jefferson: Indeed I tremble for my country when I reflect that God is just; that his justice cannot sleep forever. [25]

H. Inquirer: If you gentlemen will favor me with another meeting tomorrow, we will adjourn now. I should like to meet with you again to accomplish the second purpose of my inquiry – a better acquaintance with George Washington.

8

MEET THE
COMMANDER-IN-CHIEF

"The general is one of the most important characters in the world;
upon him depend the liberties of America" *John Adams*

Humble Inquirer: Good morning, ladies and gentlemen –
founders of our nation and other eye-witnesses to these
events. Continuing yesterday's discourse, I trust you will give
me a better understanding of the life and times of George Washington
and your reasons for naming this man the "Father of our Country." I
hope to gain some insight into the manly qualities requisite to the President of the United States.

Assembled here today are both friends and former enemies of
George Washington.

Permit me to introduce our first guests. These two have traveled a
long path from the great council fires of their fathers in the land of
shades. One is the chief of all the Indian warriors who brought down

General Braddock of the mighty British army, but could not bring down the young Colonel Washington. With the chief is one of his warriors.

Let us briefly recall the scene of the Battle of Fort Duquesne on the river, Monongahela.

The British and Americans had marched into a trap set for them by the French and Indians in a shallow ravine near the fort. A sudden hail of musket balls from the invisible enemy, concealed in the dense trees, began to decimate the British ranks.

The withering fire continued; and soon, of General Braddock's three aides, one lay dead and another mortally wounded. His only remaining aide, the young Colonel Washington, was alone left to carry the General's orders to all parts of the battlefield.

When Braddock fell from his horse mortally wounded, every mounted officer but Washington had been shot dead from the saddle. Washington had two horses shot from under him and four bullet holes in his coat, but not so much as a scratch upon his body. In the face of blazing musket fire, Washington remounted and, with the 30 remaining Virginians, covered the panicked retreat of the routed British.

First, let the Indian warrior tell his story. Then the chief will repeat his experience as he personally related it to George Washington some years after the battle.

The Favorite of Heaven

Indian Warrior: Washington was never born to be killed by a bullet! I had seventeen fair fires at him with my rifle, and after all could not bring him to the ground! [1]

Indian Chief: I am a chief and ruler over my tribes. My influence extends to the waters of the great lakes and to the far blue mountains. I have traveled a long and weary path that I might see the young warrior of the great battle.

It was on the day when the white man's blood mixed with the streams of our forests that I first beheld this chief [Washington]. I called on my young men and said, mark yon tall and daring warrior? He is not of the red-coat tribe ... he hath an Indian's wisdom, and his warriors fight as we do ... himself alone is exposed. Quick, let your aim be certain, and he dies.

Our rifles were leveled, rifles which, but for you [Washington], knew not how to miss ... 'twas all in vain, a power mightier far than we, shielded you. Seeing you were under the special guardianship of the Great Spirit, we immediately ceased to fire at you.

I am old and soon shall be gathered to the great council fires of my fathers in the land of shades, but ere I go, there is something bids me speak in the voice of prophecy. Listen!

The Great Spirit protects that man [pointing at Washington], and guides his destinies . . . . he will become the chief of nations, and a people yet unborn will hail him as the founder of a mighty empire. I am come to pay homage to the man who is the particular favorite of Heaven, and who can never die in battle. [2]

H. Inquirer: Your words were indeed the voice of prophecy, great chief of Monongahela. The white man would extend his rule from the great waters toward the rising sun, to the great waters beyond the far blue mountains toward the going down of the sun – to the great icy waters far beyond the Great Lakes, to the great icy waters far beyond the place where the sun hangs low in the midday sky. In this vast land would be many nations; and George Washington was soon to become the father of the greatest of them all.

Great chief, all tribes would suffer much in this expansion of the white man's rule – the white, the black, and the first people to live on this land – your people most of all. But, alas, 'twas ever so from the first family of people to live on the earth, even in a state of nature – brother against brother, tribe against tribe.

I have seen it written in the white man's holy book, "The Lord is high above all nations." Wise chief, you have understood that it is best we leave the founding of nations to the supreme wisdom of the Great Spirit.

In my own veins, great chief, flows a little of the blood of the Cherokee; and, I can only say this:

Let us forgive all peoples of all times for our sins against one another, else we shall go on hating and killing one another 'til the last setting of the sun. Only let us choose men like the great Washington to rule. For such men know that they also will be judged by The Great Spirit who is high above all nations.

In Service to His Country

H. Inquirer: Coming events would soon prove Reverend Samuel Davies' premonition correct, "I may point out to the public that heroic youth, Colonel Washington, whom I cannot but hope Providence has hitherto preserved in so signal a manner for some important service to his country."

Soon his Majesty's redcoats would be marching, not against the Indians, but against our countrymen at Concord. If there were a man among you, "a particular favorite of Heaven," he must step forward now.

It was April, 1775. The poorly-trained, under-supplied, and disorganized Minutemen had harassed and driven a battalion of the British army from Concord back to Boston and were holding them under siege. All of you must have been solemnly aware that our militia merely held a lion by the tail, and the British lion would not be caged for long.

Having passed the point of no return in your rebellion against the tyrant king, you must have been haunted by a sense of impending doom. Where in the colonies could be found a man able to form an army strong enough to throw off the despotic yoke of the British Crown?

Even the much respected George Washington had little formal education, little formal instruction in military strategy, and relatively light and sporadic military experience. Yet the Continental Congress unanimously appointed him Commander-in-Chief of the Continental army.

I venture a guess that you appointed him on the strength of his character alone; or, perhaps you held the same conviction as the Indian chief, "The Great Spirit protects that man and guides his destinies."

It was not my good fortune to know George Washington as you know him. Nor could I find a suitable historian of the late twentieth century to acquaint me. I was privileged, however, to discover an able historian at mid-nineteenth century. This historian holds a decent respect for our nation's founders and our founders' God.

I have taken the liberty to invite him to our assembly. And now it is with great pleasure that I call historian George Bancroft from the year, 1858, to profile George Washington.

A Self-Made Man

George Bancroft: Washington was then [in 1775] forty-three years of age. In stature he a little exceeded six feet; his limbs were sinewy and well proportioned; his chest broad; his figure stately, blending dignity of presence with ease. His complexion was florid; his hair dark brown. . . . His dark blue eyes, which were deeply set, had an expression of resignation, and an earnestness that was almost sadness.

At eleven years old, left an orphan to the care of an excellent but unlettered mother, he grew up without learning. Of arithmetic and geometry he acquired just knowledge enough to be able to practice measuring land; but all his instruction at school taught him not so much as the orthography or rules of grammar of his own tongue. His culture was altogether his own work, and he was in the strictest sense a self-made man; yet from his early life he never seemed uneducated.

At sixteen he went into the wilderness as a surveyor, and for three years continued the pursuit, where the forests trained him, in meditative solitude, to freedom and largeness of mind; and nature revealed to him her obedience to serene and silent laws. In his intervals from toil, he seemed always to be attracted to the best men, and to be cherished by them. . . .

Courage was so natural to him, that it was hardly spoken of to his praise; no one ever at any moment of his life discovered in him the least shrinking in danger; and he had a hardihood of daring which escaped notice, because it was so enveloped in superior calmness and wisdom.

His hand was liberal; giving quietly and without observation, as though he was ashamed of nothing but being discovered in doing good. He was kindly and compassionate, and of lively sensibility to the sorrows of others. . . . While he was prodigal of himself; he was considerate of others; ever parsimonious of the blood of his countrymen.

The Essence of His Character

George Bancroft: His faculties were so well balanced and combined, that his constitution, free from excess, was tempered evenly with all the elements of activity, and his mind resembled a well ordered commonwealth. . . He had in his composition a calm, which gave him in moments of highest excitement the power of self-control, and enabled him to excel in patience, even when he had most cause for disgust.

In secrecy he was unsurpassed; but his secrecy had the character of prudent reserve, not of cunning or concealment.

Profoundly impressed with confidence in God's Providence, and exemplary in his respect for the forms of public worship, no philosopher of the eighteenth century was more firm in the support of freedom of religious opinion; none more tolerant, or more remote from bigotry; but belief in God and trust in His overruling power, formed the essence of his character.

Divine wisdom not only illumines the spirit, it inspires the will. Washington was a man of action, and not of theory or words; his creed appears in life, not in his professions, which burst from him very rarely, and only at those great moments of crisis in the fortunes of his country, when earth and heaven seemed actually to meet, and his emotions became too intense for suppression; but his whole being was one continued act of faith in the eternal, intelligent, moral order of the universe. Integrity was so completely the law of his nature, that a planet would sooner have shot from its sphere, than he have departed from his uprightness, which was so constant, that it often seemed to be almost impersonal.

The purity of his will confirmed his fortitude; and as he never faltered in his faith in virtue, he stood fast by that which he knew to be just; free from illusions; never dejected by the apprehensions of difficulties and perils that went before him, and drawing the promise of success from the justice of his cause. Hence he was persevering, leaving nothing unfinished; free from all taint of obstinacy in his firmness; seeking, and gladly receiving advice, but immovable in his devotedness to right.

Supporting the "Glorious Cause"

George Bancroft: Washington was offered a command when there was little to bring out the unorganized resources of the continent but his own influence, and authority was connected with the people by the most frail, most attenuated, scarcely discernable threads; yet vehement as was his nature, impassioned as was his courage, he so restrained his ardor, that he never failed continuously to exert the attracting power of that influence, and never exerted it so sharply as to break its force.

Washington saw at a glance the difficulties of the position to which he had been chosen. He was appointed by a government which, in its form, was one of the worst of all possible governments in time of peace, and was sure to reveal its defects still more plainly in time of war.

The congress had no ability whatever to enforce a decree of their own; they had no revenue, and no authority to collect a revenue; they had none of the materials of war; they did not own a cannon, nor a pound of powder, nor a tent, nor a musket; they had no regularly enlisted army, and had even a jealousy of forming an army, and depended on the zeal of volunteers, or of men to be enlisted for less than seven months. There were no experienced officers, and no methods projected for obtaining them.

Washington saw it all. He was in the enjoyment of fame; he wished not to forfeit the esteem of his fellow-men; and his eye glistened with a tear, as he said in confidence to Patrick Henry on occasion of his appointment: "This day will be the commencement of the decline of my reputation."

But this consideration did not make him waver. On the sixteenth of June, he appeared in his place in congress, and after refusing all pay beyond his expenses, he spoke with unfeigned modesty: "As the congress desire it, I will enter upon the momentous duty, and exert every power I possess in their service, and for the support of the glorious cause. But I beg it may be remembered by every gentleman in the room, that I declare, with utmost sincerity, I do not think myself equal to the command I am honored with."

The next day, the delegates of all the colonies resolved unanimously in congress "to maintain and assist him and adhere to him, the said George Washington, Esquire, with their lives and fortunes in the same cause."

Commander of America's Armies

George Bancroft: By his commission, he [Washington] was invested with the command over all forces raised or to be raised by the United Colonies, and with full power and authority to act as he should think for the good and welfare of the service; and he was instructed to take "special care that the liberties of America receive no detriment."

Washington knew that he must depend for success on a steady continuance of purpose in an imperfectly united continent, and on his personal influence over separate and half-formed governments, with most of which he was wholly unacquainted; he foresaw a long and arduous struggle; but a secret consciousness of his power bade him not to fear; and whatever might be the backwardness of others, he never admitted for a moment the thought of sheathing his sword or resigning his command, till his work of vindicating American liberty should be done.

To his wife he unbosomed his inmost mind: "I hope my undertaking this service is designed to answer some good purpose. I rely confidently on that Providence, which has heretofore preserved and been bountiful to me."

His acceptance at once changed the aspect of affairs. John Adams [looked] with complacency upon "the modest and virtuous, the amiable, generous, and brave general" as the choice of Massachusetts.

H. Inquirer: Do any of you gentlemen remember your words and thoughts at the time of General Washington's appointment?

Benjamin Franklin:(*a toast*)
To George Washington, Commander of the American armies, who like Joshua of old, commanded the sun and the moon to stand still and they obeyed him. [3]

John Adams: [His] appointment will have a great effect in cementing the union of these colonies. The general is one of the most important characters in the world; upon him depend the liberties of America. [4]

H. Inquirer: And not for your generation alone, Mr. Adams, but for your posterity (I sincerely hope) for as long as the world shall stand.

"A Man of God"

H. Inquirer: Ms. Potts?

Ruth Anna Potts: In 1777, while the American army lay at Valley Forge, a good old Quaker by the name of Potts [General Washington's landlord at Valley Forge] had occasion to pass through a thick woods near headquarters. As he traversed the dark green forest, he heard at a distance before him, a voice which as he advanced became more fervid and interested.

Approaching with slowness and circumspection, whom should he behold in a dark bower, apparently formed for the purpose, but the Commander-in-Chief of the armies of the United Colonies in the act of devotion to the Ruler of the Universe!

At a moment when Friend Potts, concealed in the trees, came up, Washington was interceding for his beloved country. With tones of gratitude that labored for adequate expression he adored that exuberant goodness which, from the depth of obscurity, had exalted him to the head of a great nation, and that nation fighting at fearful odds for all the world holds dear. . . .

Soon as the General had finished his devotions and had retired, Friend Potts returned to his house, and threw himself into a chair by the side of his wife.

"Height! Isaac!" said she with tenderness, "thee seems agitated; what's the matter?" [5]

Isaac Potts: Indeed, if I appear agitated 'tis no more than what I am. I have seen this day what I shall never forget. Till now I have thought that a Christian and a soldier were characters incompatible; but if George Washington be not a man of God, I am mistaken, and still more shall I be disappointed if God do not through him perform some great thing for this country. [6]

First in the Hearts of His Countrymen

James Madison: George Washington, who uniting to the endowments of the hero the virtues of the patriot, and exerting both in establishing the liberties of his country, has rendered his name dear to his fellow citizens, and given the world an immortal example of true glory. [7]

Major Henry Lee: First in war, first in peace, and first in the hearts of his countrymen. . . [8]

George Bancroft: All hearts turned with affection towards Washington. This is he who was raised up to be not the head of a party, but the father of his country.

There have been soldiers who achieved mightier victories in the field, and made conquests more nearly corresponding to the boundlessness of selfish ambition; statesmen who have connected with more startling upheavals of society; but it is the greatness of Washington, that in public trusts he used power solely for the public good; that he was the life, the moderator, and stay of the most momentous revolution in human affairs, its moving impulse and its restraining power.

This is also the praise of Washington; that never in the tide of time has any man lived who had in so great a degree the almost divine faculty to command the confidence of his fellow-men and rule the willing. Wherever he became known, in his family, his neighborhood, his country, his native state, the continent, the camp, civil life, the United States, among common people, in foreign courts, throughout the civilized world of the human race, and even among the savages, he, beyond all other men, had the confidence of his kind.

Finding the colonies disconnected and dependent, he left them such a united and well ordered commonwealth as no visionary had believed to be possible.

He studied his country and conformed to it. His countrymen felt that he was the best type of America, and rejoiced in it, and were proud of it. They lived in his life, and made his success and his praise their own. [9]

H. Inquirer: Exceedingly well done, Mr. Bancroft. All accounts confirm the accuracy of your historical record and profile of George Washington.

May we soon see the day when our educators will have done with their foolish obsession with social, cultural, and political correctness; when humanist courts will have proven the futility of their efforts to suppress Christianity; when your fine history books will be reprinted and once more read in every American classroom.

To Remotest Ages

H. Inquirer: I recall the words of General Washington, upon re-signing as Commander-in-Chief of the Continental Army, the momentous task accomplished: "I consider it an indispensable duty to close this last act of my official life by commending the interests of our dearest country to the protection of Almighty God, and those who have the superintendence of them to his holy keeping." [10]

Mr. Mifflin, do you recall your response to General Washington on occasion of his resignation?

Thomas Mifflin: (*Signer of the Constitution, President of Congress,* – in reply to Washington's resignation speech)

Having defended the standard of liberty in this new world; having taught a lesson useful to those who inflict and to those who feel oppression, you retire from the great theatre of action, with the blessings of your fellow-citizens; but the glory of your virtues will not terminate with your military command; it will continue to animate remotest ages. [11]

H. Inquirer: Let us hope so, Mr. Mifflin, let us sincerely hope so.

Perhaps it will be so, if we can somehow overcome the academic treachery of the twentieth century.

King George of America?

H. Inquirer: So ended the War for American Independence.

George Washington held America and the hearts of the people in his hand. A story has persisted for over two centuries that the officers and soldiers of the Continental Army, with the approval of the people, would have crowned George Washington, King George of America. Only his abhorrence of the thought prevented them.

Thomas Jefferson: The moderation and virtue of a single character [Washington] prevented this Revolution from being closed, as most others have been, by a subversion of that liberty it was intended to establish. [12]

H. Inquirer: Gentlemen, having been taught early American history before treacherous professors of the twentieth century trashed it – and before cynics became the scourge of America – I share your high esteem for the "Father of our Country."

I should consider it the highest honor, if I might have an audience with our first President.

Could you, who personally know him, possibly be persuaded to arrange such an audience? Who knows whether he will again rise to the aid of his countrymen from the pleasant shades of Mount Vernon.

Before I depart, please permit me to express my heart-felt gratitude to all who have contributed to my understanding of your Christian faith, your courage, and your concepts of government. Our founding fathers' faith in God and passion for liberty for themselves and their posterity will now be evident to all honest people after hearing your own words.

Reverend Witherspoon, in dismissing this assembly, will you please offer a short prayer for us.

Rev. John Witherspoon: (*Signer of the Declaration of Independence, President of Princeton University*): God grant that in America true religion and civil liberty may be inseperable and that the unjust attempts to destroy the one, may in the issue tend to the support and establishment of both. [13]

H. Inquirer: Amen.

9

GEORGE WASHINGTON SPEAKS

"I am sure that never was a people, who had more reason to acknowledge a Divine interposition in their affairs, than those of the United
States; and I should be pained to believe that they have forgotten that
agency, which was so often manifested during our Revolution, or that
they failed to consider the omnipotence of that God who is alone able
to protect them." *George Washington*

Humble Inquirer: Mr. President, from the remnant of a grateful posterity, I bring you choice greetings from the dawning
of the twenty-first century.

Overlooking the peaceful Potomac from your back verandah, I must
say your home is one of the most pleasant retreats in all our fair land.
My reception here has been most cordial.

You, sir, and Mrs. Washington are ranked as the nation's most gracious and most popular hosts. Your diary, I am told, records an incred-
ible 423 house guests for the year 1785.

George Washington: [My home] is a well resorted tavern [inn], as scarcely any strangers who are going from north to south, or from south to north, do not spend a day or two at it. [1]

Mrs. Washington is well and desires her compliments may be presented to you. We wish the happiness of your fireside, as we also long to enjoy that of our own at Mount Vernon. [2]

H. Inquirer: So much of your time and happiness you sacrificed to the service of your country, Mr. President. Your posterity has been blessed by that sacrifice for over two centuries.

You will be pleased to know, sir, that your home at Mount Vernon has been restored and is being maintained as a national shrine in near original condition. In the caring hands of the Mount Vernon Ladies' Association it receives over a million visitors each year. My sincere prayer for these visitors is that they will imbibe the same spirit of civility, hospitality, and devotion to God and country that filled this great house when you and Mrs. Washington lived here.

George Washington: Our wishes, you know, were limited; and I think that our plans of living will now be deemed reasonable by the considerate part of our species. Her wishes coincide with my own as to simplicity of dress, and everything which can tend to support propriety of character without partaking of the follies of luxury and ostentation. [3]

I had rather glide gently down the stream of life, leaving it to posterity to think and say what they please of me, than by any act of mine to have vanity or ostentation imputed to me. [4]

A Sincere Believer

H. Inquirer: I was privileged to sit in your pew at Pohick Episcopal Church recently and hear a good sermon by a visiting minister from England, whose name I cannot recall. I am informed that you helped to build Pohick church, regularly attended divine services and recited the Apostle's Creed, and served as vestryman for 20 years.

Some twentieth-century theologians, not able to reconcile your terminology with theirs in speaking of God, seek to cast a shadow on your Christian orthodoxy. But please take no offense, sir, some of these theologians are ignorant of the damage they are doing. Others are more Humanist than Christian and deliberately seek to damage the Christian foundations of our republic.

While strolling over the grounds of Mount Vernon, I observed this inscription above your final earthly resting place: "I am the Resurrection and the Life, sayeth the Lord. He that believeth in Me, though he were dead yet shall he live. And whosoever liveth and believeth in Me shall never die" John 11:25.

Assurance of resurrection from the dead by faith in Jesus Christ is strong evidence of Christian orthodoxy. You are surrounded by a great cloud of witnesses, testifying to the genuineness of your faith.

To quote just one, John Marshall, fellow revolutionary soldier and later Chief Justice of the United States has this to say: "Without making ostentatious professions of religion, he [Washington] was a sincere believer in the Christian faith, and a truly devout man." [5]

With these comments, sir, I shall simply let you speak for yourself.

On God's Providential Care

H. Inquirer: Two Indian warriors, in my meeting with your compatriots, related an amazing story concerning the preservation of your life in the Battle of Fort Duquesne. After countless attempts to bring you down, they gave up the effort, convinced that you were under the special care of "The Great Spirit." Is this a true story, sir, or merely the superstition of savages?

George Washington: By the all-powerful dispensations of Providence, I have been protected beyond all human probability or expectations; for I had four bullets through my coat, and two horses shot under me, yet escaped unhurt, although death was leveling my companions on every side. [6]

H. Inquirer: Reverend Muhlenberg, Lutheran pastor near Valley Forge was heard to say, "The Lord God has also singularly, yea, marvelously, preserved him [Washington] from harm in the midst of countless perils, ambuscades, fatigues, etc., and has hitherto graciously held him in His hand as a chosen vessel." [7]

Perhaps the Indian chief spoke true prophecy when proclaiming that George Washington could never die in battle.

George Washington: (remembering the war) No history, now extant, can furnish an instance of an Army's suffering such uncommon hardships as ours have done, and bearing them with the same patience and Fortitude. To see Men without Clothes to cover their nakedness, without Blankets to lay on, without Shoes, by which their Marches might be traced by the Blood from their feet, and almost as often without Provisions as with; Marching through frost and Snow, and at Christmas taking up their Winter Quarters within a day's March of the enemy, without a House or Hutt to cover them till they could be built and submitting to it without murmur, is a mark of patience and obedience which in my opinion can scarce be paralleled. [8]

The singular interpositions of providence in our feeble condition were such, as could scarcely escape the attention of the most unobserving; while the unparalleled perseverence of the Armies of the U States, through almost impossible suffering and discouragement for the space of eight long years, was little short of a standing miracle. [9]

Disposed at every suitable opportunity to acknowledge publicly our infinite obligations to the Supreme Ruler of the Universe for rescuing our Country from the brink of destruction; I cannot fail at this time to ascribe all the honor of our late success to the same glorious Being. [10]

I am sure that never was a people, who had more reason to acknowledge a Divine interposition in their affairs, than those of the United States; and I should be pained to believe that they have forgotten that agency, which was so often manifested during our Revolution, or that they failed to consider the omnipotence of that God who is alone able to protect them. [11]

H. Inquirer: May we never forget, sir. And may the people forever stand ready to defend their liberties against enemies without and tyrants within, with heartfelt obedience to God, who alone can protect us.

On Political Ambition

George Washington: Where is the man to be found, who wishes to remain indebted, for the defense of his own person and property, to the exertions, the bravery, and the blood of others? [12]

H. Inquirer: In the White House, sir. It took much corruption of time and party for enough people to become so ungrateful or deceived; but in 1992 they elevated such a man to the Presidency, – or better stated, they lowered the Presidency to such a man. This man received less than a majority of the popular vote; but, the Electoral College – an outdated system by the end of the twentieth century – elected him.

So far as I know, sir, you are the only person ever elected unanimously to the Presidency, and that without political campaigning, or the interference of a political party.

George Washington: It appears to me, that it would be a favorable circumstance, if the character of Candidates could be known, without their having a pretext for coming forward themselves with personal applications. We should seek to find the Men who are best qualified to fill offices. [13]

H. Inquirer: Political campaigning has been totally corrupted by the end of the twentieth century. Ad men "sell" candidates as a product. This method requires huge sums of money; and, elections are more bought by the biggest spender than won by the best character.

To elect the President in 1996, huge sums were contributed by special-interest groups; and, the winner's party accepted millions of dollars from a foreign government known to be at political enmity with the United States. You can imagine, sir, the kind of government we get from this political cesspool.

Ignoring the damage done by political snake oil salesmen, Congress will not act to reform campaign laws. They, too, like to build their campaign "war chests." from whatever source will contribute.

It seems that soon after your administration, men began to clamor for election to public office. In any case, so it is in my generation – for what reasons, I cannot tell.

George Washington: All see, and most admire, the glare which hovers round the external trappings of elevated office. To me there is nothing in it, beyond the lustre which may be reflected from its connection with power of promoting human felicity. [14]

Pride and dignity of office. . . . God knows has no charms for me. . . for I can truly say I had rather be at Mount Vernon with a friend or two about me, than to be attended at the Seat of Government by the Officers of State and the Representatives of every Power in Europe. [15]

Small indeed must be the resources for happiness in the mind of that man, who cannot find a refuge from the tediousness of solitude but in a sound of dissipation, the pomp of state, or the homage of fellowmen. [16]

On the Media

H. Inquirer: Sir, I think you have been describing the man elected to the Presidency in 1992. But journalists convinced the people that respectable character in elected officials is not essential, and millions of otherwise good people were deceived into voting for the man.

It seems that you also had your share of problems with the media, as you confided in Oliver Wolcott, "There is little dependence on newspaper publications, (which take whatever complexion the editors please to give them)."

Twentieth-century technology, called television, allows us to both see and hear the news continually, 24 hours a day, and in our own homes. With the ability to see with one's own eyes, one would think it possible to get the story straight. But television editors are no different from newspaper editors.

Television broadcasts, as well as newspapers, take whatever complexion the editors please to give them. This is accomplished by what they show and what they do not, and from what perspective. With this medium, omissions, tone of voice, and bodily gestures carry a powerful interpretation of the news. Apparently not much has changed in the media in two centuries except technology, which makes mass manipulation instantly possible.

On Motivation to Public Service

H. Inquirer: I am convinced, sir, that your service to your country was not motivated by pride nor vain glory. Clearly you were not motivated by money. The record shows that you served eight years as Commander-in-Chief of the Continental Army and eight years as President of the United States, a total of 16 years without pay.

George Washington: When I was first honored with a call into the service of my country, then on the eve of an arduous struggle for its liberties, the light in which I contemplated my duty, required that I should renounce every pecuniary compensation. From this resolution I have in no instance departed. [17]

H. Inquirer: But you never insisted that others serve the public without pay.

George Washington: The compensations to the officers of the United States, in various instances, and in none more than in respect to the most important stations, appear to call for legislative revision. The consequences of a defective provision are of serious import to the Government. [18]

H. Inquirer: Congress, being in charge of their own compensation, are paying themselves pretty well. Not that their salaries are exorbitant; but, considering perks, privileges, and pensions, they do quite well for themselves.

I have come to question the wisdom of allowing any public official to set his own salary out of the public till. Perhaps questions of pay and term limits for Congress should be returned to the authority of state legislatures, as it was under the Articles of Confederation.

Campaign laws, likewise, for representatives to Congress might be handled better by the state represented. "If you cannot vote, you cannot contribute money to the campaign" might be a good rule, accompanied by limits on individual contributions within the represented district. Special interests outside the district would be excluded. Nor could wealthy persons within the district buy elections. Hence our offices might be filled with talent and virtue rather than wealth and corruption.

George Washington: It would be repugnant to the vital principles of our Government, virtually to exclude from public trusts, talents and virtue, unless accompanied by wealth. [19]

H. Inquirer: Not all men share your selfless devotion to their country, Mr. President. Can you tell us what motivated yours?

George Washington: After a consciousness that all is right within and an humble hope of approbation of Heaven . . . nothing can, assuredly, be so grateful to a virtuous man as the good opinion of his fellow citizens Tho' the partiality of mine led them to consider my holding the Chief Magistry as a matter of infinitely more consequence than it really is; yet my acceptance must be ascribed rather to an honest willingness to satisfy that partiality, than to an overweening presumption upon my own capacity. [20]

It would be peculiarly improper to omit . . . my fervent supplication to that Almighty Being who rules over the universe . . . who presides in the councils of nations . . . and whose providential aids can supply every human defect. [21]

H. Inquirer: (*musing silently*) Could this farmer be elected President at the beginning of the twenty-first century? He has no college degree, no experience in civil administration, no political organization, no campaign manager, no PAC money; he speaks of God's abilities, not his own; and he would rather be home at Mount Vernon. He must possess some quality greater than all these, perhaps some strength of character hard to find in twentieth-century America, but essential to building public confidence.

George Washington: Whenever a government is to be instituted or changed by Consent of the people, confidence in the person placed at the head of it, is, perhaps, more peculiarly necessary. [22]

H. Inquirer: I have no doubt about it, sir. I believe you were placed Providentially in a unique position, at the exact time and place in world history: first, to liberate the colonies, then, to preside over the writing of the Constitution, organizing and limiting the powers of the federal government.

On the Foundation of Government

George Washington: Of all the dispositions and habits which lead to political prosperity, Religion and morality are indispensable supports. In vain would that man claim the tribute of Patriotism, who should labour to subvert these great Pillars of human happiness, these firmest props of the duties of Men and citizens. And let us with caution indulge the supposition, that morality can be maintained without religion. [23]

H. Inquirer: Twentieth-century cynics ridicule the tribute of patriotism. And since the middle of the twentieth century, Christianity – the "indispensable support" of our nation – has been under attack by the Supreme Court and by anti-Christian administrators and legal organizations, enforcing the Court's decree. While Christianity is suppressed, Humanism, an atheistic philosophy, is given free course in all public institutions. Humanists admit to the difficulty of maintaining a necessary level of morality without the support of religion. They think they can create some sort of morality through education.

George Washington: Whatever may be conceded to the influence of refined education on minds of peculiar structure, reason and experience both forbid us to expect that National Morality can prevail in exclusion of religious principle. [24]

H. Inquirer: I understand that when you speak of religion, you mean Christianity, the only significant religion of our nation's founders. It is the consensus of the founders that the principles of Christianity are the foundations of the United States.

On Christianity and the Constitution

George Washington: No people can be bound to acknowledge and adore the invisible hand which conducts the affairs of men, more than the people of the United States. Every step by which they have advanced to the character of an independent nation, seems to have been distinguished by some token of providential agency; and in the important revolution just accomplished in the system of their united government [the Constitution], the tranquil deliberations, and voluntary consent of so many distinct communities, from which the event has resulted, cannot be compared with the means by which most governments have been established, without some return of pious gratitude.

These reflections, arising out of the present crisis, have forced themselves too strongly upon my mind to be suppressed. You will join me, I trust, in that there are none, under the influence of which the proceedings of a new and free government can more auspiciously commence. [25]

H. Inquirer: I join you, sir, in grateful acknowledgment of God, who guided the establishment of our free, self-governing republic, upon the eternal principles of Christianity. I can see clearly the Presbyterian and the Congregational order in our Constitutional system.

I recall the words of Alexander Hamilton, your Aide-de-Camp during the war, who was later called "Ratifier of the Constitution:"

For my own part, I sincerely esteem it [the Constitution] a system which without the finger of God, could never have been suggested and agreed upon by such a diversity of interests.... In my opinion, the present constitution is the standard to which we are to cling. Under its banner bona fide must we combat our political foes, rejecting all changes but through the channel itself provided for amendments. By these general views of the subject have my reflections been guided.

I now offer you the outline of the plan they have suggested. Let an association be formed to be denominated "The Christian Constitutional Society," its object to be first: the support of the Christian religion. second: The support of the United States. [26]

As we enter the twenty-first century, I think the political foes of the Constitution would brand such a Christian Coalition the "Radical Religious Right." My own preference is that a system be devised for filling public office and executing official duties, without the interference of political parties. If we must have political parties, there should be one party whose sole purpose is to maintain our Christian foundations and the integrity of our common-sense, plain English Constitution. Such a party might be denominated "The Constitutional Party."

The twentieth-century political monopoly, the Democratic and the Republican parties, despite their idealized names, gives mostly lip service to the stated purpose. Although, at the end of the twentieth century, in my studied opinion, the Republican Party is the more reliable of the two.

George Washington: My creed is simply, 1st. That the general Government is not invested with more Powers than are indispensably necessary to perform the functions of a good government; and, consequently, that no objection ought to be made against the quantity of Power delegated to it.

2nd. That these Powers (as the appointment of all Rulers will forever arise from, and at short intervals, recur to the free suffrage of the People) are so distributed among the Legislative, Executive, and Judicial Branches, into which the general Government is arranged, that it can never be in danger of degenerating into a monarchy, an Oligarchy, an Aristocracy, or any other despotic or oppressive form, so long as there shall remain any virtue in the body of the People. [27]

H. Inquirer: But let us suppose that the smoldering enmity between the Federalists and Antifederalists, aggravated by the institution of slavery and sectional animosities, should break into a horrible Civil War. And suppose that, in that war, the last precept of the Antifederalists should be crushed, and that the Constitution should be altered, not by the informed consent of the governed, but by conquest of war.

Let us suppose further that by a series of political appointments, our federal courts should become filled with judges of a particular social and political bent, incompatible with the common-sense, plain English of the Constitution, and having an inclination to despotism.

Time would prove Thomas Jefferson's foresight to be correct. The Judicial branch would become a despotic oligarchy, and the seed of dissolution of the federal government would be planted in that branch, if the Executive and the Legislative branches were not diligent to prevent them.

On Religion, Morality, and Government

George Washington: I would not be understood . . . to speak of consequences which may be produced, in the revolution of ages, by corruption of morals, profligacy of manners, and listlessness for the preservation of the natural and unalienable rights of mankind; nor for the successful usurpations that may be established at such an unpropitious juncture, upon the ruins of liberty, however providently guarded and secured, as these are contingencies against which no human prudence can effectually provide. [28]

H. Inquirer: It naturally follows, then, that the first sign of despotism in the federal government is a sign of moral degeneracy in the people; that is to say, immorality produces listlessness for the preservation of God-given rights, and renders the people incapable of self-government.

As John Adams stated it, "Our Constitution was made only for a moral and religious people. It is wholly inadequate to the government of any other."

George Washington: Of all the dispositions and habits which lead to political prosperity, Religion and morality are indispensable supports. The mere Politician, equally with the pious man ought to respect and cherish them. A volume could not trace all their connections with private and public felicity. [29]

No Country upon Earth ever had it more in its power to attain these blessings than United America. Wondrously strange then, and much to be regretted indeed would it be, were we to neglect the means, and to depart from the road which Providence has pointed us to, so plainly; I cannot believe it will ever come to pass. The great Governor of the Universe has led us too long and too far on the road to happiness and glory, to forsake us in the midst of it. By folly and improper conduct, proceeding from a variety of causes, we may now and then get bewildered; but I hope and trust that there is good sense and virtue enough left to recover the right path before we shall be entirely lost. [30]

H. Inquirer: So do I, Mr. President, so do I.

George Washington: With slight shades of difference, you have the same Religion, Manners, habits and political Principles. [31]

H. Inquirer: This was true in your day, Mr. President, and for the next century and a half, when America was known as a Christian nation. But beginning in the nineteenth century and gaining power in the twentieth, a deviant religious and political philosophy has caused America to veer seriously off her original path.

By the end of the twentieth century, this philosophy, at enmity with our Christian principles, is entrenched in high public office. Its official suppression of Christianity, and the steady stream of immorality it pours into American homes via television, have made it increasingly difficult for the Church to inculcate those virtues that make a free people self-governing.

Observing these conditions, sir, my fear is not that God will forsake America, but that America shall forsake God. Still, I share your hope that the good people will rise up and put down the despots that oppose our Christian foundations, pervert our Constitution, and destroy our liberties.

George Washington: If I could now conceive that the general government might ever be so administered as to render the liberty of conscience insecure, I beg you will be persuaded that no one would be more zealous than myself to establish effectual barriers against the horrors of spiritual tyranny, and every species of religious persecution. The liberty enjoyed by the people of these states of worshipping God agreeably to their consciences, is not only among the choicest of their blessings, but also of their rights. [32]

H. Inquirer: I believe that you and the other founders of the nation so revered this bedrock human right that you considered it requisite to all other liberties – that losing religious liberty places all other liberties at extreme risk. In any case you placed freedom of religion as Number One in the Bill of Rights.

On Christianity and the Courts

H. Inquirer: No would-be despot in the federal government dared meddle with the people's religion until the middle of the twentieth-century. Then, in defiance of the First Amendment, the Supreme Court, began a crusade to eradicate Christianity and the Bible from all public places in America.

The most common victims of this tyranny are the little children in public schools. I could relate thousands of cases of religious tyranny, in its many forms, by the end of the century. Just one case will illustrate the point. In 1995, a judge in Mississippi was hailed into federal court for refusing to remove the Ten Commandments from his court house walls.

George Washington: Let it simply be asked where is the security for property, for reputation, for life, if the sense of religious obligation desert the oaths, which are the instruments of investigation in Courts of Justice? [33]

H. Inquirer: I know not, sir, and apparently, neither does the Supreme Court. In another case, a murderer was released upon his next victim because the prosecuting attorney quoted the Bible to the jury.

While the Court seems determined to destroy freedom of religion and the right to bear arms, other liberties are pushed to the extreme, until the intended sublime becomes the ridiculous. Every vile speech and lewd action is sanctioned, under guise of freedom of speech. Known criminals are released to prey upon the people if there is the slightest supposed infringement of their fourth amendment rights.

It seems that the judges are so confused (or reprobate) that they bind that which should be free and loose that which should be bound. Has our jurisprudence gone mad, or what?

George Washington: Liberty, when it degenerates into licentiousness, begets confusion, and frequently ends in Tyranny or some woeful catastrophe. [34]

H. Inquirer: The assault on religious liberty started a chain reaction, which is destroying or perverting all other liberties – either by the Court's ridiculous overindulgence, or by unconstitutional government infringement. Removing the linchpin – religious liberty – is causing the whole structure to collapse, all liberties falling as a line of dominos.

George Washington: If I could have entertained the slightest apprehension that the Constitution framed in the Convention, where I had the honor to preside, might possibly endanger the religious rights of any ecclesiastical society, certainly I would never have placed my signature to it. [35]

10

POLITICS AND THE
FIRST PRESIDENT

"It is a fact too notorious to be concealed, that Congress is rent by
party, that much business of a trifling nature and personal concernments withdraws their attention from matters of great national interest at this critical period. . .the common and continual mischiefs of
the spirit of Party are sufficient to make it the interest and the duty
of wise People to discourage and restrain it." *George Washington.*

Humble Inquirer: As America's first President, Mr. Washington, and presiding over a new nation like none before it in
history, you had no precedent to guide you. It must have
been an awesome and sometimes baffling experience.

George Washington: There is scarcely any part of my conduct which
may not hereafter be drawn into precedent. Under such a view of the
duties inherent to my arduous office, I could not but feel a diffidence
[lack of confidence] in myself on the one hand; and an anxiety for the

Community that every arrangement should be made in the best possible manner on the other. If after all my humble but faithful endeavours to advance the felicity of my Country and mankind, I may indulge a hope that my labours have not been altogether without success, it will be the only real compensation I can receive in the closing of life. [1]

H. Inquirer: I repeat my conviction that God placed you in a unique position at a momentous time and place in world history, among other things, to set precedents for future Presidents in godly character – in selfless devotion, in wisdom, in humility, in integrity, in morality, in good manners, in marital fidelity. No wonder your countrymen named you the "Father of our Country."

George Washington: Still I hope I shall always possess firmness and virtue enough to maintain (what I consider the most enviable of all titles) the character of an honest man. [2]

On Moral Leadership

H. Inquirer: I think moral leadership from the President is essential if we are to maintain that level of national morality necessary for self-government. Few, if any, of our Presidents have attained your level of moral integrity. None have so completely commanded the respect of their countrymen as you did. While our nation may have many leaders, it can have only one Father.

Some of our Presidents have had a temporary lapse into marital infidelity; but, none, to my knowledge, to compare with the Presidents elected in 1960 and 1992.

In 1960, an unabashed and unrepentant womanizer was elected President. This man had no regard for his marital vows, which may be basic to moral integrity. He was the political idol of the 1960s generation – the same generation that rebelled against moral authority, cast off moral restraints, and started our societal slide into moral depravity. That same decade the official assault on our Christian foundations began in earnest. Let the honest conclude what are the connections.

In 1992, a man of like moral character, the political idol of his generation, was elected President. This man's character was known to the voting public; but the media shrugged it off as not an issue. His party assigned a "bimbo squad" to hush the truth, and branded Christian objectors as "The Radical Religious Right." The media loved the man and dutifully heralded his message, "It's the economy, stupid."

The first official act of this President was to officially sanction sodomy. He has also adamantly supported that evil institution, abortion – even vetoed a bill, outlawing partial-birth abortion, which had passed the Senate with only one vote short of a two-thirds majority.

Are we about to slip deeper into the dark abyss of moral depravity, when we shall no longer be able to govern ourselves?

Regarding sodomy, we found the following in your military records:

> Lieutt. Enslin of Colo. Malcolm's Regiment tried for attempting to commit sodomy, with John Monhort a soldier . . . found guilty of the charges exhibited against him, being breaches of 5th. Article 18th. Section of the Articles of War and do sentence him to be dismiss'd the service with Infamy. His Excellency the Commander in Chief [George Washington] approves the sentence and with Abhorrence and Detestation of such Infamous Crimes orders Lieutt. Enslin to be drummed out of Camp tomorrow morning by all the Drummers and Fifers in the Army never to return; The Drummers and Fifers to attend on the Grand parade at Guard mounting for that Purpose. [3]

What shall be our end if we continue to elect leadership devoid of moral integrity, and the courts continue to sanction immoral behavior under the guise of protecting liberty?

George Washington: We shall be left nearly in a state of Nature, or we may find by our own unhappy experience, that there is a natural and necessary progression, from the extreme of anarchy to the extreme of Tyranny; and that arbitrary power is most easily established on the ruins of Liberty abused to licentiousness. [4]

H. Inquirer:(*musing silently*)
Are our rulers abysmally ignorant of these things, or could they be deliberately demoralizing the people, so that they may rule with arbitrary power?

On Constitutional Balance of Power

George Washington: [The] Constitution, is really in its formation a government of the people; that is to say, a government in which all power is derived from, and at stated periods reverts to them. [5]

The basis of our political systems is the right of the people to make and to alter their Constitutions of Government. [6]

The power under the Constitution will always be in the People. It is entrusted for certain defined purposes, and for a certain limited period, to representatives of their own chusing; and whenever it is executed contrary to their Interest, or not agreeable to their wishes, their Servants can, and undoubtedly will be, recalled. [7]

H. Inquirer: Government of the People, by the People, for the People, as a later President would state it. But the Constitution did not give the people the power of recall over elected representatives; and, federal judges are not elected by the people, but appointed to the courts for life by the President.

The words of Thomas Jefferson have proven to be accurate, "Impeachment is scarcely a scarecrow." So there is little chance for the people to depose tyrants on the federal bench.

George Washington: I have always believed that an unequivocally free and equal Representation of the People in the Legislature, together with an efficient and responsible Executive, were the great Pillars on which the preservation of American Freedom must depend. [8]

H. Inquirer: Then you agree with Jefferson that the Supreme Court is not the final arbiter of the Constitution, as has become the system in the twentieth century. Rather, the primary responsibility to interpret and uphold the Constitution rests with the people's elected representatives, the President and the Congress. The Constitution is, after all, the property of the people, not the possession of any functionary, elected or appointed.

On Judicial Despotism

H. Inquirer: Mr. President, a condition has arisen in the twentieth century anticipated by only a few of the founders, most notably Mr. Jefferson and Mr. Madison. The Judicial branch has cast off its traditional judicial restraint; and, anxious to enforce their own concepts of social and political correctness, have usurped both the lawmaking power of the Legislature and the enforcement power of the Executive.

Neither the Executive nor the Legislative branch seems inclined to stop this usurpation of power. I sometimes think the creation of Congress has become its master, unrestrained by the elective process.

George Washington: The complete organization of the Judicial Department was by the Constitution to the ulterior [later] arrangement of Congress. [Congress] will be pleased therefore to let a supreme regard for equal justice and the inherent rights of the citizens be visible in all your proceedings on that important subject. [9]

It is important, likewise, that the habits of thinking in a free Country should inspire caution in those entrusted with the administration, to confine themselves within their respective Constitutional spheres; avoiding in the exercise of the Powers of one department to encroach upon another. The spirit of encroachment tends to consolidate the powers of all the departments in one, and thus to create, whatever the form of government, a real despotism. [10]

H Inquirer: In our elective system, it is difficult for a President or the Congress to become despotic. The Judiciary is quite another matter, being appointed for life and being considered the final arbiters of the Constitution, rarely, if ever, opposed by the President and/or the Congress.

A judicial despotism in America? Is it possible?

George Washington: A just estimate of that love of power, and proneness to abuse it, which predominates in the human heart is sufficient to satisfy us of the truth of this position. The necessity of reciprocal checks in the exercise of political power; by dividing and distributing it into different depositories, and constituting each the Guardian of the Public Weal against invasions by the others, has been evinced by experiments ancient and modern; some of them in our country and under our own eyes. To preserve them must be as necessary as to institute them.

If in the opinion of the people, the distribution or modification of the Constitutional powers be in any particular wrong, let it be corrected by an amendment in the way which the Constitution designates. But let there be no change by usurpation; for though this, in one instance, may be the instrument of good, it is the customary weapon by which free governments are destroyed. [11]

H. Inquirer: I am coming to agree with those who are calling for term limits for federal judges, and for a Constitutional amendment to effect the same. Perhaps term limits would not be necessary if Congress would exercise its impeachment power over federal judges who profane the Constitution.

On "Party Spirit" in Politics

George Washington: It is a fact too notorious to be concealed, that Congress is rent by party, that much business of a trifling nature and personal concernments withdraws their attention from matters of great national interest at this critical period. When it is also known that idleness and dissipation takes place of close attention and application, no man who wishes well to the liberties of his Country and desires to see its rights established, can avoid crying out where are our Men of abilities? Why do they not come forth to save their Country?

Let this voice my dear Sir call upon you – and others; do not from a mistaken opinion that we are about to set down under our own vine and fig tree and let our hitherto noble struggle end in ignominy; believe me when I tell you there is danger in it. [12]

H. Inquirer: What can I say, sir? It is ingrained in human nature to feather one's own nest. There are always too few George Washingtons among us.

Mr. President, in making its own rules, Congress has allowed what is, to me, a strange development. When this strange rule was first instituted, I cannot tell. I only know I cannot find it in the Constitution. It is called "party control of Congress," and is so commonly accepted that the phrase is used generously by the media. One or the other of the two viable political parties is also said to be in control of the White House at any given time.

In the elections of 1994, the Democratic party, which had been "in control of Congress" for 40 years, lost the majority to the Republican party; so,the media announced that the Republican party is now "in control of Congress." It seems that Congress has made rules for its own operation such that the political party having the most members in Congress dictates the proceedings of that body. Where this mode of controlling our Executive and Legislative bodies comes from, I do not know – but certainly not from the Constitution.

George Washington: The alternate domination of one faction over another, sharpened by the spirit of revenge natural to party dissention, which in different ages and countries has perpetuated the most horrid enormities, is itself a frightful despotism. [13]

H. Inquirer: What an interesting observation. Party control of government is, itself, a form of despotism.

George Washington: But this leads at length to a more formal and permanent despotism. The disorders and miseries, which result, gradually incline minds of men to seek security and repose in the absolute power of an Individual; and sooner or later the chief of some prevailing faction more able or more fortunate than his competitors, turns his disposition to the purposes of his own elevation, on the ruins of Liberty.

Without looking forward to an extremity of this kind (which nevertheless ought not to be entirely out of sight) the common and continual mischiefs of the spirit of Party are sufficient to make it the interest and the duty of wise People to discourage and restrain it. [14]

H. Inquirer: Then we would have better government without the interference of political parties. How does our partisan system weaken good government?

George Washington: It serves always to distract the Public Councils and enfeeble Public administration. It agitates the Community with ill founded jealousies and false alarms, kindles the animosity of one part against another, foments occasionally riot and insurrection. It opens the door to foreign influence and corruption, which finds a facilitated access to the government itself through channels of party passions. Thus the policy and the will of one country, are subjected to the policy and will of another. [15]

On the Danger of Political Parties

H. Inquirer: I quote from the *Fort Worth Star Telegram*, October 16, 1996, "The controversy over an Indonesian banking family's donation to President Clinton's re-election campaign has spread to the contributor's homeland, where public figures called yesterday for a criminal investigation."

Indonesian Mohammedans saw this act of foreign influence and corruption as a criminal act, but the Democratic Party in America does not.

Subsequently, Congress opened an investigation of the incident and discovered that the Democratic Party had actually received millions of dollars from Communist China, a despotic government, known to be at enmity with the United States. The investigation also brought out that the Republican Party, the party then "in control of Congress," had also taken lesser donations from foreign governments. That party neither could come to court with clean hands.

Can politicians be prevented from forming people into political parties?

George Washington: This spirit, unfortunately, is inseperable from our nature, having its roots in the strongest passions of the human Mind. It exists under different shapes in all Governments, more or less stifled, contrould, or repressed; but, in those of the popular form it is seen in its greatest rankness and is truly their worst enemy. [16]

One of the expedients of Party to acquire influence, within particular districts, is to misrepresent the opinions and aims of other Districts. You cannot shield yourselves too much against the jealousies and heart burnings which spring from these misrepresentations. They tend to render Alien to each other those who ought to be bound together in fraternal affection. [17]

H. Inquirer: The last half of the twentieth century has witnessed a great churning about of the population, so that some of the artificial regional prejudices have been lost to politicians. However, political parties, like lawyers and editors, are not such as to let the people be bound together in fraternal affection. Economics, race, religion, and social issues are rich ground for political parties to create strife and ill will for partisan gain.

George Washington: I have already intimated to you the danger of Parties in the State, with particular reference to the founding of them on Geographical discriminations. Let me now take a more comprehensive view, and warn you in the most solemn manner against the baneful effects of the Spirit of Party generally.

There is an opinion that parties in free countries are useful checks upon the Administration of Government and serve to keep alive the spirit of Liberty. This within certain limits is probably true, and in Governments of Monarchical cast Patriotism may look with indulgence, if not in favor, upon the spirit of party. But in those of the popular character, in Governments purely elective, it is a spirit not to be encouraged.

From their natural tendency, it is certain there will always be enough of that spirit for every salutary purpose. And there being constant danger of excess, the effort ought to be, by force of public opinion, to mitigage and assuage it. A fire not quenched; it demands a uniform vigilance to prevent its bursting into flame, lest instead of warming it should consume. [18]

On Politics and Bad Government

H. Inquirer: Until my recent study of these matters, I was under the impression that the people elected representatives to Congress, each representative with equal status, independent of each other and all organizations, with the sole purpose of representing the interests of their constituents, with due regard for the best interests of the whole United States. That, sir, is the only impression I can get from the Constitution.

Well over one third of the people claim no political party affiliation. Where is their representation in "party control of Congress"?

George Washington: All obstruction to the execution of Laws, all combinations and Associations, under whatever plausible character, with real design to direct, controul, counteract, or awe the regular deliberation and action of the Constituted authorities are destructive of this fundamental principle and of fatal tendency. They serve to organize faction, to give artificial and extraordinary force; to put in place of the delegated will of the Nation, the will of a party; often a small but artful and enterprising minority of a Community; and according to the alternate triumphs of different parties, to make the public administration the Mirror of the ill concerted and incongrous projects of faction, rather than the organ of consistent and wholesome plans digested by common councils and modified by mutual interests.

However combinations or Associations of the above description may now and then answer popular ends, they are likely, in the course of time, to become potent engines, by which cunning, ambitious, and unprincipled men will be enabled to subvert the Power of the People and to usurp for themselves the reins of Government; destroying afterwards the very engines which have lifted them to unjust dominion. [19]

H. Inquirer: Mr. President, you have described the system pretty well as it operates at the end of the twentieth century, in both the Executive and the Legislative branches, and, in course of time, in the Judicial branch as well, because of political Executive appointment. Our federal government has become a polyglot of factions, political parties, lobbyists, special-interest pressure groups and organizations, all driven by campaign money of questionable character.

No individual has yet risen to dictatorship; but a condition possibly more odious has developed. The government that actually touches our daily lives is a vast bureaucracy created by Congress, filled with petty tyrants, armed with fill-in-the blanks acts of Congress, and having broad regulatory powers. In theory this bureaucracy is under the authority of the President; but, as a practical matter, because of continuous litigation, it is more under the control of the Judiciary. In short, we are governed by an out-of-control bureaucracy and a judicial oligarchy which has declared, "We are under a Constitution, but the Constitution is what the judges say it is."

Congress seems blind to our circumstances. They seem to be preoccupied with building their campaign "war chests," partisan wranglings, and promoting their political parties. How shall we ever return to the simplicity of the Constitution?

On Making Congress Work

George Washington: Party disputes and personal quarrels are the great business of the day whilst the momentous concerns of an empire, a great accumulated debt, ruined finances, depreciated money . . . are but secondary considerations and postponed from day to day, from week to week as if our affairs wore a most promising aspect. [20]

H. Inquirer: In the vernacular, sir, you've "hit the nail on the head" again.

It seems to me that State Legislatures could devise a plan for electing representatives to Congress that would preclude the interference of political parties. Congress could do likewise for electing the President.

Congress surely could exclude unelected political party hacks from the legislative process. Unfortunately, the only two viable political parties are already firmly entrenched and monopolizing the political process. One or the other of these two parties is in control of State Legislatures, the Congress, and the White House at any given time.

How shall we ever break the stranglehold of political parties on the elective and administrative process and get back to the simplicity of the Constitution?

George Washington: For Heavens sake who are Congress? [21]

H. Inquirer: Good question, sir.

George Washington: Are they not the Creatures of the People, amenable to them for their Conduct, and dependant from day to day on their breath? [22]

H. Inquirer: I believe that is the way it was intended to be, sir.

George Washington: Congress are in fact, but the People; they return to them at certain short periods; are amenable at all times for their conduct, and subject to a recall at any moment. [23]

H. Inquirer: Occasionally a rotten Congressman will fail in a bid for re-election; but I have never heard of one being recalled, a reflection on his constituents, I suppose. Actually a recall process is not available to the people.

George Washington: My political creed . . . is, to be wise in the choice of Delegates, support them like Gentlemen while they are our representatives, give them competent powers for all federal purposes, support them in the due exercise therof, and lastly, to compel them to close attendance in Congress during their delegation. [24]

H. Inquirer: One of the most comical scenes I have witnessed was a Congressman babbling away to an empty hall. I do believe, sir, if we all adopted your political creed and pursued it with conviction, most of our problems with our elected representatives would be solved.

George Washington: These things under the present mode for, and the termination of elections, aided by annual instead of constant

Sessions, would, or I am exceedingly mistaken, make us one of the most wealthy, happy, respectable and powerful Nations, that ever inhabited the terrestrial Globe, without them, we shall in my opinion soon be every thing which is the direct reverse of them. [25]

On Limiting Congressional Sessions

H. Inquirer: Annual sessions instead of constant sessions? Please explain.

George Washington: Annual sessions would always produce a full representation, and alertness at business. The Delegates, after a recess of 8 or 10 Months would meet each other with glad Countenances; they would be complaisant; they would yield to each other as much as the duty they owed to their constituents would permit; and they would have oppertunities of becoming better acquainted with the Sentiments of them [their constituents] and removing their prejudices during the recess.

Men who are always together get tired of each others Company; they throw off the proper restraint; they say and do things which are personally disgusting; this begets opposition; opposition begets faction; and so it goes till business is impeded, often at a stand. I am sure (having the business prepared by proper Boards or a Committee) an Annual Session of two Months would dispatch more business than is now done in twelve; and this by a full representation of the Union. [26]

H. Inquirer: Did you say two months, sir, a session of two months? In two months they could dispatch more business than is now done in twelve? I had thought it would take a session of at least six months, after which time they would be up to more mischief than legitimate business; but, I bow to your greater wisdom.

Perhaps they hang around Washington to collect money from lobbyists, to run the President's business, or to build and protect their personal fiefdoms.

Two months, you say! There is a stirring among the people – fed up with partisan wrangling, pork barreling, tax increases, and passing more laws than we can digest – to limit sessions to six months – a good idea whose time has definitely come.

Two months, you say? Perhaps six months is necessary. But then, after more than two centuries of lawmaking, surely we have about all the laws we need. They just cannot be spending all that time making laws. What they need, I think, is more time to repeal at least half the laws we have already; so I will vote for six-month sessions.

On Term Limits

George Washington: There are other points on which opinions would be more likely to vary. As for instance, on the ineligibility of the same person for President, after he should have served a certain course of years. Guarded so effectually as the proposed Constitution is, in respect to the prevention of bribery and undue influence in the choice of a President: I confess, I differ widely myself from Mr. Jefferson and you, as to the necessity or expediency of rotation in that appointment.

There cannot, in my judgment, be the least danger that the President will by any practicable intrigue ever be able to continue himself one moment in office, much less perpetuate himself in it; but in the last stage of corrupted morals and political depravity: and even then there is as much danger that any other species of domination would prevail. Though, when a people shall have become incapable of governing themselves and fit for a master, it is of little consequence from what quarter he comes.

Under an extended view of this part of the subject, I can see no propriety in precluding ourselves from the services of any man, who on some great emergency shall be deemed universally, most capable of serving the Public. [27]

H. Inquirer: Because of sincere agreement on the issues, as well as great respect for your person and station, sir, rarely would I disagree with the Father of our Country.

For nearly a century and a half, Presidents followed your precedent, and declined to serve for more than eight years. Then, in 1932, a man was elected President of the United States in the middle of a deep economic depression. I cannot relate all the details; but, in the public view, this man fed the people when they were hungry. He was elected for a second term; and, as the end of his second term drew near, a despicable madman in Europe was drawing the whole world into a horrendous war.

It seemed expedient under the circumstances not to change Presidents at that time, so, he was elected for a third term. The war lasted for four dark years; and he, being a wartime President and very popular with the people, was elected for the fourth term; although he was too incapacitated to negotiate the peace in the best interests of the United States. Within a year after his third re-election, he died in office.

From this experience we learned that there can be a combination of circumstances – popularity, political power, and party spirit – effecting a popular election not in the best interest of the people. In 1951 an amendment was added to the Constitution limiting the President to two terms, thus honoring the precedent you set a century and a half earlier.

In 1992, a man was elected President by 43 percent of the popular vote. Defying all logic, the man was re-elected in 1996. Under a system which can elect a President without the expressed will of the majority, and considering the man's character, it is a comfort to know that he can hold the office no more than eight years.

When Congressmen have the power to determine their own pay and benefits, when they have ceased to be citizen legislators and become lifetime professional politicians it is difficult to persuade them to pass laws that are right for the people if those laws are threatening to their egos, their power, or their life of ease and luxury on the public payroll. In a word, they are willing enough to regulate the people, but not themselves.

When political parties are in control of Congress; when great sums of money are required to conduct political campaigns; when high-paid lobbyists stand ready to supply these large sums of money for the election of Congressmen who look after their special interests; the rising voice of the people cries, "Term limits for Congress." For reasons noted, it will be difficult to persuade Congress to pass this law.

When politically-appointed federal judges usurp the power deposited in the Legislature and form themselves into a judicial oligarchy, wisdom says term limits for federal judges is necessary to protect the people from judicial despotism.

So, Mr. President, on principle, I wholeheartedly agree that good and talented people should not be excluded from serving the public. But, under the conditions of late twentieth century politics, I believe wisdom requires us to override principle with practicality. This, I believe to be an honorable exception to the rule; for, in this case, preferring practicality over principle upholds the more basic principle of virtue.

The people, if they wish to remain free, must find ways to remove scoundrels from office when deception and intrigue cause the elective process to fail.

11

HOPE FOR A
HAPPY NATION

*"Almighty God, We make our earnest prayer. . . that
Thou wilt most graciously be pleased to dispose us all to do justice,
to love mercy, and to demean ourselves with that charity, humility,
and pacific temper of mind which were the characteristics
of the Divine Author of our blessed religion, and without an
humble imitation of whose example in these things we can never
hope to be a happy nation. George Washington.*

George Washington: I wish the Constitution which is offered
had been made more perfect, but I sincerely believe it is the
best that could be obtained at the time. [1]

Humble Inquirer: By and large, it has served us well, sir. It is only
when tyrants ignore it or pervert its common-sense language that it is
turned against us.

On Slavery

H. Inquirer: I do wish that slavery could have been abolished in the beginning of the Union. I know that "peculiar institution" haunted many of the founders as you established the nation. What could possibly be more incompatible than slavery with the concepts of liberty?

Although you inherited slaves yourself, your conscience was evidently troubled.

George Washington: Would to God a like spirit would diffuse itself generally into the minds of the people of this country; but I despair of seeing it. Some petitions were presented to the Assembly, at its last Session, for the abolition of slavery, but they could scarcely obtain a reading. To set them afloat at once would, I really believe, be productive of much inconvenience and mischief; but by degrees it certainly might, and assuredly ought to be effected; and that too by legislative authority. [2]

H. Inquirer: I cannot conceive of a system in which one man holds another in bondage to devour all the substance of his labor. On the other hand, I can imagine the dilemma of one born a slave holder in a system that offers no alternative for the slave, yet bearing the consciousness of the inhumanity of it.

What would a slave do, being set free in a system that offers him no alternative means of livelihood – a system in which he might be captured and sold again into slavery on a distant plantation?

George Washington: I hope it will not be conceived from these observations, that it is my wish to hold the unhappy people in slavery. I can only say that there is only one proper and effectual mode by which it can be accomplished, and that is by Legislative authority; and this, as far as my suffrage will go, shall never be wanting. [3]

H. Inquirer: You demonstrated the benevolence of your heart, Mr. President, when you bequeathed freedom to your slaves in your Last Will and Testament. But tragically, the slaves were not to be set free by legislative authority. Only 70 years later, half a million men, North and South, would die unnecessarily in a horrible Civil War to end that "peculiar institution." Casualties of that war equaled the eighth part of the entire population of the United States at the time of your 1790 census.

Lost liberties added to the tragic toll of lost lives. Constitutional amendments, deemed necessary to legally free the slaves, grant them citizenship, and assure their civil liberties, opened the door to perpetual harassment of all the people by the federal government. Oh, that this blotch upon the American soul had never been!

And so, the curse of the "peculiar institution" is still with us as we approach the twenty-first century. Some black people, forgetting that the white man spent his blood and his fortune to set them free, remember only the white man who held them in slavery, and spew their hatred on all people of light complexion.

Others, blaming the sin of slavery on the Christian religion, turn to the Mohammedans, not understanding that it was the principles of Christianity that goaded the white man – some voluntarily – to release their slaves, and others to fight and die for their liberty.

Other black people are perpetually angry and will not be reconciled because of agitators among them who foment hatred and strife for their own political or economic gain. Some demand that the United States cede to them several States for the establishment of a separate black nation, many of whose citizens I would foresee fleeing back to ours.

Some turn to crime and degrading immorality, creating a blotch upon the reputation of all their kin. Perhaps the most to be pitied are those who are content to be eternal dependents of the federal government, thrusting their own legs back into the shackles of slavery more odious than the former kind.

Fortunately, others of African descent take their place alongside citizens of all races. They are good, productive citizens, a credit to their race, bearing their part of the load and reaping their share of the nation's benefits.

In 1995, the Southern Baptists formally repented – publicly begging forgiveness from the black people – for condoning slavery in the ante-bellum South and for any anti-black sentiment since that time. Perhaps an official national repentance for slavery and other abuses of people of all races would do much to cleanse the national soul. Having done this, I know nothing more to do than to expect that all people shall be proud citizens of this great republic, contributing their talents and labor, and reaping their share of her benefits.

On Crime and Punishment

H. Inquirer: If I may offer one more criticism of our Constitution it is this: I wish the framers could have clearly defined "cruel and unusual punishment."

In my day I have seen the Court flip flop over the issue of capital punishment. At one time the death penalty was declared "cruel and unusual punishment" so that the most vile murderer could not be put to death. "Lock 'em up and throw away the key" became the supposed punishment for the most heinous criminals.

Our courts have become so soft on crime today that unpleasant prison conditions are declared "cruel and unusual punishment." As prisons overflow with criminals of one class or another, the courts demand that they be released. Why? Because prison crowding is considered to be "cruel and unusual punishment."

Ridiculous demands of incarcerated criminals, with the complaisance of the courts, are too numerous to relate to you. Judges even demand that prisons supply law libraries so that criminals can learn legal procedures and bring frivolous lawsuits against the people.

At the end of the twentieth century, we are a society ruled (and ruined) by lawyers. I am not sure whether the silly stance of judges regarding crime and punishment is a perverted favoritism for criminals over their victims, or simply a method to rob taxpayers and stuff the pockets of lawyers.

These recycled thugs, who routinely repeat their crimes, are a boon to law business. Never mind their terror to the people. It is truly maddening to have such fraud and treachery perpetrated upon us in the name of defending our Constitution. It is more likely that the Constitution has been abandoned; and, the judges are wading deeper into the dismal swamp, with no law to guide them.

I do not wish, sir, to belabor the point; but we know from your military records that you did not regard public whipping as "cruel and unusual punishment."

George Washington: For the most atrocious offenses, (one or two Instances only excepted) a Man receives no more than 39 Lashes; and these perhaps (thro' the collusion of the Officer who is to see it inflicted) are given in such a manner as to become rather a matter of sport than punishment; but when inflicted as they ought, many hardened fellows who have been the Subjects, have declared that for a bottle of Rum they would undergo a Second operation; it is evident therefore that this punishment is inadequate to many Crimes it is assigned to. [4]

H. Inquirer: It seems a fitting punishment for abusers of women and children. After the second or third application "well laid on," brute beasts among men might get the message that such crimes are the business of society, not of the victims only.

But, now as then, light punishment is not sufficient to deter the most heinous criminals. The death penalty (which you, sir, did not see as "cruel and unusual punishment" for the most heinous crimes) is the only just response to unmitigated murder. The same confirmation can be found in Thomas Jefferson's legal code for Virginia.

Not being a lawyer, sir, you probably never wrote a legal code; but, being an administrator of justice, perhaps you have an opinion of one.

George Washington: A short and simple code, in my opinion, tho' I have the sentiments of some of the Gentlemen of the long robe against me, would be productive of happy consequences, and redound to the honor of this or any Country which shall adopt such. [5]

H. Inquirer: Apparently lawyers and judges have not changed much in two centuries. They love to occupy our legislatures as well as our courts, and there enact a super abundance of complicated or nebulous laws. Then, they can wrangle over these laws ad infinitum, stuffing their pockets with fees – at taxpayers' expense more often than not – under the system which they have devised. In 1997, our state legislature enacted (can you believe this?) 1,000 new laws. We cannot possibly be aware of all these laws – let alone obey them!

I say these things, sir, with all due respect to that minority of lawyers who perform an honest and necessary service to the people.

On Taxes

H. Inquirer: And now, I would value your thoughts on our taxes and public debt.

George Washington: It is essential that you should practically bear in mind, that towards the payment of debt there must be a Revenue; that to have Revenue there must be taxes, that no taxes can be devised which are not more or less inconvenient and unpleasant. [6]

H. Inquirer: Nothing is certain but death and taxes, I have heard it said.

Economists tell me, sir, that as we approach the twenty-first century, Americans are required to pay 53 percent of their incomes to support local, State, and federal governments – if we take into account federal regulations and mandates.

Put another way, Americans are required to pay all their earnings from January 1 to July 4 to the government before they can claim any as their own (a new spin on Independence Day, I suppose.)

If it were not for the government's benevolence that allows us to keep 47 percent out of each paycheck, I tell you, sir, we would starve long before we paid our annual tax bill! Now I ask you, sir, is that not a bit much?

George Washington: There is a danger that a commercial and free people, little accustomed to heavy burthens, pressed by impositions of a new and odious kind, may not make a proper allowance for the necessity of the conjuncture, and may imagine, they have only exchanged one tyranny for another. [7]

H. Inquirer: That pretty well sums up the state of mind of American taxpayers in late twentieth century. And, although we have become numbed to these heavy burdens, and pay as sheep to the shearers, there is never an end to the demand for more money to support local, state, and federal governments.

George Washington: When the people are oppressed with Taxes, and have cause to suspect that there has been a misapplication of their money, the language of despotism is but illy brooked. [8]

H. Inquirer: True indeed, Mr. President; and if our colonial forbears could have lived during the twentieth century, I think they would have broken the back of this homebred despotism decades ago.

On Public Debt

George Washington: I entertain a strong hope that the state of the national finances is now sufficiently matured to enable you to enter upon a systematic and effectual arrangement for the regular redemption and discharge of the public debt, according to the right which has been reserved to the Government; no measure can be more desirable, whether viewed with an eye to its intrinsic importance, or to the general sentiment and wish of the nation. [9]

H. Inquirer: In August, 1995, our national debt reached $5 trillion and continues to grow by $250 billion per year, in spite of our governments' confiscation of 53 percent of our income. Is it not very likely that our money is being misappropriated?

George Washington: As a very important source of strength and security, cherish public credit. One method of preserving it is to use it as sparingly as possible; avoiding occasions of expense by cultivating peace, but remembering also that timely disbursements to prepare for danger frequently prevent much greater disbursements to repel it; avoiding likewise the accumulation of debt, not only by shunning occasions of expense, but by vigorous exertions in time of Peace to discharge the Debts which unavoidable wars may have occasioned, not ungenerously throwing posterity the burthen which ourselves ought to bear. The execution of these maxims belongs to your Representatives, but it is necessary that public opinion should cooperate. [10]

H. Inquirer: Admittedly, sir, the public is largely to blame for oppressive taxes and skyrocketing debt, ever demanding more "entitlements" from the federal government, as if there were no tomorrow, no children and grandchildren to bear the burden of our extravagance.

The state of our finances is such, I believe, that we can, in reasonable time, pay our public debt, but not if the federal government continues to spend like drunken sailors. If this is the responsibility of our representatives, Mr. President, what do you advise?

George Washington: No pecuniary consideration is more urgent than the regular redemption and discharge of the public debt; of none can delay be more injurious, or an economy of time more valuable. [11]

It is believed that the result is such as to encourage Congress to consummate this work without delay. Nothing can more promote the permanent welfare of the nation, and nothing would be more grateful to our constituents.

Indeed whatsoever is unfinished of our system of public credit, cannot be benefited by procrastination; and, as far as may be practicable, we ought to place that credit on grounds which cannot be disturbed, and to prevent that progressive accumulation of debt, which must ultimately endanger all governments. [12]

On Foreign Trade

George Washington: I know that Britain arrogantly expects we will sell our produce wherever we can find a market and bring the money to purchase goods from her; I know that she vainly hopes to retain what share she pleases in our trade, in consequence of our prejudices in favor of her fashions and manufactures; but these are illusions, which will vanish and disappoint her, as the dreams of conquest have already done. [13]

H. Inquirer: Sounds like our experience with Japan today.
You were the first to advise "buy American," Mr. President, and practiced what you preached by purchasing rough broadcloth from Connecticut mills for your suits, in preference to the finer fabrics of Europe. Yet, foreign trade that is fair to all can, I believe, bring great benefit to all.

George Washington: The Great rule of conduct for us, in regard to foreign Nations is in extending our commercial relations, to have with them as little political connection as possible. . . . Our commercial policy should hold an equal and impartial hand: neither seeking nor granting exclusive favors or preferences; consulting the natural course of things; diffusing and deversifying by gentle means the streams of Commerce; but forcing nothing. [14]

H. Inquirer: Was not commercial despotism part of what invited the British to your Boston Tea Party? Are not commercial appetites the cause of most wars?
What do you suggest, sir?

George Washington: Observe good faith and justice towards all nations. Cultivate peace and harmony with all. Religion and morality enjoin this conduct; and can it be that good policy does not equally enjoin it? It will be worthy of a free, enlightened, and, at no distant period, a great Nation, to give to mankind the magnanimous and too novel example of a People always guided by an exalted justice and benevolence.

Who can doubt that in the course of time and things the fruits of such a plan would richly repay any temporary advantages which might be lost by a steady adherence to it? Can it be, that Providence has not connected the permanent felicity of a nation with its virtue? The experiment, at least, is recommended by every sentiment which enobles human Nature. [15]

On War Among Nations

H. Inquirer: There is a condition in the world at the end of the twentieth century that I should mention.

The Mid East remains the seat of international terrorism against other nations, a nest of modern-day Barbary Coast pirates, you might say. I must confess, sir, in my opinion, such nations should be given no consideration commercially, but such as is forced upon us by our own necessity. Political connections with them, I believe, approach the rules of war.

George Washington: My first wish is to see this plague to mankind [war] banished from off the Earth, and the sons and Daughters of this world employed in more pleasing and innocent amusements, than in preparing implements and exercising them for the destruction of mankind. [16]

It is really a strange thing that there should not be room enough in the world for men to live, without cutting one anothers throats. [17]

It is time for the age of Knight-Errantry and mad-heroism to be at an end. Your young military men, who want to reap the harvest of laurels, don't care (I suppose) how many seeds of war are sown; but for the sake of humanity it is devoutly wished, that the manly employment of agriculture and the humanizing benefits of commerce, would supercede the waste of war and the rage of conquest; that the swords might be turned into plough-shares, and the spears into pruning hooks, and, as the Scripture expresses it, "the nations learn war no more." [18]

H. Inquirer: History has never refuted the words of our Lord that "there will be wars and rumors of wars" until He returns, the Prince of Peace.

Since your time, no generation of Americans has been free from war or the dark threat of war. Most American wars have been on foreign soil, most defending a just cause, most unavoidable. Every generation produces a new crop of despots, madmen, and would-be tyrants. I suppose we have no choice but to be prepared for it.

George Washington: To be prepared for war, is one of the most effectual means of preserving peace. A free people ought not only to be armed, but disciplined; to which end, a uniform and well digested plan is requisite: and their safety and interest require that they should promote such manufactories as tend to render them independent on others for essentials, particularly for military supplies. [19]

If we desire to avoid insult, we must be able to repel it; if we desire to secure peace, one of the most powerful instruments of our rising prosperity, it must be known that we are at all times ready for war. [20]

H. Inquirer: Europe has drawn us into two horrendous world wars in the twentieth century. I wish we could have stayed clear of it, as you kept the United States clear of the French Revolution; but we keep getting into Europe's squabbles.

George Washington: Europe has a set of primary interests, which to us have none, or very remote relation. Hence she must be engaged in frequent controversies, the causes of which are essentially foreign to our concerns. Hence therefore it must be unwise in us to implicate ourselves, by artificial ties, in the ordinary vicissitudes of her policies, or the ordinary combinations and collisions of her friendships, or enmities. [21]

H. Inquirer: Yet, if we had not intervened in World War II, the Russians and the Germans would have finished cutting one anothers throats, after their bloodthirsty dictators had already slaughtered millions of their own people. And (I suppose) either the German or the Russian mad despot would have gained control over all of Europe and half of Asia. From there, I think, he would have turned his madness on America; and, we would have been engulfed in an unavoidable (and possibly unwinnable) war for our liberties after all. It seems we can no longer escape the madness that Europe produces from time to time.

On Avoiding Foreign Influence

H. Inquirer: Now, sir, I must apprise you of a condition in the world of the late twentieth-century, that you could not have imagined in the eighteenth. Worldwide communication is at the speed of light; and travel, civilian or military, is greater than the speed of sound.

Man-made satellites float high in the sky, beaming pictures and messages instantly all around the world. Pictures from these satellites can tell in discernable detail what is happening at any vital point on Earth.

We have virtually shrunken the world to the size of an eighteenth-century state. Under these conditions, sir, must we still maintain the integrity of the American nation and the American people?

George Washington: Against the insidious wiles of foreign influence, (I conjure you to believe me, fellow citizens) the jealousy of a free people ought to be constantly awake; since history and experience prove that foreign influence is one of the most baneful foes of Republican government. [22]

H. Inquirer: According to our daily news broadcasts, to gain re-election to the White House in 1996, the President, Vice-President, and their party sold access to the White House to foreign influence, and that to known political enemies of the United States. This treachery, I firmly believe, is grounds for impeachment of the President and Vice-President, and dismissal of their entire cabinet. But, this offense, sir, treacherous as it may be, is not the most insidious danger to the state of our international affairs.

In the twentieth century, the United States, through no real desire for the status (at least on the part of ordinary Americans), has been thrust upon the world scene as the most powerful nation on earth. I think – because of the remnants of our Christian heritage – we also remain the most careful of human rights. We are, therefore, whether we choose it or not, given the leadership role among all the nations of the earth as we approach the twenty-first century.

History has shown that all nations that aspired to rule the world have ended in despotism and ruin – this, I believe, is because they have lusted after that which has been given to the Prince of Peace alone. And can we expect that the United States will be any different?

With what honor and integrity we discharge our responsibilities to the world depends, I believe, upon whether we are guided by the same principles our forefathers chose in establishing this free republic – the general principles of Christianity. But our record to date has been anything but encouraging.

On the United Nations

H. Inquirer: When the United Nations was organized in 1945, there was no Benjamin Franklin present to beg that deference be made to the Supreme Sovereign of the Universe, no George Washington to guide the convention on a godly path. So, the U. S. delegates decided to forego any recognition of God, for fear of offending the various religious and atheistic sentiments of the nations represented.

You will recall, sir, this question had long before been laid before our Constitutional Convention of 1787. The founders of the United States chose the upward path toward God. The founders of the United Nations chose another course.

Thus the United Nations was founded, not on the general principles of Christianity, but upon Humanism – the same man-worshipping religion which had just recently soaked the soil of Europe and Asia in human blood. That same decade commenced the internal assault on our Christian foundations, with the goal of re-establishing the United States on the same foundations as the United Nations.

The insidious wiles of foreign influence no longer refers so much to individual foreign nations; although, Communist China may some day challenge our world leadership, the same as the Communist Soviet Union did for half a century. The most insidious threat, however, comes from the United Nations – not because the U.N is more powerful, but because our rulers are gratuitously surrendering our national sovereignty, bit by bit, to this one-world system.

Already, by treaty with the U. N., large tracts of U. S. lands surrounding our National Monuments and National Parks are under United Nations authority – this under guise of protecting the environment.

This is only the beginning of our coming sorrows. In 1995, an international conference proposed that we surrender such intimate matters as parent-child relationship to international law under a World Court. Another conference tackled the monumental task of defining human gender. (Have they never heard, "Male and female, made he them?")

The wife of the President of the United States led the U. S. delegation to these conferences.

For heavens sake, are we no longer capable of protecting our own environment and rearing our own children? Do we no longer have the moral capacity to govern ourselves? Apparently our rulers think not.

No, I think this may be the right answer: Our rulers are drunken with the notion of the power of the United States, expecting to rule the world themselves, oblivious to the wiles of foreign influence.

I fear, sir, the U. S. Samson is teasing the U. N. Delilah – the U. S. fly is tempting the U. N. spider and will be caught in its insidious web.

George Washington: My policy has been . . . to be upon friendly terms with, but independent of, all the nations of the earth. To share in the broils of none. [23]

'Tis our true policy to steer clear of permanent Alliances, with any portion of the foreign world. So far, I mean, as we are now at liberty to do it, for let me not be understood capable of patronizing infidelity to existing engagements. [24]

H. Inquirer: I do believe, sir, that we as a nation have a God-given responsibility to the peoples of the world; but our present course in the United Nations is not the right course. It may be, as many believe, we should get out of the United Nations, remove that international body from American soil, and find a Christian approach to international affairs.

If we are to remain a free, self-governing people, it is imperative that we maintain our national sovereignty and respect the sovereignty of other nations. Our present course, I sincerely believe, will, in the not distant future, engulf our once-free nation in a one-world socialistic system.

I have seen with what ease our Supreme Court formed itself into an oligarchy, and how it dictates the most intimate matters of our private and public life. I have seen the federal government swallow, into its own jaws, the powers reserved to the States respectively or to the people. I foresee the next step as surrendering the American people over to the United Nations and the World Court.

> World government.
> Oh, dreadful night.
> A descent into Maelstrom!
> All powers spiraling,
> Ever accelerating,
> In circles diminishing,
> Into its vortex – a global despot.
> Sweet liberties collapsing,
> As that primordial galaxy,

Into a fathomless black hole.
O Lord, keep America,
One nation under God,
'Til He returns,
And takes the sceptre,
Whose right it is to reign!

On the Weaknesses of Democracy

George Washington: It is one of the evils of democratical governments, that the people, not always seeing and frequently misled, must often feel before they can act right, but then evils of this nature seldom fail to work their own cure. It is to be lamented, nevertheless, that the remedies are so slow, and that those, who may wish to apply them seasonably are not attended to before they suffer in person, in interest and in reputation. [25]

H. Inquirer: Playing upon this weakness of our system, enemies of our republic, by deceit and treachery, are able to unravel her fabric and weaken her foundations against the known will of the people. Little by little, day by day, termites eat at our foundations, and moths devour our fabric.

I tremble, sir, that the corruption of time and party and the listlessness of the people shall cause the structure to crumble. O, tragedy of tragedies, for what a structure it was! What a bold experiment of trust in human virtue!

George Washington: It is regretted, I confess, that Democratical States must always feel before they can see: it is this that makes their Governments slow, but the people will be right at last. [26]

H. Inquirer: I hope so, sir, I sincerely hope so. Yet I recall John Adams' dire warning, "Have you ever found in history, one single example of a Nation thoroughly corrupted that was afterwards restored to virtue? And without virtue there can be no political liberty."

We have veered so far off course, Mr. President, that many States are calling for another Constitutional Convention to amend our way out of our domestic quagmire. I am in agreement; but, who can we trust?

Where is Jefferson, Franklin, Mason, Madison? Where are Reverends Witherspoon and Sherman? Where is self-sacrificing Washington, who alone can command the confidence of the people? Who knows whether we will be amended deeper into the dismal swamp from which we so earnestly wish to escape?

George Washington: I coincide perfectly in sentiment with you, my Dear Sir, that there are errors in our national Government which call for correction, loudly I would add: but I shall find myself happily mistaken if the remedies are at hand. We are certainly in a delicate situation, but my fear is that the people are not yet sufficiently misled to retract from error.

To be plainer, I think there is more wickedness than ignorance mixed in our Councils. Under this impression, I scarcely know what opinion to entertain of a general convention. That it is necessary to revise and amend.... I entertain no doubt; but what may be the consequences of such an attempt is doubtful. Yet something must be done, or the fabrick must fall, for it certainly is tottering.

I think often of our situation and view it with concern. From the high ground we stood upon, from the plain path which invited our footsteps, to be so fallen! so lost! it is really mortifying; but virtue, I fear has in a great degree, taken a departure from us; and the want of disposition to do justice is the source of the national embarrassment; for whatever guise or colorings are given to them, this I apprehend is the origin of the evils we now feel, and probably shall labor under for some time to come. [28]

Washington's Prayer

H. Inquirer: If it were possible, my Dear Sir, I would beseech you once again to leave the pleasant shade of your own vine and fig tree at Mount Vernon and, with the blessing of Divine Providence, take the Helm of State once again in your steady hands.

My humble prayer is that our conversation will contribute in some small way to prevent those who, having denied their Creator, would erase the "Father of our Country," your Christian faith, and your God from our memory, leveling us all into their concept of social and political correctness.

And now, with great sadness I must leave you, my Dear Sir. Before I depart will you favor my generation, as you favored yours, with a prayer for pardon and blessing.

George Washington: Let us unite . . . in imploring the Supreme Ruler of the nations to spread his holy protection over these United States; to turn the machinations of the wicked to the confirming of our constitution; to enable us, at all times, to root out internal sedition, and put invasion to flight; to perpetuate to our country that prosperity, which his goodness has already conferred; and to verify the anticipations of this government being a safeguard to human rights. [28]

Almighty God, We make our earnest prayer that Thou wilt keep the United States in Thy holy protection; that Thou wilt incline the hearts of the citizens to cultivate a spirit of subordination and obedience to government; and entertain a brotherly affection and love for one another and for their fellow citizens of the United States at large.

And finally that Thou wilt most graciously be pleased to dispose us all to do justice, to love mercy, and to demean ourselves with that charity, humility, and pacific temper of mind which were the characteristics of the Divine Author of our blessed religion, and without an humble imitation of whose example in these things we can never hope to be a happy nation. [29]

Farewell to the "Best of Men"

The "Father of our Country" was called on the 14th December, 1799, by the ALMIGHTY FATHER OF HEAVEN, we hope, to the enjoyment of that rich reward which is reserved for those who *act well their part* on earth. [30]

By resolution of Congress, on the 26th of December, 1799, a funeral procession marched from Congress Hall to the German Lutheran Church. There they heard George Washington's funeral oration delivered by Major Henry Lee. Excerpts from this moving tribute to George Washington follows:

Major Henry Lee: In obedience to your will, I rise, your humble organ, with the hope of executing a part of the system of public mourning which you have been pleased to adopt, commemorative of the death of the most illustrious and most beloved personage this country has ever produced; and which, while it transmits to posterity your sense of the awful event, faintly represents your knowledge of the consummate excellence you so cordially honor.

Desperate indeed is any attempt on earth to meet correspondingly this dispensation of Heaven; for, while with pious resignation we submit to the will of an all – gracious Providence, we can never cease lamenting, in our finite view of Omnipotent Wisdom, the heart – rendering privation for which our nation weeps.

When the civilized world shakes to its centre; when every moment gives birth to strange and momentous changes; when our peaceful quarter of the globe, exempt as it happily has been from any share in the slaughter of the human race, may yet be compelled to abandon her pacific policy, and to risk the doleful casualties of war: What limit is there to the extent of our loss? None within the reach of my words to express; none which your feelings will not disvow.

The founder of our federate republic – our bulwark in war, our guide in peace, is no more! Oh that this were but questionable! Hope, the comforter of the wretched, would pour into our agonizing hearts its balmy dew. But, alas! there if no hope for us; our Washington is removed forever!

Possessing the stoutest frame, and purest mind, he had passed nearly to his sixty-eighth year, in the enjoyment of high health, when, habituated by his care of us to neglect himself, a slight cold, disregarded, became inconvenient on Friday, oppressive on Saturday, and, defying every medical interposition, before the morning of Sunday, put an end to the best of men.

An end did I say? – his fame survives! – bounded only by the limits of the earth, and by the extent of the human mind. He survives in our hearts, in the growing knowledge of our children, in the affections of the good throughout the world; and when our monuments shall be done away; when the nations now existing shall be no more; when even our young and far-spreading empire shall have perished, still will our Washington's glory unfaded shine, and die not, until love of virtue cease on earth, or earth itself sinks into chaos.

He best understood the indissoluble union between virtue and happiness, between duty and advantage, between the genuine maximums of an honest and magnanimous policy, and the solid rewards of public prosperity and individual felicity; watching with an equal and comprehensive eye over this great assemblage of communities and interests, he laid the foundations of our national policy in the unerring, immutable principles of morality, based on religion, exemplifying the pre-eminence of a free government; by all the attributes which win the affections of its citizens, or command the respect of the world.

When before was affection like this exhibited on the earth? Turn over the records of ancient Greece! Review the anals of mighty Rome! Examine the volume of modern Europe; you search in vain. America and her Washington only afford the dignified exemplification.

Such was the man for whom our nation mourns! Methinks I see his august image, and hear, falling from his venerable lips, these deep-sinking words:

"Cease, sons of America, lamenting our seperation: Go on, and confirm by your wisdom the fruits of our joint councils, joint efforts, and common dangers. Reverence religion: diffuse knowledge throughout your land; patronize the arts and sciences; let liberty and order be inseparable companions; control party-spirit, the bane of free government; observe good faith to, and cultivate peace with all nations; shut up every avenue to foreign influence; rely on yourselves only; be American in thought and deed. Thus will you give immortality to that union which was the constant object of my terrestrial labors. Thus will you preserve undisturbed to the latest posterity the felicity of a people to me most dear; and thus will you supply [if my happiness is now aught to you] the only vacancy in the round of pure bliss high Heaven bestows." [31]

Our Country mourns her Father

Rev. J. T. Kirkland: The virtues of our departed friend were crowned by piety. He is known to have been habitually devout. To Christian institutions he gave the countenance of his example; and no one could express, more fully, his sense of the Providence of God, and the dependence of man. [31]

President John Adam: For his fellow-citizens, if their prayers could have been answered, he would have been immortal. It remains for an affectionate and grateful people, in whose heart he can never die, to pay suitable honors to his memory. [31]

Samuel Livermore: (*President of the Senate Pro Tempore*): Let his countrymen consecrate the memory of the heroic general, the patriotic statesman, and the virtuous sage; let them teach their children never to forget that the fruit of his labors and his example are their inheritance.

On this occasion it is manly to weep. To lose such a man, at such a crisis, is no common calamity to the world: our country mourns her Father. [34]

President John Adams: His example is now complete, and it will teach wisdom and virtue to magistrates, citizens, and men, not only in the present age, but in future generations, as long as our history shall be read. [35]

H. Inquirer: Weep, my generation, with your noble ancestors. The Father of your Country and his timeless example can live only when our true history is faithfully written and faithfully taught. Weep for your children; for, while you sleep, treacherous professors rob them of their American birthright.

(To the assembly of mourners at German Lutheran Church)
My brothers and sisters of yesterday, I weep with you on occasion of our mournful loss, and my soon departure back to my own generation. Before I depart, President Jefferson, will you be pleased to offer the same prayer for my generation that you prayed for yours.

President Thomas Jefferson: Almighty God, who has given us this good land for our heritage; we humbly beseech Thee that we may always prove ourselves a people mindful of thy favor and glad to do Thy will. Bless our land with honorable ministry, sound learning, and pure manners.

Save us from violence, discord, and confusion, from pride and arrogance, and from every evil way. Defend our liberties, and fashion into one united people the multitude brought hither out of many kindreds and tongues.

Endow with Thy spirit of wisdom those to whom in Thy Name we entrust the authority of government, that there may be justice and peace at home, and that through obedience to Thy law, we may show forth Thy praise among the nations of the earth.

In time of prosperity fill our hearts with thankfulness, and in the day of trouble, suffer not our trust in Thee to fail; all of which we ask through Jesus Christ our Lord, Amen. [36]

Recommended Reading for Chapters 5 through 11

Bancroft, George, *History of the United States*, (Boston: Little, Brown, and Company, 1858) Volume VII, pp. 393-403.
The profile of George Washington is taken from this fine old history book.

Barton, David, *The Myth of Separation*, (Aledo, TX: Wallbuilder Press, 1992).
This and a number of other related books can be obtained from the Wallbuilders Press. Mr. Barton, an able lecturer on these matters, can be reached at the same address.

Federer, William J., *America's God and Country*, (Coppell, TX: Fame Publishing, Inc., 1994).
This is a must-have reference book for the lecturer, writer, teacher, researcher and patriots at large. Every minister of the gospel should own a copy. We have used it liberally in our foot-note references; because, it often gives several references to more primary source documents. Copies can be obtained by con-tacting Fame Publishing, Inc. at the above address.

Mayo, Bernard, *Jefferson Himself*, (Charlottesville, VA: The University Press of Virginia, 1970).

Barton, David, *The Bulletproof George Washington*, (Aledo: TX: Wallbuilder Press, 1990).
For the account of the Battle of Fort Duquesne.

Washington, George, *Rules of Civility and Decent Behaviour in Company and Conversation*, (Mount Vernon, VA: The Mount Vernon Ladies Association, 1989).

Allen, W. B., *George Washington*, (Indianapolis, IN: Liberty Fund, Inc., 1988).
A collection of George Washington's letters and speeches. (Most of George Washington's quotes are taken from this source.)

Millard, Catherine, *Rewriting America's History*, (Camp Hill, PA: Horizon House Publishers, 1991.)
> A most informative book on the trashing of our early American history. Must reading for those who wish to be informed about revisions taking place in America today.

Hickey, W., *The Constitution*, (Philadelphia: T. K. & P. G. Collins, 1853) pp. 247-257.
> George Washington's funeral oration. This oration by Major General Henry Lee is also recorded in the Congressional Record. The complete oration is included as Appendix A at the back of this book.

PART II

NO OTHER GODS

"Thou shalt have no
other gods before me."
The Bible, Exodus 20:3

12

MASTERS OF DECEIT

"Had the people, during the Revolution, a suspicion of any attempt to war against Christianity, that Revolution would have been strangled in its cradle." House Judiciary Committee, 1854

While the foreign tyrant overthrown in the War for Ameri can Independence has long since faded into history, the potential United Nations' threat to our national sovereignty cannot not be overlooked.

The tyrant that most threatens America today, however, is not a foreign nation. Our nation's geographical advantages and economic strength make takeover by a foreign power most unlikely – unless, how-ever, America's true strength is first destroyed from within.

In Section One of this book, the Founding Fathers reminded us of who and what we were as Americans. In their own words, they defined the foundations upon which they established our nation. For nearly two centuries America stood secure upon those bedrock foundations.

In our land today, however, a persistent uneasiness pervades our sense of national well-being. Something seems to be basically wrong. A persistent majority of informed Americans sense that we, as a people, are not as safe, not as educated, not as happy, not as hopeful, not as free as we once were. And our income, in real dollars, is diminishing. Is our country, in spite of her economic strength, on the wrong tracks?

If the greatest present threat to our God-given liberties is not a foreign power, what is it? Could there be a despotic tyrant within our own borders?

The answer is a resounding, Yes; and, the time has come to expose and evict the insidious American tyrant that has been ruling the nest for several decades.

The Cuckoo's Nest

To better understand the American tyrant within, we look to the character and tactics of the cuckoo bird.

The cuckoo does not build its own nest. Silently, as a thief in the night, it studies the host bird that it intends to deceive and steal its nest. While the marked victim goes about its business, building a nest and preparing to raise its family, the impostor watches from a nearby perch.

Perhaps from the weariness of its labor, or its attention to other matters, the victim relaxes its vigil, and leaves its nest unguarded for a moment too long. On silent wings, the cuckoo moves in, and, undetected, deposits its own egg in the nest, to which it had contributed not one straw.

The host pair, stupefied by instinct and deceived by the bandit, begin to warm and care for the alien egg. In time, alongside their own eggs, the cuckoo egg hatches into a baby chick. The host birds are delighted, deceived into believing it to be their very own.

Having stolen surrogate parents and nursemaids, the cuckoo contributes not one morsel to the care of its own offspring. The cuckoo chick, likewise a born thief, is more aggressive and demanding than the native brood; so, the deceived pair feed it more and more, to the neglect of their own.

The cuckoo chick, a despotic bird, has an innate instinct to push with its head against whatever is near it; and, soon it begins to push the true-born chicks over the edge of their own nest. They fall to the ground and die, one by one. Thus the deceived parents, ignorant of the tyrant within, have destroyed their own posterity.

With the true owners of the nest now dead, the cuckoo has full control. The deceived parent birds work feverishly for the cuckoo's survival and the extinction of their own kind. Thus the cuckoos, those masters of deceit, contribute nothing. Instead, by cunning craftiness, they enslave the real builders, devour their substance, and destroy their posterity, replacing them with a population of their own kind.

Oh, the power of wicked deceit. The deceived birds could have evicted the cuckoo from the nest at any time and saved their own posterity. Deceived into stupidity, however, they destroyed their own children and enslaved themselves to a despotic master.

Life in Christian America

Just over two centuries ago, your ancestors founded a safe and prosperous homeland – these United States of America.

- They laid down strong foundations on "the general principles of Christianity."
- They erected a sound superstructure based on their European/ American culture.
- They wove the general principles of Christianity into the fabric of the American government, as the people had woven them into the fabric of the American culture.
- They bound this American nest together with the strong cords of the English common law, the English language, and "the general principles of English and American liberty."
- Then they deeded it all to you.

In this American homeland, basic Christian virtues empowered a free people to govern themselves. In this American family of virtues, the sanctity of marriage and the resulting family grew strong. With a firm respect for God and the Bible, the secure family unit fostered:

- the sanctity of human life
- the work ethic
- honesty, integrity
- accountability
- self-discipline
- respect for law and order
- respect for oneself and others

All was well in the American nest. People were free to choose their own lifestyle, so long as it did not invade the God-given rights of others. A virtuous lifestyle was not imposed by law, and only the most basic level of morality needed to be enforced. Why? Because virtue was honored and immorality frowned upon in the American culture.

Americans were free to exercise their religious faith just about anywhere and anytime they pleased, "provided he doth not disturb the public peace or others in their religious worship." Some schools had the Ten Commandments posted on the wall, and the school children sang "Joy to the World, the Lord is Come" at Christmastime. They sometimes heard a simple prayer of thanksgiving at convocations and ball games.

"Family" meant a man and a woman, in the bond of holy matrimony (usually the only marriage for both), and their biological offspring, consisting of two and a half children on average. Children were highly valued and not considered by the parents to be a "burden," even in unexpected pregnancies. Killing babies in the womb was not only illegal but considered unthinkable by all respectable citizens.

"Love" meant that blissful feeling a man and woman have when contemplating the lifelong relationship of a happy marriage. This kind of love was based, not on sex alone, but on mutual respect, affection, and commitment. Respect, affection and commitment extended beyond the home to embrace relatives, neighbors, and countrymen.

Divorce, single moms, deadbeat dads, child abuse, and spousal abuse were rare occurrences and discussed only amid shock and embarrassment. Such topics were avoided in polite company as were such subjects as birth control methods, premarital sex, and sexual preferences. Even comedians and entertainers were discreet with sexual innuendoes and remarks. "Gay" referred to a happy and free state of mind, not to devious sexual behavior.

Before television was invented, the family spent their evenings in family activities, conversation, games, and reading. Early TV programs were centered around two-parent families and their normal, everyday problems – which were always resolved with positive effects. Sitcoms and movies in those days left viewers feeling entertained – not indoctrinated, offended, or degraded.

In this "once-was" family, it was usually the husband who worked outside the home. His one income covered the family's needs quite well, since the wife worked full time managing the affairs of home and family. This one-worker home was possible because only a small fraction of family income was required for taxes. The government had not yet become a burdensome taskmaster, seeking to confiscate their paychecks and direct their lives at every turn.

People were not imprisoned in their own homes because of the threat of drugs, crime, and violence. In most towns, doors were left unlocked, and people freely and fearlessly walked the streets at night.

The schools were not continually demanding more money for less education. The children were happier and healthier with both biological parents, usually in a quiet and secure home environment, and under the constant care of Mom.

Johnny and Jane

Mom and Dad sent the kids off to public school with confidence. It was not necessary to constantly monitor the school system, nor did the schools need to hire public relations experts to convince Mom and Dad that the kids were being educated according to their family values. Why not? Because home, church, school, and government were in agreement as to how to bring up Jane and Johnny.

Except for occasional disagreements – which might lead to fisticuffs (Johnny) or hair pulling (Jane) – violence was unheard of at school and uncommon at home. Johnny, but never Jane, might be seen, hidden from the school principal, puffing awkwardly and dizzily on a cigarette, or recovering from a chew of Brown's Mule. (Jane had not yet "come a long way, baby.") Drugs and weapons at school was unheard of and unthinkable.

When they graduated from high school, Jane and Johnny could easily read their diplomas. Upon graduation, they were well prepared for college or the work place. They entered the adult world reasonably well adjusted and generally followed their parents' footsteps – with one exception.

Now Jane, as well as Johnny, had to go to work outside the home. By this time, the federal government had initiated programs that increased taxes and prices such that one income could no longer meet their family's needs.

Nevertheless, Jane and Johnny kept a healthy respect for God, country, and their fellow man, and stood ready to defend their American homeland against tyrants without. But, alas, this young couple did not see the tyrant cuckoo in the American nest.

Then, beginning in the 1960s, this now middle-aged couple watched in stunned disbelief as their children, one by one, began to fall from the American nest. And with each casualty their virtues, their education, and their liberties perished.

What went wrong, or rather, who did it and why?

Exposing the Impostor

To answer these questions, let's go back to the year, 1933.

In that year, 34 men got together and wrote the statements of faith and the missions program for their atheistic, man-worshipping religion. They called their religion "Humanism" and their statements of faith and mission the "Humanist Manifesto."

The Humanist statements that follow are highly condensed and powerful. Read them carefully and thoughtfully.

First, Humanists will reveal what they believe religiously. These are more than religious doctrines of a few philosophers, however. They also define Humanist educational, social, and political goals and strategies for America and the world.

With this information we will understand why our country has veered onto the wrong tracks. It will become clear to you that our government – and other social and cultural institutions – are being systematically switched from their original Christian foundations to another religion.

As we look beyond the carefully crafted statements of Humanist Manifestos I and II, the ugly face of the impostor will come into focus. It will become evident that the gradual switch from Christianity to Humanism has developed into a full-grown monster.

Does this mean the beginning of the end for our free, self-governing republic? The answer will be determined by the American people. Will they continue to feed the beast or will they decide to strangle the cuckoo in the nest.

What is Humanism?

As we set out on our fact-finding expedition, put yourself in the place of the Liberator, who will be putting forth the questions we should all be asking.

All answers are taken from the writings of the authors of Humanist Manifesto I and II and other Humanists and quoted exactly from these written documents.

The Liberator: (to American Humanists)
Sirs, we would know something of the religion you call Humanism. First of all, just what is Humanism?

Humanist Manifesto I: (dated 1933)
Humanism is a philosophical, religious, and moral point of view. [1]

The Liberator: Then, we can say candidly, our discussion will be about religion, morality, and politics.
Since Humanism is a religion, we must accept it by faith, if we are to accept it at all. Some things cannot be proven by using our natural senses alone.
I tend to agree with John Adams, American founding father and philosopher, who wrote: "It has been long, very long a settled opinion in my Mind that there is now, never will be, and never was but one being who can Understand the Universe. And that it is not only vain but wicked for insects to pretend to comprehend it." [2]
How does Humanism deal with these questions, unfathomable to the natural mind?
To facilitate our inquiry, let us begin with the Cardinal Doctrines of Humanism.

Doctrine 1
Atheism

H. Manifesto I: Religious humanists regard the universe as self-existing and not created. [3]

The Liberator: Then you are atheists, rejecting the one Being who can understand the universe.
Creation – the making of something from nothing – is inconceivable to the human mind. Can we agree with John Adams that this is a question transcending the capabilities of the human mind, which is trapped in a realm with limits of time and space?
At what time did the universe become self-existing – if such was the case – and, was there time before that? Can we comprehend the

endless expanse of the universe, or define the substance that marks its boundaries, or know what is beyond that? Should we not leave the question of creation where we found it – locked in mystery, or better stated, in the realm of faith, beyond our natural comprehension?

Let us not classify ourselves with Mr. Adams' vain and wicked "insects."

For my part, I regard the biblical explanation far superior to all others, ancient or modern. While the Bible does not provide much detail, it does present a plain statement – one that requires faith to believe: "In the beginning God created the heaven and the earth" (Genesis, Chapter 1)

All of us possess the ability to believe – the necessity to believe. And we have the freedom to choose, with consequences, what we believe.

Do you, sirs, wish to be considered as enemies of our Declaration of Independence – the Charter and Birth Certificate of our nation? Do you really mean to place yourselves in direct opposition to the founders of our nation? In denying the Creator you do just that.

America's founding fathers vindicated our patriot ancestors and justified the existence of our republic by authority of "the laws of nature and nature's God." They declared man's revered "unalienable rights," to be "endowed by their Creator," which you deny.

Will you deny America's right to exist and give up your rights as Americans?

Doctrine 2
The Advent of Man

H. Manifesto I: Humanism believes that man is a part of nature and that he has emerged as the result of a continuous process. [4]

The Liberator: The "continuous process," – sometimes called the Theory of Evolution – was advanced by Charles Darwin, the English biologist. The theory goes something like this:

Hundreds of millions of years ago – too far distant in ages past to prove anything – a molecule of dead matter, in a pool of primordial soup, sprang to life all by itself. Whence came the dead matter and the primordial soup? Darwin could not tell.

Anyway, (so the theory of evolution goes) this molecule of

self-created life formed itself into a living cell, and – over a period of millions and millions more years – changed itself into a variety of many-celled living organisms. After millions upon millions more years, one of these self-created organisms crawled out of the primordial soup onto dry land.

How the primordial soup changed itself into the total environment of land, water, and air, friendly to the human species, Darwin could not tell.

Anyway, according to Darwin's speculation, one of these land creatures, over a period of many more millions of years changed itself into an intermediate being, similar to an ape; and, this being, in progressive stages, changed itself into modern man – all by itself.

Darwin knew his Bible and, for many months, while lying upon his deathbed, avidly read the Book of Hebrews. Reading that Book caused him to exclaim, "Christ Jesus and his salvation. Is not that the best theme?" [5]

Darwin believed in the Creator, affirming, "There is a grandeur in this view of life, with its several powers, having been originally breathed by the Creator into a few forms or into one." [6]

According to Darwin, himself, it was his followers who put the atheistic spin to his theory of evolution. He wrote:

I am well aware, that scarcely a single point is discussed in this volume on which facts cannot be adduced, often apparently leading to conclusions directly opposite to those at which I arrived. . . . I was a young man with unformed ideas. I threw out queries, suggestions, wondering all the time over everything; and to my astonishment the ideas took like wildfire. People made a religion of them. [7]

Those who made a religion of Darwin's theory were the nineteenth century rationalists, looking for a doctrinal excuse to slide into total man-worship.

"For although they knew God, they neither glorified him as God nor gave thanks to him, but their thinking became futile and their foolish hearts were darkened." Thus, as often happens, the mind-ramblings of a good man have brought evil upon mankind.

The religion that Darwin mentioned is the religion you, sirs, have adopted as a cardinal doctrine of religious Humanism. And, unlike Darwin, to my knowledge, none of your kind has ever expressed any regret for leading multitudes away from their Creator. On the contrary, you insist that school children must accept this religious theory as fact, if they are to become true scientists and understand the physical universe.

University professors and public school teachers routinely teach this religion to school children. Public television broadcasts it daily by way of nature programs. *Kratt's Creatures,* a public television nature program expertly designed for children, outrightly teaches this religion as fact to our children. And all this religious indoctrination is sponsored by government at taxpayer expense.

A Monstrous Hoax

Although lauded as scientific reasoning, the whole concept of evolution is a monstrous hoax. The absurdity of the concept is proven by an indispensable axiom of scientific discovery – the law of cause and effect. In true science – physical, social, or political – every existing condition must have had a creating cause.

The evolutionists' primary design is to destroy opposition to their agenda. (If conditions are evolving and not created by willful acts, then it must follow that the end results are inevitable and irresistible. In which case, all opposition might just as well surrender to the evolutionists' will.)

So what is the truth of the matter? Simply this: The evolutionary process does not exist. All existing conditions – biological, physical, social, and political – did not evolve. They were caused by willful acts. In a word, these conditions were created, not evolved.

So, how did the first life form come into being? What was it made of and where did that substance come from? When was there nothing that became something, and how? Again, sirs, our limited human mind is standing at the threshold of faith. Every human being must accept some things by faith, or become mindless of them. By faith, you have accepted the way of atheism and death. The wise choose the way to life, by faith in the Bible record.

Doctrine 3
The Nature of Man

H. Manifesto I: Holding an organic view of life, humanists find that traditional dualism of mind and body must be rejected. [8]

The Liberator: Humanists "find that traditional dualism of body and mind must be rejected." How did you "find" it? By "holding an organic view."

In other words, sirs, you adopted a "view" of man by faith, and then "found" a religious doctrine based on faith in that view. You would have been more honest to say, "Humanists *believe* the traditional dualism of mind and body must be rejected."

I understand you to say that man is nothing more than organic matter, having no spiritual part to his being. Of course, we cannot see the spiritual part of our being.

"The wind blows wherever it pleases," said Jesus, "You hear its sound, but you cannot tell where it comes from or where it is going. So it is with everyone born of the Spirit" (*John 3:8* NIV).

So where are we? Right back to the door of faith. Please don't think me disrespectful, sirs; but I choose to enter this door with Jesus Christ, not with religious Humanists. You too would be wise to choose Christ – to choose life instead of death.

Doctrine 4
Science – The Highest Authority

H. Manifesto I: Humanism asserts that the nature of the universe depicted by modern science makes unacceptable any supernatural or cosmic guarantees of human values. [9]

The Liberator: This religious dogma of Humanism is a little difficult to decipher. Modern scientists are well aware that they have not answered the great issues of life. They have merely unlocked some secrets of the physical universe – as they found it already existing – and have learned to make useful devices out of materials already provided. They have done a marvelous job; and, it was not necessary to deny the existence of God to do so.

With all due respect, sirs, I think it is pseudo-scientists like yourselves (psychologists, psychiatrists, sociologists, and philosophers) who are at war with God Almighty. I think you are on a head trip, seeking to use physical science to bolster your atheistic religious concepts.

At any rate your statement, "supernatural or cosmic guarantees of human values," does not come through clearly. For a clearer statement of your value system, I shall take up the question with Humanist Manifesto II a little later.

Doctrine 5
Religious and Social Evolution

H. Manifesto I: Humanism recognizes that man's religious culture and civilization, . . . are the product of a gradual development due to his interaction with his natural environment. [10]

The Liberator: So far as I know, this is true of all naturalistic religions, including your own. However, you are overlooking one shining exception.

Go to the scriptures of the Hebrews, both Old and New Testaments. You will not find a religion being developed by their interaction with nature, unless you have a rather undisciplined imagination. You will find rather a system of belief and values with all the indications of an unfolding revelation, coming not from nature, but – as our nation's founders stated it – from nature's God.

In social science, the concept of evolution destroys a fundamental principle of decent society – the principle of responsibility and accountability. (According to social evolution, no one is responsible for the condition. It simply evolved without a cause.) The concept of evolution, therefore, is the humanist doctrine most destructive of decent society.

Evolutionists will claim that the present "wave of globalism" is evolving and, therefore, irresistible. Not so! Like all conditions, it is being created by willful acts which can be resisted and overcome.

H. Manifesto I: We are convinced that the time has passed for theism, deism, modernism, and the several varieties of "new thought." [11]

The Liberator: Among other things, that statement impresses me as being rather pompous and bigoted. You have convinced yourselves that your religion is superior to all religions of all mankind of all ages, past and present.

Sirs, this should come as no surprise to you: A human being will not be without a god of some kind for long. We are not created that way. Man desires to be the center of his universe; but, he must have a god to place him there.

Man is your god; Self is your savior; and Science is your gospel. Man is corruptible and fallible; and, Science is too sterile, too impersonal, too cold, too dead.

H. Manifesto I: It follows that there will be no uniquely religious emotions and attitudes of the kind hitherto associated with belief in the supernatural. [12]

The Liberator: You are a cool lot, all right. So make way for New Age.

Secular and scientific Humanism is swiftly being outpaced by New Age Humanism. New Age replaces your science gospel with a hodge podge of all the gods of ancient mystical religions and spiritualism, whose time, you were convinced, had passed.

You say all is material. They say all is spirit.

Rejecting the plain truths of the Bible, man-worshipping religions take many strange forms.

Humanism and the Bible

The Liberator: All the world's religions have ancient roots. Did Humanism first appear in 1933, or is it older?

H. Manifesto I: As old as human civilization itself. It has its roots in classical China, Greece, and Rome. [13]

The Liberator: I think the Bible and other ancient writings date Humanism and human civilization much older than the classical period.

The Bible depicts Humanism in the story of the fall of Adam and Eve – the earliest account of an impostor robbing the nest. This incident, describing the beginning of Humanism, predates any written record: ". . . in the day ye eat thereof, then your eyes shall be opened, and ye shall be as gods" (Genesis, Chapter 3).

The story of these human "gods" continues in the Bible and other ancient writings. It is essentially the story of a fallen race, engaged in murderous wars of pillage or conquest – in worship of mystical spirits or their most powerful men and women (real and imagined) – and in other practices degrading to the individual and to their society.

The Apostle Paul, about 60 A.D., gives us a brief, and not so complimentary, view of ancient Humanism.

> For although they knew God, they neither glorified him as God nor gave thanks to him, but their thinking became futile and their foolish hearts were darkened. Although they claimed to be wise, they became fools and exchanged the glory of the immortal God for images made to look like mortal man and birds and animals and reptiles. Therefore God gave them over in the sinful desires of their hearts to sexual impurity and the degrading of their bodies with one another. They exchanged the truth of God for a lie, and worshipped and served the created things rather than the Creator – who is forever praised. (*The Bible, Romans* 1:21-25, NIV).

Thus Humanists were concisely defined nearly 2000 years ago as those who "worshipped and served created things rather than the Creator." This definition, I believe, is valid for Humanism in all its forms, ancient and modern. In times ancient and modern "created things" refers to man and his inventions.

I think Christianity is your real anathema. Am I right?

Humanism and Christianity Irreconcilable

H. Manifesto I: We consider the religious forms and ideas of our fathers no longer adequate. [14]

The Liberator: Some of you have striven to include our nation's founders under your anti-Christian umbrella. Having failed in this, you simply reject their God, and their Christian concepts of society, law, and government.

You would destroy the works of the founding fathers and rebuild this nation upon your atheistic religion. You are very much like the nest-robbing cuckoos. You contributed nothing to build the American nest. You simply intend to steal it and fill it with your own kind.

But, to me, your last statement tacitly admits that you do, indeed, understand that our nation's founders were Christian. You are at war with Christianity as we shall soon clearly see.

You have proclaimed your enmity against our nation's founders, their Christian religion, and the free, self-governing republic they founded upon their religion. So now, what do you propose?

The Humanist Agenda for America

H. Manifesto I: A socialized and cooperative economic order must be established. [15]

The Liberator: Religiously, you are Atheists. Economically, you are Socialists. This explains your long-standing admiration for the Soviet Union.

How well I remember the hue and cry of Humanists in the media, in Congress, and elsewhere when President Reagan correctly labeled the atheistic socialist Soviet Union an "evil empire."

Human rights, which you pretend to champion, were viciously trampled by that Humanist regime.

H. Manifesto I: The goal of humanism is a free and universal society in which people voluntarily and intelligently cooperate for the common good. Humanists demand a shared life in a shared world. [16]

The Liberator: I think I see a contradiction of concepts here. "Humanists demand" and "voluntarily cooperate" are incompatible mindsets.

This is a high-minded statement, sirs, with very pretty words. But, with all due respect, it is purely pie in the sky.

A one-world socialist system, based on your man-worshipping religion – which is what you propose – was the Soviet Union. That evil empire was to stand only 60 more years after you wrote Humanist Manifesto I. Then it fell under the weight of its own incompetence and despotism. Yet your pipe dream of worldwide socialism and forced redistribution of wealth (or poverty) is undiminished.

You fill our ears with pretty words; but, your religion accomplishes the very opposite of what you say. It leads to the most barbarous despotism.

Go to Socialist Nazi Germany and the Communist Soviet Union for proof. Before the ink was dry on your *Humanist Manifesto I*, these two man-worshipping systems were slaughtering millions of their own people. Then they turned all of Europe and Asia into a human slaughterhouse.

Humanist despots of the twentieth century have butchered more people than all other religious wars of human history combined, yet you stumble blindly onward, hell-bent to restructure America and the world on your wicked Humanist worldview.

13

THE SUBVERSION
REAFFIRMED

"As in 1933, humanists still believe that traditional theism, especially faith in the prayer-answering God, assumed to love and care for persons, to hear and understand their prayers, and to be able to do something about them, is an unproved and outmoded faith."
Humanist Manifesto II

L et us now move ahead to 1973 and have a talk with the signers of Humanist Manifesto II. In this discussion, we will ask for a progress report on the Humanist religion and for clarification of its value system.

We have tallied the list of signers of Humanist Manifesto II and find the following:

90 Humanist and Ethical Organization Members/Officers
78 University Professors
22 Psychologists/Psychiatrists/Humanist Counselors

21 Writers/Lecturers
14 Unitarian-Universalist Ministers
9 Business Consultants
4 Medical Doctors
2 Jewish Rabbis
2 School Teachers
2 Military/Chaplain
2 Planned Parenthood
1 National Association for Repeal of Abortion Laws
1 Founder, National Organization for Women
1 National Women's Conference
1 Committee for Fair Divorce and Alimony Laws
1 Americans United for Separation of Church and State
1 Public Policy Training Institute
1 National Committee for an Effective Congress
1 Hoover Institute
1 Overseas Development Council
1 United Nations Representative
1 Mediator Fellowship Officer
1 Sensory Awareness Center
1 Mathematician
1 Scientist
1 Economist [1]

The Liberator: (*to American Humanists*) Since you are an atheistic association, it seems rather strange that Unitarian ministers and Jewish rabbis would join your ranks.

Humanism and Apostate Christians and Jews

Humanist Manifesto II: (*dated 1973*)
Many within religious groups, believing in the future of humanism, now claim humanist credentials. [2]

The Liberator: From the beginning of their nationality, some Jews, stiff-necked and uncircumcised in heart, have rejected the God of Abraham, Isaac, and Jacob – but Jewish rabbis?
I believe there is a story behind the falling away of the Unitarians. I think the story might be titled, *From Puritanism, to Congregationalism, to Unitarianism, to Atheism: How the Mighty are Fallen.*

Your core group appears to be made up primarily of university professors, writers, Unitarian ministers, abortionists, political scientists, and pseudo-scientists (psychologists, psychiatrists, and sociologists). I can see feminism, socialism, secularism, liberalism, multi-culturalism, and globalism – even apostate Christianity and Judaism – all represented in your ranks.

Humanism and America's Moral Decline

The Liberator: All indicators show America to be a degenerating society, – morally, educationally, and politically.

It is said of John Dewey – most noted signer of Humanist Manifesto I – "John Dewey's fame is primarily as an educator, his reputation ranging from that of the foremost theorist of education of our time to that of the chief instigator of the moral breakdown of American civilization." [3]

I am convinced that Dewey is guilty on both counts. Dewey's "progressive schools" probably laid the groundwork for the sorry state of American education today. You are now teaming public education with your Humanist religion to complete the moral, social, and political degradation of America.

This brings us to the question of morals, ethics, and values. Perhaps you can clarify a statement from Humanist Manifesto I: "Humanism asserts that the nature of the universe depicted by modern science makes unacceptable any supernatural or cosmic guarantees of human values." [4]

The Humanist Value System

H. Manifesto II: We affirm that moral values derive their source from human experience. Ethics is autonomous and situational, needing no theological or ideological sanction. [5]

The Liberator: Morally speaking, sirs, humanity has experienced it all. From your reasoning it would follow that anything goes; that there is neither right nor wrong by any reliable standard.

Have you not confessed that human experience has revealed the depth of human brutality? Don't we all know the other fellow is capable of doing us wrong by some reliable standards that we all know from "the laws of nature and nature's God?" Does not the other fellow know that we are capable of the same offenses?

Is there one among us who actually believes the other fellows' whims and fancies are a reliable foundation for our system of values, a guide for conduct in our society, the underpinning of our law and government? Are you actually telling us that these human whims and fancies are the foundation of your religious values?

Your code of ethics is easy to write. It has just two parts: "autonomous ethics" and "situational ethics."

Autonomous Ethics

The Liberator: Your doctrine of "autonomous ethics" declares everyone to be his own god and, therefore, his own supreme authority:

"I am God."
"Whatever is, is right."
"If it feels good, do it."

Go to any degraded neighborhood in any big city. How would you describe it? Crime ridden, drug infested, impoverished, and prostituted. There you will see the ultimate expression of your principle of "autonomous ethics."

With all due respect, sirs, you are dreaming again.

As long as you "do thy neighbor no harm," as Samuel Adams stated it, and as long as our nation remains on Christian foundations, you may pretty well "do your own thing" without interference from the law.

On the other hand, what will be the result if you convert the American people to your concept of "autonomous ethics" without the sanction of the Bible? Our society will degenerate into anarchy, a microcosm of which may be seen in our inner cities. Such a society – with you and me included – will soon be ruled by a master. Man in society cannot be his own god for long.

Let's get real! Your religion can only lead to tyranny, in which some elitist oligarchy or some despotic master will decide, situation by situation, what is right or wrong!

Situational Ethics

The Liberator: Is it right or wrong? It strictly depends upon the situation, so says "situational ethics." And "autonomous ethics" says that each person may evaluate the situation and decide upon his own authority alone whether his actions are right or wrong.

Place your "situational ethics" in a courtroom.

The Menendez brothers, of mature age, confessed to shooting their own mother with a shotgun. They walked out of the house and left her for dead. Re-entering the house and finding their mother still alive, they finished her off with a second blast from the shotgun.

Were they guilty of murder? Your "situational ethics" says it all depends. A jury, deliberating under your value system, could not find these confessed murderers guilty! We are not talking mitigating circumstances here.

This is a value system gone cuckoo. There is no "situational" justice.

Many are the dead, the maimed, the robbed, the abused, the abandoned, the impoverished, the broken, the terrorized because of your "autonomous and situational ethics."

Was there a wrong committed against these? Their killers, robbers, and abusers didn't think so. They merely did what pleased them in the given situations. After all, were they not their own gods, accountable to no one but themselves?

According to your religion, there was no Bible with authority to guide, no God to give account to, no "supernatural guarantees of human values."

The American liberties that you enjoy, sirs, and seek to destroy by licentiousness, come not from twentieth century Humanism, but from a free republic established under God, within the societal moral boundaries sanctioned by the Bible.

Do you honestly believe you can destroy this republic and build a better society under world government, founded upon the shifting sand of human nature? But why bother to speak to you of honesty? Your honesty would be "situational" and totally unreliable.

Your ethics, sirs, is planted firmly in mid air. It has no honesty, no integrity, no character, no stability, no dependability, no accountability.

Rejecting a simple Bible restraint, "Thou shalt not steal," Humanists can, with no compunction, steal every institution and every organization in America. If you were not dressed up in the fine garments of intellectualism, you would be seen as the most scurrilous of characters.

You, like the President you elected in 1992, must continually test the air to see which way the wind is blowing, so you can decide which virtue seems inconvenient and, therefore, dispensable for the moment. I suppose this continual testing of the air is why you think it necessary to form yourselves into ethical societies.

Situational ethics is the very heart and soul of the con artist. Yet you claim to highly value the unrestrained liberty of the individual.

Unrestrained Personal Liberties

H. Manifesto II: The preciousness and dignity of the individual person is a central humanist value. We reject all religious, ideological, or moral codes that denigrate the individual, suppress freedom, dull intelect, dehumanize personality. We believe in maximum individual autonomy consonant with social responsibility. [6]

The Liberator: Those are pretty words, very pretty words. With all due respect, sirs, if we wish not to "denigrate the individual, suppress freedom, dull intellect, and dehumanize personality," the religion we must reject is your own.

When your legal arm, the American Civil Liberties Union, comes to court under your religious banner, we find that you stand for absolute freedom of expression, regardless of how it might denigrate the individual. At the same time, social responsibility goes out the window.

It should be evident to logical minds that situational ethics and social responsibility are not compatible concepts. Unrestrained release of debased instincts, which you call "rights," is your forte – not social responsibility. You are no doubt the most socially irresponsible association in America today.

But then, I must remember that situational ethics allows you to lie when you think the situation calls for it. Of what value, then, is "situational" social responsibility?

You care nothing for the "preciousness" of the unborn. Your sixth statement supports the killing of conceived human life in the womb. [7]

This method of birth control and population control has now degenerated to partial-birth abortion. With the baby alive and fully born except for the head, the abortionist severs its spinal column and draws out its brains, sometimes saving its body parts for medical purposes. I must apologize for this gruesome word picture, but I must be candid.

On November 8, 1995, President Clinton had opportunity to stop this grisly, inhuman practice, but he refused. On that very same day a man was hailed into a Florida court for mistreating a dog. If convicted, he could face a 15 year prison term. Such is the "ethics" of Humanist America.

Since you are champions of the "preciousness and dignity of the individual person," I would expect you to oppose such practices as using tissue from aborted babies for medical research and other medical purposes.

H. Manifesto II: We would resist any moves to censor basic scientific research on moral, political, or social grounds. [8]

The Liberator: (*musing silently over memories of Auschwitz, Joseph Mengele, Nazi Germany*)

You approve suicide (killing oneself), and euthanasia (killing of other individuals whose condition you do not specify). [9]

Shadows of Jack Kevorkian, ("Doctor Death"), Derek Humphrey, and his Hemlock Society pervade your doctrine. Yours is a religion of death, not life; of degradation, not "preciousness and dignity of the individual person."

You support no-fault divorce, and make no effort to discourage the breakup of biological families. You do not seem to care for the "preciousness and dignity" of the children from broken homes, traumatized by this curse on American society, or their abandoned mothers, left in poverty, often dependent upon taxpayers for their support.

You couch your support for sodomy in words of "preciousness and dignity of the individual person," but your legal arm defends the most vile and open displays of this degrading lifestyle.

In short, sirs, you are selective in the individuals you recognize as precious. Your humanitarianism must contribute to your ultimate goal. Of what value is "situational" humanitarianism?

Humanism: Failed but Unrepentant

The Liberator: Forty years have passed since your Humanist predecessors issued Humanist Manifesto I, defining their atheistic religious beliefs and spelling out their agenda for America. They rejected our nation's founders, their Christian religion, their free enterprise economic system, and their concepts of law and government. I suppose they presumed themselves wiser than the founding fathers and able to devise a better system.

Tell us, sirs, has the Humanist religion, which they instituted in America, reached their glorious goals?

H. Manifesto II: Events since then make that earlier statement seem far too optimistic. [10]

The Liberator: Please explain.

H. Manifesto II: Nazism has shown the depths of brutality of which humanity is capable. Other totalitarian regimes have suppressed human rights without ending poverty. [11]

The Liberator: Marxist humanism, which you so long admired in the Soviet Union has let you down, hasn't it?

When you signed Humanist Manifesto II in 1973, you could not have known that the Humanist Soviet empire would collapse under the weight of its own incompetency and despotism just 17 years later.

Humanist China continues to oppress her own people, as you well know. Secular social nationalism (Nazism) is little more than the same despotism behind another humanist mask.

These are all man-worshipping systems. I sincerely hope you have learned what our founding fathers knew over two centuries ago – Government without God is always tyranny.

Humanist Manifesto I preached the gospel of science. Do you think science has proven to be a satisfactory gospel?

H. Manifesto II: In learning to apply the scientific method to nature and human life, we have opened the door to ecological damage, overpopulation, dehumanizing institutions, totalitarian repression, and nuclear and biochemical disaster. [12]

The Liberator: You have agreed, sirs, 40 years of Humanist experimentation has failed. Why not take this opportunity to turn around and return to the faith of your fathers, to affirm this nation under God, whose Providence alone, with our intelligent cooperation, can save us?

I firmly believe, sirs, the Bible has the answers to all our personal, social, and national problems. But if we reject its timeless principles, invent and re-invent our own do-it-yourself value system, we will only wander deeper into the wilderness. Without confidence in an unchanging magnetic north, our compasses, no matter how well we design them, will never direct our course.

H. Manifesto II: As in 1933, humanists still believe that traditional theism, especially faith in the prayer-answering God, assumed to love and care for persons, to hear and understand their prayers, and to be able to do something about them, is an unproved and outmoded faith. [13]

The Liberator: Because of the dismal failure of Humanist Manifesto I, and your refusal to return to the Truth, you were forced to re-write Humanist Manifesto. You called this re-written version, Humanist Manifesto II.

In reality, you must revise and re-write continually because your religion is based on the shifting sand of human nature. Metaphorically speaking, you have declared there is no magnetic north; and, you have thrown away your compass.

Your "I am God" mentality makes "Self" supreme and allows you no chance to see your error and change your mind. Such a mentality, unrepented, is destined to self-destruct. And you will take America down with you, if you are not successfully opposed.

Your last statement singles out Christians and orthodox Jews for attack. I think you realize that Christianity and the Bible alone is preventing your design for America. Destroy these great pillars of American liberty, and who shall save us from some despot, rising to power from the dissipated ruins of our once virtuous society?

H. Manifesto II: We can discover no divine purpose or providence for the human species. No deity will save us; we must save ourselves. [14]

The Liberator: With all due respect, sirs, after 60 years of tinkering with your do-it-yourself salvation kit, our society is nearer the brink of ruin or revolution.

Over 350 armed militia groups exist in the United States, intent on disrupting or bringing down our government. And worse – we have just begun to suffer the horrors of made-in-America terrorism. Americans never even dreamed of these things until you started the erosion of our Christian foundations, pushing the more fragile personalities into irrational and irresponsible conduct.

You have confessed the depth of brutality to which humanity is capable. This is the same humanity, sirs, upon which you base your religion.

Your man-god has failed you. Your science-gospel has failed you. Your self-savior will surely fail you too.

In vain you declare man capable of saving himself. You need to save yourselves and your country from the madness of Humanism, by returning to the faith of your fathers.

The Many Masks of Humanism

The Liberator: Your religion appears to be the philosophical/religious head of a many-tentacled organism, with a global secular/socialist mission. From your list of organizations, it appears that you have created an "ism" and one or more organizations for each of your social and political aims.

Humanist Manifesto II: Many kinds of humanism exist in the contemporary world. The varieties and emphases of naturalistic humanism include "scientific," "ethical," "democratic," "religious," and "Marxist" humanism. Free thought, atheism, agnosticism, skepticism, deism, rationalism, ethical culture, and liberal religion all claim to be heir to the humanist tradition. [15]

The Liberator: Sirs, what company you keep!
Some varieties, I recognize.
Marxist humanism has been plotting the seditious overthrow of our free American republic for most of the twentieth century. Some, if not all of the other varieties, I believe, have been their fellow travelers.

All, I am sure, stand for an America radically different from the one our founders gave us – the one that served us so well for over two centuries.

Just where do humanist loyalties lie?

Humanism and the New World Order

H. Manifesto II: The best option is to transcend the limits of national sovereignty and to move toward the building of a world community. [16]

The Liberator: The Humanist dream of a one-world secular/socialist government has not changed since 1933.

Would radical notions such as La Frontera, a proposed cultural region encompassing the southwestern United States and northern Mexico, be compatible with your goal?

H. Manifesto II: It [world government] would not exclude pride in national origins and accomplishments nor the handling of regional problems on a regional basis. [17]

The Liberator: You have no problem, then, with illegal aliens pouring across our borders and devouring our substance through every kind of federal welfare program?

H. Manifesto II: Extreme disproportions in wealth, income, and economic growth should be reduced on a worldwide basis. [18]

The Liberator: You seem to favor forced redistribution of wealth on a world-wide scale – shadows of Marx, Lenin, and Stalin of the fallen Soviet Union. As I understand it, the American way to distribute wealth has always been to work for it. But, I suppose, this concept was developed in the American workplace and not in the ivory halls of academia.

The United States, then, would be required to surrender her culture, her sovereignty, and her wealth to the transnational – that is to say, the one-world government?

H. Manifesto II: This [world government] would appreciate cultural pluralism and diversity. [19]

The Liberator: You are the source of "multi-culturalism," "bilingualism," and "diversity" with which you are presently indoctrinating our school children. You must destroy our unique American culture before you can create the "international child of the future."

You will tear our unique American culture into its many ethnic components. Then you will regionalize America ethnically under your New World Order.

Do we get to keep our American laws?

Humanism and the World Court

H. Manifesto II: We look to the development of a system of world law and world order based upon transnational federal government. [20]

The Liberator: This must be the reason Hillary Clinton and her U.S. team have been flitting from one international conference to another, laboring over such knotty international problems as defining human gender and how American parents must raise their children. The goal of these conferences, I strongly suspect is to turn such personal matters over to a World Court. And considering what your U. S. Supreme Court has done to us over the last several decades, may Heaven save us from a World Court!

As I have observed power shift and concentrate from the local to the state to the federal government, I have seen personal liberties slowly dwindle away. It seems the higher the level of government, the bigger and more intrusive the bureaucracy, and the more tyranny required to enforce its laws, to the demise of individual liberty. I believe this was also what America's founders were trying to prevent.

Are you out of your minds, sirs? Human history is strewn with the corpses of societies that lost their culture and their freedom to foreign conquering powers. But, to my knowledge, never was there a people in history – free, strong, and prosperous – yet foolhardy enough to gratuitously offer up their wealth, their liberty, and their government to a weaker foreign power. You will never sell this scheme to Americans, sirs, unless you first deceive them into insanity.

Humanism Summed Up

The Liberator: In a word, what is the sum of your religious principles?

H. Manifesto II: They are a design for a secular society on a planetary scale. [21]

The Liberator: (*musing silently in disbelief*)
A one-world secular/socialist order. Ghosts of Marx, Lenin, Stalin. Do religious Humanists actually love these would-be global despots? Will these people never learn?

H. Manifesto II: We . . . reaffirm a commitment to the building of world community, at the same time recognizing that this commits us to some hard choices. [22]

The Liberator: Your religion does, indeed, force us into hard choices. Religious liberty is precious to all of us – yours as well as ours. Certainly I would have no right nor inclination to berate your religion as I have done, except for these things:

- Your religion is, in reality, a religious mission to destroy our time-tested Christian foundations and replace them with your amoral, Godless worldview. You would eradicate Christianity completely from the fabric of American society and government.
- Your religion is an agenda for social and political action, leading to religious, social, and political tyranny.
- Your religion is a plan of action by which you would destroy our people's virtues and our nation's sovereignty, then surrender us over as political and economic pawns to a one-world socialist government.
- Your plan of action is subversive, as we shall soon see.

The Lowest Common Denominator

The Liberator: A question has puzzled me for years: As Christianity strives to elevate the individual – and thereby society and government – to a higher plane morally, mentally, economically, socially, and spiritually, why does religious Humanism push liberties downward to licentiousness and inhuman practices? I think our discussion has given me the answer.

Your announced goal is a one-world secular society, ruled by a one-world secular/socialist government. To fit every person in the world into this scheme, you must first level all of us to the lowest common denominator.

- You do not have the economic power to raise anyone's economic status; so, you would redistribute America's wealth and lower everyone to the lowest economic common denominator.
- You do not have the moral character to raise anyone's moral standard; so, you would reduce everyone to the lowest moral common denominator.

- You do not have the values to raise anyone's educational level; so, you are dumbing down education to the lowest common denominator.

In short, you have no power to elevate, only to degrade. This, sirs, is the mark of tyrants.

If We Wish to Remain Free

The Liberator: Despite your high-minded words, your religion is a religion of failure. Your words speak of high ideals; but, your accomplishments are negative and degenerate. You accomplish the opposite of what you say. And should you ever succeed in reducing all of us to the lowest common denominator – mentally, morally, economically, and socially – you would then hand us over as puppets to a one-world government. Thus you would have accomplished, by deception and subterfuge, what your Marxist compatriots have not been able to accomplish by military force.

Only Christianity stands between you and your diabolical goal.

I can only speculate as to the hard choices you see for Humanists. But I know what hard choices you are forcing upon the people.

If we, as Americans, wish to remain free, we must learn to recognize your religion – in whatever institution it may be at work and behind whatever mask it may be hiding. We must realize there is no more time for delay. You have proclaimed the twenty-first century as the century of Humanism; and, century 21 is only months away.

Had the people today and understanding of the war against their God-given liberties, they would strangle the Humanist cuckoo in the American nest.

14

MINISTERS OF
ANOTHER SORT

"These teachers must embody the same selfless dedication as the
most rabid fundamentalist preachers, for they will be ministers of another sort, utilizing a classroom instead of a pulpit."
The Humanist Magazine

Τhe socialist agenda of the nineteenth century gave way to the
communist conspiracy of the twentieth. The designs of these
political systems have now been exposed and are seldom mentioned today.

These subversive systems, however, were merely different political
expressions of the same religious worldview that furnishes common
doctrines and a common agenda for Humanists of many stripes and
colors. The outrage against liberty never ceases – it simply changes
names and faces.

The design against American liberty is always the same: The overthrow of our free, self-governing republic and the Christian worldview
upon which it stands.

As the twenty-first century dawns upon us, the deadly virus of religious Humanism has been spread throughout the American society and body politic. To see how this has been accomplished, we continue our discussion with Humanist Manifesto I.

The Purpose and Program of Humanism

H. Manifesto I: Religious Humanism maintains that all associations and institutions exist for the fulfillment of human life. [1]

The Liberator: That doesn't seem to be such a bright new revelation. So, what is your point?

H. Manifesto I: The intelligent
Evaluation,
Transformation,
Control, and
Direction of such associations and institutions, . . .is the
Purpose and Program
Of Humanism. [2]

The Liberator: What a contemptible, arrogant statement! What intellectual tyranny! What a world-class, elitist con job!

You assume that you alone have the intelligence to direct American institutions – institutions that were built centuries before you instituted your Humanist religion in America – and which fared much better without you.

But what an ingenious, diabolical plan! To propagate your religion, you will not build churches, temples, synagogues, schools, or universities as others have done. Like worthless cuckoos of birddom, you are simply stealing our universities, courthouses, legislative halls, government buildings of all kinds, newsrooms, even some churches and once-Christian organizations, but most of all our public classrooms.

Stealthily you are planting your own offspring in our institutions, which were built by our Christian ancestors. Your offspring are pushing from the American nest all the Christian values, liberties, and foundations of government held sacred by our Christian ancestors. In these stolen institutions you are substituting the doctrines of your Humanist religion.

In public institutions you are doing this at taxpayers' expense. In private and religious foundations you operate on tax-exempt contributions. Incredibly you are being paid to destroy America. Deceived people are working feverishly for you to bring about their own extinction as a virtuous, free society and as a sovereign nation.

When Humanists have full control, you will *transform*, *control*, and *direct* our once-free, self-governing United States into the jaws of a one-world secular/socialist state. Traditional morality from the Bible would see this ruse as thievery of the most colossal dimensions. But then, you have discarded traditional morality in favor of "situational ethics," which, I suppose, includes "the end justifies the means."

How great the power of wicked deceit! What an ambitious, diabolical scheme! How are you doing this to a people, 90 percent of whom claim to be Christian?

According to George Washington, "It is one of the evils of democratical governments, that the people, not always seeing and frequently misled, must often feel before they can act right."

You are taking advantage of this weakness in our system to slowly but surely destroy America. By numbing the senses of the people, you may betray them before they feel enough pain to act against you.

Let's consider some of the institutions that you are *evaluating, transforming, controlling,* and *directing* toward the *purpose* and *program* of religious Humanism. Where is your main base of operations?

Invading America's Classrooms

The Humanist: (from *The Humanist* magazine, January/February, 1983, p. 26.)
The battle for humankind's future must be waged and won in the public classrooms.

The Liberator: Mankind's future has long been shaped by several institutions: the home, the Church, the classroom. But you seem to be the first to introduce the concept of the public classroom as a battleground. By whom will your war on education be waged?

The Humanist: By teachers who correctly perceive their role as the proselytizers of a new faith; a religion of humanity.

The Liberator: A religion? It is my understanding that your legal front, The American Civil Liberties Union, persuaded your Supreme Court to outlaw the promotion of religion in public classrooms! Are your teacher converts actually ministers on a religious mission?

The Humanist: These teachers must embody the same selfless dedication as the most rabid fundamentalist preachers, for they will be ministers of another sort, utilizing a classroom instead of a pulpit.

The Liberator: What is their mission?

The Humanist: . . .to convey Humanist values.

The Liberator: Will you have special classes on the Humanist religion, or will your teachers spread your religious message along with other subjects?

The Humanist: . . . in whatever subject they teach.

The Liberator: I presume this religious indoctrination will be kept at the university level.

The Humanist: . . . regardless of the education level – preschool day care, or large state university.

The Liberator: Clearly you are violating your own demand for separation of Church and State, when you turn our public classrooms into mission fields for your religion. Perhaps you define "Church" as pertaining only to Christianity. Or maybe you simply apply your principle of "situational ethics," which allows you to lie, cheat, and steal, and your "autonomous ethics," which allows you and you alone to decide what the situation calls for – and these are the "Humanist values" you expect to convey to our school children!
Do you expect opposition to this devious scheme?

The Humanist: The classroom must and will become an arena of conflict between the old and the new.

The Liberator: What do you mean by "old?"
The Humanist: The rotting corpse of Christianity, together with

all its adjacent evils and misery.

The Liberator: Perhaps there are some besides yourselves who are ignorant enough to associate "evils" and "misery" with Christianity. But I do not believe this holds true for the vast majority of Americans. Our national roots sink deep into "the general principles of Christianity," as founding father, John Adams, stated it. And what do you mean by "new?"

The Humanist: . . . and the new faith of Humanism.

The Liberator: (*musing silently*)

Parents of America, do you understand what is happening to your school children? Do you care?

Christians – and Christian ministers – of America, are you listening? There is a religious war raging for the soul of America. Although subtle, that war is all around you. Are you in the fight? If so, on whose side?

Redirecting American Education

The Liberator: So there we have it, right from the horse's mouth, so to speak. Our school children are being dumbed down because your teacher converts are not concentrating on academics. They are busily trashing the parents' religion, their authority, and their values, and making Humanist converts of their children – "the international children of the future."

So you Humanists expected a fight in the public classroom. I'm not sure you will find much opposition. You have captured our Supreme Court, making the battle rather difficult for Christians who are long accustomed to respecting the law. And twentieth-century Christians, unlike their colonial counterparts, seem disinclined to fight for their children's future.

To date you have had a free hand to do with America pretty much as you pleased. As the American Titanic sinks, the Christian band plays on!

How are you getting control of American education? How can you use public buildings free of charge as your religious chapels and force the taxpayers to pay your religious missionaries? I think I know.

By the time John Dewey signed Humanist Manifesto I, religious

Humanism had already gained virtual control of our universities. You held advantaged positions in the nation's universities, entrusted with the development of the minds of America's youth. You violated that trust and began your religious indoctrination of future teachers, lawyers, journalists, authors, political scientists, psychologists, sociologists, and, yes, clergy.

Your tenured radical professors in America's universities turn out a steady stream of teachers indoctrinated in Humanist nonsense, derived from such accredited courses as:

"Taking Marx Seriously"
"Sexualities – From Perversity to Diversity"
"Environmental Advocacy"
"American Racism"
"Black Marxism," etc., etc.

Dedicated to propagating your religion at taxpayers' expense, your teacher/missionaries pass their Humanist ignorance along to our children and youth. Your missionary zealots have become our nation's teachers, occupying our educational system all the way from the college level down to kindergarten.

Teacher converts to your religion have transformed and controlled the most powerful union in the world. Your National Education Association, buying elections for candidates of a particular political bent, has strong-armed our federal government into creating an educational hierarchy in total control of public education.

In 1979, President Jimmy Carter and the Congress, under control of the Democratic Party, created the United States Department of Education. This was done to fulfill a promise to the National Education Association, a major force in Carter's re-election.

By 1983, you were so confident of your *transformation, control,* and *direction* of the educational hierarchy that you felt free to announce your takeover of public classrooms as chapels for your Humanist religion. You probably are pleasantly surprised that you have had so little conflict with (to use your words) "the rotting corpse of Christianity."

Using textbooks, into which you have written generous portions of your religious dogma, your teacher converts propagate your religion in all subjects, within the public classrooms of America. With scowl or biting reproof, your academic tyrants intimidate any parent's child who dares hint at anything of God or the Bible in public school.

You have ripped the Ten Commandments from school house walls and replaced them with posters promoting your religious amoral values. But you forbid our children to hear prayers at convocations and ball games, or to sing "Joy to the World" at Christmastime. (Too much of the "the rotting corpse of Christianity, together with all its adjacent evils and misery," I presume.)

Creating "International Children of the Future"

The Liberator: Your teachers in our public classrooms inculcate Darwin's theory of evolution – one of your religious dogmas – as if it were provable fact. At the same time, you successfully demand that the Bible account of the Creator and the Hebrew/Christian worldview be aggressively excluded. After declaring your atheistic worldview a religion, the Supreme Court allows you to propagate your religion in public classrooms at all levels and in all subjects.

Under the tutelage of your teacher converts, America's school children imbibe your religious ideals, such as "situational ethics," sexual "liberation," and children's "rights" against their parents. Pregnancy, abortion, and illegitimate birth among schoolgirls has soared.

Rape in school is not uncommon, rape of school teachers not unheard of. Either as gang terrorists, or in self defense against them, school children have armed themselves with guns, knives, and an assortment of other weapons. Murder is the number one killer of teenagers.

When our children enter public school each day, you pass them through metal detectors, hand them a condom, confine them in a godless environment, and teach them more of your religious principles that created these problems in the first place. More and more kids at an ever younger age, without hope, without purpose, are turning to mind-numbing drugs as an escape from the world you have created for them. Suicide is the number two killer of teenagers.

These are your hopes for dumbed-down, Goals 2000 "international children of the future" – puppet workers for your future global secular/ socialist state. This is the legacy of John Dewey and others of your Humanist forbears. This is your contribution to American education.

Yet, your touchy-feely curriculum encourages students to feel good about themselves even as their educational accomplishments plummet. Then you waste school funds on public relations experts to convince parents that everything is just fine down at the schoolhouse. Parents, many deceived by your propagandists, work feverishly to help you destroy their values in their own children and convert them to religious Humanism.

Citizens at large, stupefied by long-standing trust in school teachers and administrators – working hard to pay their school taxes, reassured by your public relations personnel, and misled by the media – rarely bother to vote in school board elections or to monitor their public schools. Thus you have a free hand to demand more and more money from taxpayers to purchase more and more Humanist ignorance for our school children.

This is public education in Humanist America as we approach the new millennium. But the long arms of Goals 2000, Educate America Act have not yet encircled all our school children. Many have escaped to private schools, mostly conducted by Christian organizations.

And fortunately there is a remnant of Christian America in our public schools. Not all public school teachers and administrators have been corrupted by your religion. Many stay in the public schools to earn a living and salvage what they can from the shambles of your design for American education. Sixty-two percent of public school teachers and administrators save their own kids by sending them to private schools. [3]

If you have your way, private schools will not long escape the tentacles of your secular/religious organism. Goals 2000, if not strangled in the cradle, will bring all education, public and private, under your power through the federal government. The Humanist cuckoo will then be in full control of the American education nest.

Re-directed education can go a very long way in fulfilling your *program* and *purpose* for the demise of America. But you need to *transform*, *control*, and *direct* several other institutions as well.

Programming America's Entertainment

The Liberator: I am told that our entertainment industry was created by immigrant Jews – who may have been slack in keeping the commandments – but held a healthy respect for their adopted country and the institutions, religion, and sensibilities of her people.

In the early days, Hollywood generally handled morals, ethics, and values in a manner agreeable to the traditional American value system – values generally sanctioned by the Jewish Old Testament. Christianity, also, was generally handled with respect.

Hollywood was never a great purveyor of high moral values, but in "the good old days" the shows were not disgustingly vile. Today the entertainment industry has now cast off all moral restraint and has become perhaps the most influential propagator of your Humanist religion. [4]

Playwrights, actors, artists, and their bosses were not difficult to convert to your religion. They had long since lived on the edge of societal restraint. "Situational ethics" was made to order for Hollywood and dominates American sitcoms. It is difficult to say whether public education or the entertainment media is doing more to infuse the American mind with your Humanist value system. Our natural need for entertainment makes us easy to manipulate through drama and music; and, America's appetite for entertainment has become insatiable.

Hollywood knows that the baser instincts of human nature are easily aroused, and that their arousal is extremely profitable. Thus, as other parts of your *program* have destroyed social restraints, the entertainment industry has degenerated from the sometimes sublime to the pornographic.

The Humanist belief in absolute freedom of expression has released Hollywood to pour out a steady stream of immorality, vulgarity, violence, and incivility. Television and movies have contributed inestimably to your *program* of leveling all Americans to the lowest moral common denominator. The music industry has largely followed the same course.

The Hollywood troupe, although they would sometimes produce a good show, were never personally adept at marriage, home, and family. How do we know? Their often immoral and adulterous lives are an open book and constant fodder for the scandal writers and weekly tabloids.

By displaying a steady diet of irresponsible sexual activity on screen, cable, and networks, the entertainment industry has probably helped Humanism more than any other institution:

- To destroy the traditional family;
- To instigate the abuse of women and children;
- To encourage teen sex and teenage pregnancy;
- To swell welfare rolls;
- To fill abortion mills.

By your Humanist value system, America has two and a half million irresponsible conceptions of human life every year – all abandoned by the males that sired them. Every year one and a half million of these babies are put to death in their mothers' wombs. Most of the others, mother and child, are cast upon the taxpayers for public support.

Abandoned mothers and traumatized children, however, do not concern you. After all, the stable, traditional American family stands in the way of your *program* and *purpose* for America's downfall.

Hollywood's War on America

The Liberator: Hollywood has found another gold mine in arousing the violent side of human nature. So a steady stream of crime and violence flashes across the movie and TV screens and through the "boom boxes" of America. The violent upsurge in crime and the countless victims left in its wake don't concern you at all. On the contrary, your legal arm is quick to the rescue of Hollywood and your criminal "clientele" with cries of "absolute freedom of expression" for Hollywood and "criminal's rights" for thugs. This too weakens America for your *program* and *purpose.*

Hollywood does not hesitate to assist you in reviling God Almighty, Himself. Some films coming out of Hollywood are so blasphemous and disgusting to American sensibilities, sirs, that I will not discuss them here. Instead I will recommend Michael Medved's eye-opening and aptly-named book, *Hollywood vs. America.* An equally appropriate title would have been *Hollywood: The Entertainment Branch of Religious Humanism.*

You now control the Walt Disney Company. You have turned this once family-oriented institution into one of the chief purveyors of everything vile in your amoral value system. Disney's TV series, *Nothing Sacred,* is nothing less than a Humanist broadside attack against Christianity in general and Catholics in particular. (Catholics of America, are you listening?)

The main character in *Nothing Sacred*, portrays a Catholic priest whose value system and "ministry" is repugnant to practically every tenet of the true Catholic faith. Indicative of Hollywood's attitude toward Christianity, this character was nominated to receive a Golden Globe award as best actor in serious drama.

In 1996, Empower America, a watchdog group, appealed for help in petitioning Time Warner, a powerful entertainment conglomerate, to stop recording music of the most abominable character. Examples were submitted of the rap music of 2 Live Crew, Nine Inch Nails, Tupak

Shakur, and Snoop Doggy Dog. Common decency forbids a repetition of the vile words of this so-called "music." In the appeal was a quote from a current issue of *U. S. News and World Report:*

> Like a junkie quivering for a fix, Time Warner simply can't resist cashing in on the amoral singers who work tirelessly to tear the culture apart, glorifying brutality, violence, and the most hateful attitudes toward women the public has ever seen, ranging from rape to torture and murder.

I have not heard of The National Organization for Women, one of your front organizations, making any move against these vile abusers of women. Perhaps NOW's assignment in your *program* and *purpose* for America is confined to promoting abortion and sodomy. Or possibly they were occupied at the time in psycho-sexually analyzing Dr. Seuss' *The Cat in the Hat.* [5]

Your high-minded intellectualism would never allow you to publicly endorse these abominations. But the fact remains: It is your war on Christianity, your basic contempt for America's history and traditional culture, and the widespread acceptance of your "situational ethics" that makes these things possible.

Some Flew Over the Cuckoo's Nest

The Liberator: Yet much of the blame must be laid on weak Christians. Hollywood stars, flaunting immorality and indecency, entice them to your theaters, where they adore their silver screen idols more than their Creator, "who is forever to be praised."

As if starving for entertainment, they imbibe your values and become more Humanist than Christian. They deposit their Christian money in Humanist bank accounts and unwittingly contribute to your destructive *program* for America.

According to Hollywood, the entertainment media simply acts out, in drama or music, what society has already chosen to do. Hollywood, they insist, has no responsibility for degeneracy in America, they simply re-enact it for entertainment.

Does the entertainment industry, in fact, have a powerful impact on the mind and does it play a major role in shaping the society we live in? "The Hollywood blockbuster had been playing for about 20 minutes when one of the characters took a gunshot in the face, the camera lingering on the gory close-up. Fifteen rows from the big screen, a little girl – no more than six years old – began shrieking. Her mother hissed, 'Shut up,' and gave her a stinging slap." *The Reader's Digest*, September, 1997, pages 37-38, tells the rest of the story.

From the front page of *Fort Worth Star Telegram*, December 18, 1997, we read, under the headline, *Japan cartoon off air after children fall ill* – "Nearly 600 children were rushed to hospitals Tuesday night after watching the program *Pokemon*, [pocket monsters]." Is a Humanistic Hollywood helping you shape our society for your *program* and *purpose* for America? You bet, it is. The Humanist cuckoo rules the entertainment nest.

Humanist education and Humanist entertainment together cannot fully accomplish your *purpose* for America. Hollywood has corrupted millions of Americans for you. Others – of more firm resolve – are more selective in their viewing. They refuse to indulge themselves in the degrading and blasphemous. The wisest fly over the cuckoo's nest, shunning your theaters altogether and turning off the degrading TV programs.

Media Mouthpieces

The Liberator: To complete your *program* and *purpose* for America you needed mass communication with a persuasive voice.

You now own the network news media; and, journalists indoctrinated in your religion, fill key positions – reporters, editors, producers, newsmen, and anchormen. Manipulation – not accurate reporting – is often their goal. By the language they use, by what they report and refuse to report; by how they cover a story and interpret events, they keep your Humanist principles before the masses. Your converts in the media praise your endeavors, cover up your failures, and ridicule those who resist you. At the same time, they hide your *program* and *purpose* for America.

Your news media makes certain that emissaries of religious Humanism appear to be the voice of that segment of society they presume to represent. Your selected "ism" gets the press.

• The media makes feminism appear to speak for the women of

America.

- Radical environmentalism is made to appear to be the voice of all who are concerned about wasting and polluting the planet.
- Liberalism is made to appear to be the people's choice in public affairs.
- Liberal religion is presented as the voice of Christianity.

The media, those great disturbers of the peace, search far and wide for some conflict, some tragedy, some confrontation. Speeches, rallies, and parades by one of your "isms" are magnified many times over, while seldom is heard a word from mainstream America. Thus by deceit, omission, and distortion, the media makes you roar like a lion and appear far more significant than you really are.

By magnifying the voice of a minority, the media makes the minority appear to speak for the majority. Those who resist your radical extremism, are labeled radical extremists.

The media rushes to the rescue of any tentacle of your Humanist organism, as evidenced by its coverage of Hollywood. [6]

The media has moved its self-appointed role as "fourth branch of government" into your Humanist camp. Journalists, indoctrinated in your religion, promote candidates who are compatible with your views and with issues you endorse

Public officials who resist your *program* and *purpose* feel the acid of your editorials and political commentaries. Other officials – no matter how immoral, dishonest, or greedy – who are agreeable to your worldview are praised and their character weaknesses ignored.

The people's respect for your media mouthpieces is just slightly higher than their respect for your lawyers, who rank lowest of all professions. Your situational ethics has destroyed the credibility of network media. The Humanist cuckoo occupies the media nest.

Reconstituting the Church

The Liberator: It is unlikely, sirs, that you could ever destroy America in the presence of an informed Church – faithfully grounded in the Bible and American history, and committed to Christ's Great Commission. I dare say, then, that you have some *program* and *purpose* for the Christian institution also.

H. Manifesto I: (1933) Certainly religious institutions, their ritualistic forms, ecclesiastical methods, and communal activities must be reconstituted as rapidly as experience allows, in order to function effectively in the modern world. [7]

The Liberator: But your religion is anti-Christian to the core. How can you conquer the Church? Will you *evaluate, transform, control,* and *direct* the Church also? Have you planted religious Humanists within her councils?

H. Manifesto II. (1973) Many within religious groups, believing in the future of Humanism, now claim Humanist credentials. [8]

The Liberator: Evidence of your invasion of the Church abounds:

- When the National Council of Churches joined atheist Madalyn Murray O'Hare in petitioning the Supreme Court to outlaw prayer in school.
- When a Methodist minister in Fort Worth denies cardinal doctrines of Christianity, and another in Washington, D.C., preaches global socialism.
- When a Lutheran woman seeks the aid of People for the American Way (another of your legal fronts), in forbidding children to pray at school.
- When a United Church of Christ minister heads the Americans United for Separation of Church and State.

In such cases, we know that more is being "reconstituted" than "ritualistic forms, ecclesiastical methods, and communal activities." These are but a few examples of the Humanist virus which possibly infects all Christian denominations to some extent.

Wolves in Sheep's Clothing

A solicitation letter, dated October, 1997, from Barry W. Lynn, Executive Director of Americans United for Separation of Church and State, prompts the following response:

The Liberator: I received your letter, Mr. Lynn, soliciting my support for Americans United. Why should I support your organization?

Barry Lynn: Give Americans United the resources we need to fight back against the Religious Right. Get back the satisfaction of knowing you're helping to put the heat on Pat Robertson and his Christian Coalition.

The Liberator: Why should I fight these people?

Barry Lynn: One of our staff members . . . wrote a whole book about Robertson. . . . It's chock full of the extreme, bizarre things Robertson has said over the years.

The Liberator: I think all of us get our foot in our mouth at times. I also have observed Mr. Robertson over the years. My observation is that Pat Robertson:

- Preaches a gospel of morality, life, and hope;
- Feeds the hungry;
- Ministers to the sick with prayer and medical help;
- Reports the news from a Christian perspective;
- Surveys political candidates as to their values and agenda and informs the people of their responses;
- Informs the people as to the voting record of their representatives in Congress.

I cannot see the dangerous threat to our liberties in these activities. As a matter of fact, Mr. Robertson seems to be doing what Humanist Manifesto II declared that Christianity has ceased to do.

Barry Lynn: You know the folks I'm talking about. My quarrel is with the self-appointed "family values" brigade who call separation of church and state a lie and yammer about making America a "Christian" nation. . . . We'll fight them in courts of law, courts of public opinion and through the media. We'll take them on anywhere. . . . I've dedicated my life to stopping them – from Pat Robertson, Jerry Falwell, James Dobson and Pat Buchanan – right on down to their foot soldiers.

The Liberator: I detect a great deal of hatred in your declaration of war on these Christians, Mr. Lynn. Where are you coming from?

Barry Lynn: Please understand one thing: Americans United's quarrel is not with religious Americans. Far from it. I'm a Christian minister myself, and many of AU's members are people of faith.

The Liberator: It is rather hard for me to understand: If you are a Christian minister for real, why have you declared war on Christianity as the religion undergirding the government of our nation? From many authorities, we know that our colonial forbears were almost 100 percent Christian in worldview, that the founders were unified on "the general principles of Christianity" – and that Christianity, to paraphrase George Washington, has been our government's "indispensable support."

I recall running across the name of your organization somewhere, Mr. Lynn. Ah yes! Americans United for the Separation of Church and State was a signer of Humanist Manifesto II in 1973. This explains your declared war on Christianity.

Humanist Manifesto II defines you not as Christian, Mr. Lynn, but, I think rather contemptuously, as "liberal religion."

"Many in religious groups," said Humanist Manifesto II, "believing in the future of Humanism, now claim Humanist credentials." You belong to that apostate part of Christianity that is seriously infected with the Humanist virus. Your kind needs to decide, Mr. Lynn, what you will be – either fish or fowl.

With all due respect, sir, I must call you what you now are – what I believe Christ would call you – "wolves in sheep's clothing."

Little by little, conference by conference, ministers like you who have imbibed large portions of religious Humanism in your Schools of Religion, lead their churches to cave in to the demands of radicals such as the Black Panthers, outlaw gangs, feminists, and homosexual activists. Deluding themselves that their self-effectuated piety is Christ-like, they do severe damage to Christianity and the moral foundations of our society and government.

The colonial Church, which shaped American culture and laid the foundations for America's government, was made of better stuff.

The Homosexual Ultimatum

The Liberator: The assault on the Church by militant homosexuals, unleashed by the societal and political successes of religious Humanism continues to intensify.

Congressman William Dannemeyer of California has heard all the moral, religious, and legal arguments of militant homosexuals firsthand. His expose of the homosexual ultimatum to Christians and Jews follows:

Jews and Christians have been homophobes for the better part of 3,000 years, persecuting homosexuals more than any other minority in the history of Western civilization. But now the tide has turned. We have at last "come out," and in so doing we have exposed the mean-spirited nature of Judeo-Christian morality. You have been narrow-minded and self-righteous. But with the help of a growing number of your own membership, we are going to force you to recant everything you have ever believed or said about sexuality.

Here are some of the things you will be expected to affirm, in the process of renouncing love, marriage, and family:

- Henceforth homosexuality will be spoken of in your churches and synagogues as a "honorable estate."

  You can either let us marry people of the same sex or better yet abolish marriage altogether.

  You will also be expected to offer ceremonies that bless our sexual arrangements, whether or not you retain marriage as something to be celebrated in your churches.
- You will also instruct your young people in homosexual as well as heterosexual behavior.

  If any of the older people in your midst object, you will deal with them sternly.
- We will in all likelihood want to expunge a number of passages from your Scriptures and rewrite others.

Warning: If all of these things do not come to pass quickly, we will subject orthodox Jews and Christians to the most sustained hatred and vilification in recent memory. We have captured the liberal establishment and the press. We have already beaten you on a number of battlefields. And we have the spirit of the age on our side. You have neither the faith nor the strength to fight us, so you might as well surrender now. [9]

I confess, sirs, I was tempted to question Congressman Dannemeyer's credibility. For most of us, these incidents happen in some far away part of the nation. We do not feel; so, we cannot see. And then one day, we find our liberties destroyed and ourselves bound by some tyrannical government policy vexatious to our moral values.

Beware the Militant Homosexual

The Liberator: Even as I was writing this, an appeal for help came in the mail from a beleaguered church in Madison, Wisconsin. Here is their story:

> The pastor of the church is a 17 year veteran in the Madison fire department. His offense was sharing some tracts with fellow firemen. The tracts stated that homosexuality is immoral and sinful according to the Bible. This exercise of free speech rights set off a firestorm of retaliation by the homosexual community that is threatening the pastor's job as fireman, his church, his home, and his family.
>
> Madison's fire chief ordered that the pastor be suspended for three months without pay and that he attend a pro-homosexual "diversity" training class.
>
> Never mind that all manner of publications are distributed at the fire stations – including pornographic and pro-homosexual materials.
>
> More than 300 militant homosexuals broke into the pastor's church service – chanting, "Crush the Christians! Bring back the lions!" These militants also urinated on the hallway floor, while those outside threw rocks at the church windows. Police arrived but refused to intervene.
>
> Radical homosexuals from the hate group, the Lesbian Avengers, vandalized the pastor's home in the middle of the night, trying to break in and leaving pink triangle stickers with graphic homosexual references pasted to the walls and windows.
>
> A radical homosexual group from the University of Wis-

consin admits to paying for the attack on the pastor's home, yet the police did nothing to bring them to justice.

Now, openly homosexual elected officials – city, county, and even state – are insisting that the pastor be fired from his fireman job, even though he has been an excellent fireman in Madison for over 17 years.

It might be noted in passing that the person you elected in 1992, as his first official act as President of the United States, gave sodomy the official blessing of the U. S. government. Being a man without moral convictions in matters of sexuality, he continues to embrace the militant homosexual movement, a strong element in his political successes.

Many ministers will cave in to homosexual demands and pressure their congregations to wallow in self-condemnation and beg forgiveness for their "mean-spirited, narrow-minded self-righteousness;" because they dared, with Christian love, to uphold the moral standards of the Bible.

Many congregations will quietly absorb the homosexual lifestyle into their churches, pretentiously giving it Christian status. You will be pleased.

You advocate total sexual liberation for all forms of homosexuality. Presumably you understand that such liberation will further adulterate the moderating influence of Christianity and weaken the moral foundations of American society and government.

Not a Pretty Picture

The Liberator: It might be well to allow the Apostle Paul to continue his description of a thoroughly corrupted Humanist society. Alert observers will see America's current course in his word picture, vividly painted nearly 2000 years ago:

Because of this, [their rejection of God and their worship of man] God gave them over to shameful lusts. Even their women exchanged natural relations for unnatural ones. In the same way the men also abandoned natural relations with women and were inflamed with lust for one another. Men committed indecent acts with other men, and received in themselves the due penalty for their perversion. Furthermore, since they did not think it worthwhile to retain the knowledge of God, he gave them over to a depraved mind, to do what ought not to be done. They have become filled with every kind of wickedness; evil, greed and depravity. They are full of envy, murder, strife, deceit and malice. They are gossips, slanderers, God-haters, insolent, arrogant, and boastful: they invent ways of doing evil; they disobey their parents; they are senseless, faithless, heart-less, ruthless. Although they know God's righteous decree that those who do such things deserve death, they not only con-tinue to do these very things but also approve of those who practice them. *(The Bible, Romans 1:26-32 NIV)*.

The Apostle Paul observed that Humanistic societies degenerate into open sexual depravity and rebellion against common decency.

Trends in America today affirm this. Such people are no longer capable of self-government and are ready for a master – perhaps the global master in the world of your Humanist dreams.

But your Humanist plants in the Church are deceiving many into rejecting these dire warnings. According to *World* magazine (February, 1995, page 24), top leaders in the Episcopal church have already rough-drafted a new *Book of Common Prayer*, complying with the demands of homosexuals.

Christians who are made of the same stuff as their colonial Chris-tian ancestors should draw a line in the sand, and, either put the Hu-manist impostors out of their churches or get out themselves. Your media will brand such Christians "the Radical Religious Right."

Cuckoos in the Church Nest

The Liberator: Cuckoos in the Church nest, whom Humanists hail as liberal religion, position themselves in the National and the World Councils of Churches, on whose rolls are familiar and long-respected denominations. [10]

These impostors are allowed to *transform*, *control*, and *direct* these councils. They write "official" statements, vainly attempting to Chris-tianize your Humanist values, and rubber stamp them for God. [11]

They take untold millions of dollars from American churches and divert these monies to your treacherous cause. Disregarding the objec-tions of millions of church members, they pass themselves off as the voice of American Christendom. The media gives them favorable press, while, at the same time, bashing uncooperative Christians as the "Radical Religious Right."

Possibly all divisions of Christianity have been infected to some extent with the Humanist virus. Christian openness to "whosoever will" makes churches vulnerable to infiltration by alien worldviews. Therefore, eternal vigilance on the part of Christians, both clergy and laity, is imperative if our churches are to remain true to the Bible, and our people are to remain free and self-governing.

Some of the adulterating of Christianity is by wicked design. Some is by ignorance of the fact that religious Humanism and Christianity are mutually exclusive and cannot be reconciled.

So you see Christianity as a "rotting corpse," do you? Christianity is a "rotting corpse," sirs, only to the extent that it has been infected with the Humanist virus.

Orthodox Judaism to a lesser degree, because of fewer numbers, is also a bulwark against your demoralizing of America. But, the two rabbis who signed Humanist Manifesto II testify to the fact that cuckoos have also invaded the Jewish community.

After all your dumbed-down education, the demoralizing influence of Hollywood, the bias of the media, and the apostasy of liberal religion, you still need the force of law to fulfill your *program* and *purpose* for America.

Wax in Their Hands

The Liberator: Lawyers are not trained to find and defend truth. They are trained to manipulate facts, words, and people to win their argument.

The Humanist doctrine of "situational ethics," therefore, is made to order for the legal profession. It is a rather frightful thought that lawyers, thus conditioned, fill our public-interest law firms, our legislatures, and our judgeships, making and interpreting the laws that control our daily lives.

By the time you published Humanist Manifesto in 1933, lawyer converts to your religion had already advanced to positions on the U.S. Supreme Court. One of them, Chief Justice Charles Evans Hughes, while governor of New York, had announced the judicial despotism that was soon to follow: "We are under a Constitution, but the Constitution is what the judges say it is." [12]

This despotic grab for power by the Supreme Court marked the beginning of the end for Constitutional government – jurisprudence based on what the Constitution plainly means. Since that time, we have moved steadily deeper into judicial despotism – jurisprudence based on whatever sitting judges may construe the Constitution to mean. By this twisted logic, these manipulators of facts, words, and people made themselves, not the Constitution, the Supreme Law of the Land.

As Thomas Jefferson had predicted, the Constitution became "a thing of wax in their hands." And, we might add, their perversion of the Constitution became a despotic yoke on our necks.

"Useful Tools for Social Change"

The Liberator: The American Civil Liberties Union predated your Humanist Manifesto I by 13 years. Like yourselves, its founder, Roger Baldwin, was a communist sympathizer. [13]

Baldwin declared in 1933, "civil liberties, like democracy are useful only as tools for social change." [14] Judging from the social activism of the Supreme Court for the last half century, the Court has come to the same mindset as Baldwin.

Roger Baldwin's concepts for social change were identical to the signers of Humanist Manifestos I and II. So, the American Civil Liberties Union was fathered in sedition and deceit. Its 75 year history has proven it to be the dutiful offspring of its father.

Humanist converts from your law schools have filled ACLU ranks from its inception. The ACLU, from the beginning, has been the legal arm of religious Humanism, promoting and defending in totality your *program* and *purpose* for America – the collapse of the United States of America and the creation of a one-world secular society under a one-world secular/socialist state.

Two main thrusts can be detected in the legal actions of the ACLU:

1. Promoting and protecting the religious concepts of Humanist Manifesto I and II in every American institution, public and private.
2. Attacking and erasing all traces of Christianity and the Bible from the same institutions.

Before Humanists can fulfill their treacherous dream for America and the world, you must first destroy the Biblical underpinnings of American society, law, and government and replace those destroyed foundations with religious Humanism.

Born of thieves and liars, the ACLU promotes your subversive mission under pretense of defending civil liberties.

A Snake in the Grass

The Liberator: We have in hand a letter from the U. S. Justice Foundation relating to a legal action in Hemet, California, typical of the ACLU.

When parents of an eleven year old schoolboy learned of his teacher's secretive classroom discussions about AIDS, sex, and marriage, they complained to school officials. The teacher was put on administrative leave pending verification of the complaints. Forty-one specific complaints were verified.

Enter the ACLU, demanding that the teacher keep his job and suing the parents for exercising their freedom of speech rights guaranteed by the First Amendment. To you, sirs, liberties too are "situational." Their exercise must further your *program* and *purpose* for America's downfall.

The tyranny of the ACLU is not confined to the lawsuits in which it actually engages. Perhaps more overbearing is the tyranny of the constant threat of disruptive and destructive lawsuits hanging over the heads of public administrators, teachers, even ministers of the gospel.

I borrow the words of William Donohue: "Just what are principals to do, to take one issue, about the problem of school crime if every time they try to stop it, they are met with a letter, phone call, or lawsuit from the ACLU focusing on the rights of the offenders?" [15]

The ACLU, like a snake in the grass, lies ready to strike at anyone who might attempt to exercise religious liberty of a Biblical nature in any public place, and at anyone who might threaten your entrenched Humanist religion in the same places. Neither is the ACLU above moving that threat into private institutions, including churches.

With judicial accomplices in every court in the land, the ACLU is determined to keep Christians under church-house arrest until your treacherous work is done. The Church, itself, is not safe from harassment by the ACLU, which is constantly searching for an excuse to destroy the tax-exempt status of churches and the free speech rights of ministers.

As you harass the moderating influence of Christianity from America's public affairs, your perverted sense of civil liberties releases countless vile and vicious criminals to prey upon their hapless victims.

Then you force crime's victims to pay twice for your client's crimes –
once by loss of property, life and limb – and again by paying judge and
jury, prosecution and defense, incarceration and parole and, of course,
the legal fees for protecting your recycled thugs. This too is your contribution to America.

No tyrant can be more oppressive than those in the legal system
whose sympathy lies with the lawless – and not with the law-abiding –
aiding those who harass the people's predominant religion to enforce
religious Humanism. Small wonder that lawyers are at the bottom of
the list regarding the respect of the people.

Humanist lawyers and judges can never rightly interpret our Christian Constitution. Their "situational ethics" is playing havoc with our
jurisprudence. The Humanist cuckoo is gaining control of our courts
of law.

Liberating our Captive Government?

The Liberators: By mid-twentieth century, sirs, your Humanist
religion had captured the federal courts. At about that same time you
gained virtual control of the U. S. Congress.

For 40 years you controlled the Congress and the Court. Inter-
mittently during the same 40 years, you have had virtual control of
the Presidency.

With the same Humanist worldview in virtual control of all branches
of our federal government, we have lost the concept of balance of power
between the three branches. Particularly out of Constitutional control is
your Supreme Court, which has the final word on all matters, uncontested
by the Executive and the Legislative branches. Thus your plan and program for America has moved ahead virtually uncontested.

One thing you have never gained – the good people of these United
States – nor the informed consent of the governed.

On November 8, 1994, Humanist Manifesto I and II engaged the
people's forward troops. The people – at least for a short time – wrested
control of their Congress from your despotic hands, and the Second
War for American Independence began.

The Congress, under new leadership, began a faltering effort to reverse the wrong direction in which you have been leading the country.
Unfortunately, the new Congress is not yet strong enough to overcome
the veto of your President, who will hold the office from 1992 to 2000.

It is regrettable also that the new leadership in Congress shows signs of caving in to the weight of your opposition. May we see 100 courageous replacements in Congress every two years until the people have regained control of their government – then onward to the liberation of all American institutions!

You have taken your turn at governing America, sirs; and, you have dismally failed. Government – of all places – is not the place for you. So give it up, and let the good people get America back on her original course.

★ ★ ★

15

COUNTDOWN TO GLOBAL BONDAGE

"There is a way that seems right to a man, but in the end it leads to death." The Bible, Proverbs 16:25 NIV.

Early in the twentieth century, Italian Communist Antonio Gramsci, advanced a nearly fail-safe scheme for effecting the Communist takeover of the world. He termed this treacherous scheme "a long march through the institutions."

It seems very likely that American Humanists were familiar with Gramsci's teaching when, in 1933, they announced the *purpose* and *program* of Humanism – "The intelligent, *evaluation, transformation, control, and direction* of such associations and institutions. . ."

As we saw in the last chapter, American Humanists have spent most of the twentieth century in their "long march through the institutions." Today, as we approach the twenty-first century, the goal of their long march is in sight.

We have also reviewed American society and government when we were one nation under God – when Christianity was our government's "indispensable support". Only a remnant of that once-great America remains today, severely damaged by the inroads of religious Humanism.

Because of the remnant of the "general principles of Christianity" in our government and the people's general adherence to Christianity, we still are relatively free as compared to many other peoples of the world.

Our remaining liberties that we enjoy today, however, are departing at an ever accelerating pace. They will be gone tomorrow if we fail to halt and reverse the Humanist " long march through our institutions" and put our nation back on her original course. This we must do quickly before we, as a once free and self-governing people, pass the point of no return.

Let's look at life in Humanist America today after half a century of *evaluation, transformation, control and direction* by religious Humanism. Then we will preview the Humanist world as it will be tomorrow if America's religious war against Christianity is finally won by religious Humanism.

Life Today in Humanist America

The Liberator: (*to American Humanists*)
To create Humanist America as she appears today, here is what you have done to our country:

- You have ripped the Ten Commandments – the basis of all decent human society and self-government – from our schoolhouse and our court house walls.
- You have turned our public schools into chapels of the Humanist religion – moral vacuums, without prayer, without Bibles, and without Christian moderation.
- You have filled these schools with Humanist "ministers of another sort," Humanist posters, Humanist textbooks, Humanist religious dogmas, Humanist political concepts, Humanist amoral values, condoms, violent gangs, guns, knives, and metal detectors.
- Force feeding Humanist ignorance into the nation's children, you have lowered our academic achievement level from number 1 to number 17 among the developed nations of the world.

- You have taught our children to reject God, to dishonor their father and mother, to rebel against legitimate authority, to vilify our traditional American culture, and to defame our nation's Christian founders and foundations.
- You have refilled their emptied minds with ideas of liberation to every form of illegitimate and perverse sexual behavior.
- You have encouraged school children to be sexually active outside of wedlock, destroying their childhood prematurely and forever.
- You have given them condoms and told them to be careful.
- You have infected them with AIDS and other vile diseases.
- You have sent them to Planned Parenthood – one of your tax-payer-supported front organizations – for instruction in abortion without their parents' consent.
- You have cursed American soil with innocent blood from your overflowing abortion mills.
- You have raised the rate of out-of-wedlock childbirths to nearly 50 percent of all newborns.
- You have laid the burden of illegitimate birth and illegitimate parenthood on the taxpayers' shoulders.
- You have vainly attempted to assuage our children's sense of uselessness and hopelessness with mind-numbing drugs.
- You have prostituted them, intoxicated them, and caused them to sink into every form of moral depravity.
- You have filled our drug rehabilitation centers, attempting to restore the minds you have destroyed, but mostly in vain.
- You have murdered our children and youth and caused them to kill themselves.
- You have filled our divorce courts, ending 50 percent of our marriages there.
- You have destroyed the traditional American home and scattered our traumatized children to the wind.
- You have given us six million single mothers and then abandoned them and their children to their fate of poverty, dependence, and abusive treatment by live-in "boyfriends."
- You have overflowed our family courts and our child support courts in a vain effort to correct these Humanist-caused crimes against the American family.
- You have filled our mental hospitals, rape crisis centers, and shelters for battered women.

- You have cursed American soil with innocent blood unavenged by your unjust judges and juries.
- You have filled our prisons and released the overflow to terrorize our women, children, and others who cannot defend themselves against your criminal clientele.
- You have filled singles bars and gay bars.
- You have unleashed the vile fury of the sexually depraved, demanding that we normalize – that churches Christianize – sodomy.
- You have openly paraded every form of sexual depravity in our streets, flaunting this degrading lifestyle in our faces.
- You have destroyed the moral leadership of our Presidency, filling our White House with lechery, intrigue, and alleged perjury – making our Chief Executive a disgrace to his country and our country the laughingstock of the world.
- You have corrupted millions of Americans, convincing them that these things do not matter – that material things is all that counts – that "It's the economy, stupid." These are those described in the Scripture as those "whose God is their belly."

The House that Humanism Built

The Liberator: We cannot build enough prisons to hold all the criminals you have made. We cannot hire enough policemen to make our streets safe again. We cannot build enough drug rehab centers, crisis pregnancy centers, battered women shelters, divorce courts, family courts, and child support courts to mend all the lives you have broken. Still, unrepentant you bumble along, sticking Humanist bandaids on the Humanist cancer in the land.

This is the house that Humanism built. This is your contribution to America.

Some of you betrayed your country and countrymen with premeditated, treasonous intent. Your mentors, obsessed with pompous notions of their superior intelligence become blind to their own abysmal ignorance. "Professing themselves to be wise, they became fools."

Perhaps most of you were merely deceived into believing you were improving America, not destroying her. Possibly you never heard – or you were led to reject – wise old Benjamin Franklin's admonition, quoting Scripture, "Except the Lord build the house, they labor in vain that build it."

Can conditions grow progressively worse in Humanist America?

They can and will if religious Humanism finally wins the religious war against Christianity.

Is there yet time and opportunity to repent of our destructive deeds, restore our Christian foundations, and return America to her former virtue? Hopefully so. If the good people, en masse, ever awaken to the danger befalling our country and our liberties, they may in time – if God will – backtrack us out of the dismal swamp into which Humanism has led us. This will mean routing determined Humanists from every captive institution along the way.

My hope and prayer is that the words of George Washington will prove to be prophetic: "The people will be right at last."

Christians – The Chosen Enemy

The Liberator: Now, sirs, we must bring our discourse to an end. Obviously, Christians are your chosen enemy. Do you wish to make some parting remarks to them?

H. Manifesto II. The separation of church and state and the separation of ideology and state are imperative. [1]

The Liberator: Imperative to what? Imperative to your takeover and sellout of America? Church and state have never been united in our federal government. Now let us separate your ideology from state, before it is too late.

H. Manifesto II. Traditional religions often offer solace to humans, but, as often, they inhibit humans from helping themselves or experiencing their full potentialities. Such institutions, creeds, and rituals often impede the will to serve others. [2]

The Liberator: With all due respect, sirs, I think you describe your Humanist religion, not Christianity. If any of your kind have ever served others or done anything to help people to help themselves and to experience their full potentialities, your benevolent acts have escaped my notice.

What you have done is to force working people to give up their hard-earned wages in support of federal programs that encourage indolence, immorality, illegitimacy, drug abuse, and crime – systems that discourage work, destroy lives, and lock their victims in perpetual dependence upon the federal government.

You sacrifice nothing. You use government to give away other people's money; and, for designing and administering the programs, you pay yourselves handsomely from the public till.

H. Manifesto II. Too often traditional faiths encourage dependence rather than independence, obedience rather than affirmation, fear rather than courage. More recently they have generated concerned social action, with many signs of relevance appearing in the wake of the "God is Dead" theologies. [3]

The Liberator: Perhaps when you sneaked in to steal the institutions of America you expected a fight from American Christendom. What you found was an abandoned public arena and Christians withdrawn into Christianized comfort zones. We may have a point of agreement here.

While I cannot agree that Christianity has lost its will to serve others, I do hold that the abandonment of our public affairs to Humanism is the greatest corporate sin of twentieth-century Christians. The adulterating of Christianity with religious Humanism by the "God is Dead" crowd is, perhaps, equally abominable.

However, I give you this: You have raised some thought-provoking questions for American Christendom, which should be seriously and prayerfully pondered.

Now to you, sirs, I offer my sincere apology for any incivility I may have expressed toward you. It is not my intention to attack people; for they are God's creation. My anger is aroused because you are held captive by a despotic worldview damning to your souls, devastating to decent society, and destructive of our free, self-governing republic.

Your religious freedom is as precious as mine. But when your religion expresses its enmity against the faith of our fathers – and when it promotes the destruction of traditional American culture and government – it is then that I must emphatically respond.

To all of you: the signers of Humanist Manifesto II and all followers of your destructive religion; the 250,000 supporters of the American Civil Liberties Union and its 6,000 lawyers; the "liberal" Christians, who are more Humanist than Christian – God offers an open invitation to save yourselves from the madness of religious Humanism by returning to the faith of your fathers.

Those who determine to stay your destructive course to America's ruin, however, should know that your stealth tactics have been found out. Henceforward, expect open warfare with the good people of these United States.

I bid you, sirs, Good Day.

The Clinton/Tucker Takeover Plan

Now let us suppose that the American people fail to rescue their government and other institutions from Humanism's *program* and *purpose* for the United States – that religious Humanism is finally victorious over Christianity in the religious war for America's future – that American Humanists finally reach the goal they *think* they want for the world of tomorrow, a one-world secular/socialist state.

Suppose the American people permit the creation of an extensive, intrusive federal mega-bureaucracy – one similar to the plan envisioned by Marc Tucker, President of the Center on Education and the Economy. Tucker shared this plan with Hillary Clinton – a fellow board member – in an 18 page letter dated November 11, 1992.

Suppose the Clinton/Tucker Plan is implemented and enforced in the United States and every American citizen comes under the control of three departments of the U. S. Government: The Department of Education, The Department of Health and Human Services, and the Department of Labor.

Consider this very probable route to the Humanist world of tomorrow: – A world of global bondage.

Phase One: Federal Control of Education

The first phase of the final socialization of the United States was initiated in Arkansas under then Governor Bill Clinton.

Bill and Hillary Clinton, in collaboration with Marc Tucker, initiated a program of public education aimed toward the federalization of all education in America. The Arkansas pilot project culminated in the federal Goals 2000: Educate America Act.

Unable to resist federal money, the states initiate Goals 2000 throughout the country. Shortly after the year 2000, all education in America comes under control of a greatly expanded federal bureaucracy – the U. S. Department of Education.

Over the past several decades Humanist "ministers of another sort"
had been planted in America's universities, public schools, the U. S.
Department of Education, and the National Education Association.
In 1972 one of them, a Harvard professor, had brazenly declared:

> Every child who enters school at the age of 5 is mentally ill
> because he enters school with an allegiance toward our elected
> officials, our founding fathers, our institutions, the preserva-
> tion of this form of government that we have, patriotism, na-
> tionalism, sovereignty. All this proves that the children are sick,
> because a truly well individual is one who has rejected all of
> those things, and is what I would call the true international
> child of the future. [4]

After the federal takeover of America's education, these Humanist
school teachers and administrators quickly finish the task of indoctrinating "the international children of the future." In all courses, at all
levels the children are progressively converted to the doctrines and
agenda of religious Humanism:

- Following "the twentieth century model" for American history,
  Humanist teachers erase from the children's minds all knowledge of their Christian roots and the nation's Christian founders
  and foundations.
- With courses in "multiculturalism," "bilingualism," and "diversity,"
  Humanist teachers teach the children to despise the "dead white
  men" who founded their nation and prepare them to accept the idea
  of regionalizing the United States along cultural lines.
- Courses in environmentalism condition the children to accept
  the idea of lowered production, polulation control, and global
  socialism – by which everyone in the world is to be leveled to
  the lowest economic common denominator.
- In "values clarification" classes the children learn to reject all
  Christian morals, ethics, and values and to accept the Humanist
  doctrine of "situational and autonomous ethics."
- Sex education courses encourage the children to throw off the
  Christian restraint – abstinence outside of wedlock – and to experiment with all kinds of devious sexual practices.

Meanwhile the federal courts hold Christians at bay and bring all education – day care, home schooling, private schools, and Christians schools – under federal Goals 2000 control.

Phase Two: National Health and Human Services

The second phase of the final socialization of the United States is Hillary Clinton's Health Care Plan, proposed during Bill Clinton's first term as President.

Hillary's first attempt to socialize health care was defeated in the nick of time by the reform Congress elected in 1994. However, the new Republican leadership in Congress failed to address the fundamental issues threatening American liberty. Because of voter disillusionment and apathy, the Humanists regain control of both the White House and the Congress.

The Humanists move quickly to enact the Hillary Health and Human Services Act. Almost immediately, the people find their health care and welfare under the control of the second greatly expanded federal bureaucracy – the U. S. Department of Health and Human Services.

With education and health and welfare totally under federal control, the bureaucracy moves health care facilities into the local schoolhouses. Over a relatively short period of time, every pertinent detail of every man, woman, and child's personal and public life is entered into a gigantic computer database.

Phase Three: National Employment and Housing Services

Phase three of the total socialization of the United States is a federal takeover of the employment of every American citizen by a third greatly expanded federal bureaucracy – the U. S. Department of Labor.

In this phase, a federal employment office is set up in the local public schools, which become known as "one-stop shopping centers" for the care and control of every person in the United States. Employment records are entered into the computer database.

Although not mentioned in the Clinton/Tucker Plan, all housing is later placed under the control of a fourth greatly expanded federal bureaucracy – The U. S. Department of Housing and Urban Development.

Under control of the federal colossus, the people find every facet of their lives guided by bureaucrats – just as Marc Tucker had envisioned, "from the cradle to the grave." Their lives, now considered the property of the state, are literally no longer their own.

Phase Four: The New World Order

Soon after the Plan is perfected in the United States, it comes to light that American Humanists had orchestrated the process throughout, as part of their *program* and *purpose* for America and the world.

In phase four the federal government surrenders the Plan and all the people in it over to the United Nations. Government of the People, by the People, for the People perishes from the Earth.

The United States of America is only a tragic memory now – our wealth, our liberties, our national sovereignty all gone – surrendered over to a one-world tribunal.

Was Phase Four actually an unannounced part of the Clinton/ Tucker Plan? Apparently so. On October 17, 1997, Bill Clinton announced to a group of Argentine reporters, "What I'm trying to do is to promote a process of reorganization of the world so that human beings are organized in a way that takes advantage of the new opportunities of this era. [5]

The Humanist World of Tomorrow

Imagine life as it may very well become if we should wake up and find ourselves in the Humanist world of tomorrow – our coveted American liberties forever gone.

• *The United Nations re-districts the world.*
The United Nations, now in political and military control of the world, moves quickly to erase all existing national boundaries and divide the world into cultural regions within a one-world secular/socialist order. People are now confined to their assigned regions by restrictions not unlike the Soviet Iron Curtain.
• *Enter the Global Master.*
After a few years, the one-world tribunal loses control of world government. The people, indoctrinated with the Humanist concept of absolute freedom of expression and "situational ethics," become so demoralized that all possibility of representative government is lost. Unable to control a corrupted people, the World Court – in much the

same way as Germany abdicated to Hitler – turns the government over to a single despot. Now all authority resides in this one-world dictator.

• *The Dictator betrays and murders American Humanists.*

Following the example of Hitler and Stalin, the Dictator exterminates those who elevated his system to world power. He, too, believes in "situational ethics" and decides the situation calls for the elimination of all potential rivals. His Humanist mentors had trained him well: "Ethics is autonomous and situational, needing no theological or ideological sanction." [6]

• *From time to time the Dictator orders a "spiritual cleansing."*

Humanism, proclaiming "the preciousness of the individual," had promised the people absolute freedom of expression. They had believed the media pundits, "You cannot legislate morality." They learned too late what the founders knew more than two centuries ago – a people totally corrupted must be ruled by a master.

The dictator knows very well that a certain level of morality must be legislated for people too corrupt to govern themselves. They were rudely awakened when he instituted "spiritual cleansing," once practiced in the former Communist Chinese regions – imprisonment, brainwashing, torture, forced labor, and executions.

• *Population is officially controlled by forced abortion and euthanasia.*

In an attempt to achieve a balance between population and environment, the dictator moves from the days of "a woman's choice" to the Communist Chinese system of forced abortion.

"Assisted suicide" had been legalized in the United States in the early twenty-first century by "Doctor Death" – the late Dr. Jack Kevorkian. The Dictator changes "assisted suicide" to forced euthanasia for all persons who cannot support themselves, including the poor who have reached the age of 70.

Murder, both the political and the criminal kind – as well as suicide – also take a heavy toll.

• *God is not recognized in this Humanist dream world.*

Gone are our inalienable rights endowed by the Creator. All rights must be granted by the world Dictator who can, and often does, withdraw them on a whim.

• *Humanism remains the established religion.*

Subtly Humanism, in its many emphases, had been made the de facto established religion of the United States in the late twentieth and early twenty-first centuries. The Dictator later reduces the Humanist religion to one man-worshipping form. The Dictator, with the consent of the World Court, orders that he be the only object of adoration. His image is displayed everywhere; and, people are required to bow as they pass by.

• *Christianity is forced underground worldwide.*

After waiting too long to rise up and put down creeping Humanist despotism in America, Christians now worship in fear. Occasionally muffled prayers can be heard, beseeching God to give back the Christian liberties they once enjoyed. Sometimes one of their number will admonish them that God is not likely to restore that which they had not the resolve to hold. Others simply pray, "Come quickly, Lord Jesus."

• *Families no longer exist.*

"Family" is now defined as any group living together. There is no parental authority, since all persons – adult and children – belong to the state. Loving parent-child relationships are gone. Family and other social relationships have been placed under international law. This was done in international conferences beginning with those attended by Hillary Clinton in late twentieth-century. Clinton's book, *It Takes a Village*, is credited with many of the concepts of parent-child relationships later adopted into international law.

• *World government is secular and socialist.*

Wealth – or rather poverty – is distributed under a plan worked out by the World Court and approved by the Dictator. If there are those still living who remember the Communist system in the regions formerly known as the Soviet Union, they will recognize the pattern. Two classes – the politicians and the industrialists and bankers who support the political powers that be – always retain and increase their wealth. Our one-world secular/socialist government is no exception in this regard.

• *All property and means of production are owned by the world government.*

For much of the twentieth century, organized labor in the United States had been coerced into elevating Humanist visionaries to political power. The Humanist *program* and *purpose* for workers became apparent when the Dictator betrayed American Labor.

Following a plan, which extended and expanded the Goals 2000 Educate America Act, the "international children of the future" are dumbed down and trained to take their assigned workplace and labor for the government. The government in turn promises to take care of them "from the cradle to the grave."

• *Americans have little chance to resist the Dictator's will.*

The United States military had been turned over to the United Nations early in the twenty-first century. This transfer of military power was begun shortly after the U. S. Supreme Court upheld President Bill Clinton's court martial and discharge of Sgt. Michael New for refusing to serve in U. N. uniform under U. N. command.

The Dictator is now backed by the most awesome military firepower ever known to man. The largest contingent of the standing one-world army is located in the former United States of America. The World Court reasoned that the people there, having once known Christian liberty, might rise in rebellion against the New World Order.

• *Freedom of Assembly does not exist under the Dictator.*

Occasionally small hushed groups in the American regions can be heard sadly reminiscing, "Our Christian ancestors gave us the best system ever devised on this earth. How did we let it go?"

• *Americans remember how they were enticed to forget God and follow the Humanist dream.*

They agonize over their apathy that landed them in this world of Humanist dreams. Why did we allow Humanists to take over our institutions and indoctrinate our children in Humanist values? they ask themselves. How were we persuaded to concentrate all power in our federal government? they wonder. How did our federal government betray us – who were once free people – into the hands of the world tribunal?

The takeover and sellout had been so deceitful and so gradual that they had not believed and heeded the warning signs. They had squelched their own premonition of something fundamentally wrong in the land. Not seeing and often misled, they had taken no action to stop their descent from Christian liberty to Humanist global bondage.

With downcast eyes, dejectedly they leave their little hushed groups and return to their shackles of the heart and soul.

Recommended Reading for Chapters 14 through 17

Bennett, William J., *The Index of Leading Cultural Indicators*, (New York: Simon & Schuster, 1994)

Hitchcock, James, *What is Secular Humanism*, (Harrison, NY: RC Books, 1982)

Johnson, Phillip E., *Darwin on Trial,* (Washington, DC: Regnery Gateway, 1991)

Chandler, Russell, *Understanding New Age,* (Grand Rapids, MI: Zondervan Publishing House, 1991)

Feder, Don, *A Jewish Conservative Looks at Pagan America,* (Lafayette LA: Huntington House Publishers, 1993)
If you have ever thought, "Will the real Jews please stand up," get this book.

Eakman, B. K., *Educating for the New World Order,* (Portland, OR: Halycon House, 1991)
To learn how religious Humanists are stealing your kids and indoctrinating them for their one-world secular/socialist state, get this book.

Coral Ridge Ministries, *Renewing America's Schools,* (Ft. Lauderdale, FL: 1997)
Get this booklet for an insight into the ruin of our public education system and what to do about it. Contact Coral Ridge Ministries, P. O. Box 1940, Ft. Lauderdale, FL, 33302-1940.

Medved, Michael, *Hollywood vs. America,* (New York, NY: Harper Collins Publishers, 1992)
An excellent exposé of Hollywood by a Jewish movie critic.

Hattemer, Barbara, and Showers, Robert, *Touch that Dial, The Impact of the Media on Children and the Family,* (Lafayette, LA: Huntington House Publishers, 1993)

Berryhill, Dale A., *The Media Hates Conservatives, How it Controls the Flow of Information,* (Lafayette, LA: Huntington House Publishers, 1994)

Donohue, William A., *The Politics of the American Civil Liberties Union,* (New Brunswick, NJ: Transaction Publishers, 1985)
This book and its companion book, Twilight of Liberty, is "must" reading for an understanding of the history, mindset, activities, and goal of the ACLU.

Donohue, William A., *Twilight of Liberty*, (New Brunswick, NJ: Transaction Publishers, 1994)

Reisman, Judith A., *Soft Porn Plays Hardball*, (Lafayette, LA: Huntington House Publishers, 1991)

Dannemeyer, William, *Shadow in the Land, Homosexuality in America*, (San Francisco, Ignatius Press, 1989)

Kincaid, Cliff, *Global Bondage: The U.N. Plan to Rule the World*, (Lafayette, LA: Huntington House Publishers, 1995)
Kincaid updates the Humanist subversion right into the Clinton Administration.

Chenney, Lynne V., "Hijacking America's History," *Reader's Digest*, January, 1995, Page 89.
Reprints available from Reader's Digest.

Oursler, Will, *Protestant Power and the Coming Revolution*, (Garden City, NY: Doubleday & Co., Inc., 1971).

Gross, Martin L., *The End of Sanity: Social and Cultural Madness in America* (New York: Avon Books, 1997).
After writing a number of good books on government reform, Mr. Gross comes close to identifying the religious war for America's future.

16

FROM PLOWSHARES
TO SWORDS

"The time for reasoning with tyrants is past. Figuratively speaking, it
is time to whet the sword, not to sheath it." *The Liberators*

I n spite of glaring signs of societal and political decay all around us,
many will not see the sickness in our land. Insulated in their secluded neighborhoods and religious comfort zones and drawing
comfortable paychecks, they do not see the dangerous erosion of our
foundational principles. They fail to acknowledge the creeping tyranny
against our fundamental liberties.

To paraphrase George Washington: The people fail to see, are often misled, and must feel before they will take action.

Let all who think Humanist Manifestos I and II are nothing more
than religious pamphlets collecting dust on library shelves, think again.
A manifesto is a public declaration of motives and intentions.

Religious Humanists have made crystal clear their *purpose* and *program* for America and the world.

- They are now essentially in control of every American institution of power and influence, including the federal government.
- They are as near as your local public school – and, possibly, your local church.
- Their infiltration and takeover of our institutions explains why our government continues to go against the better judgment of the majority, even though the people still have the power of the ballot.

Section Two of this book has attempted to define the societal and national sickness in our land and the virus causing it. The time-tested foundations of our American liberties are Christian. The assault on this American system is by religious Humanism – which, in its many emphases, promises Americans a better life in a socialist New World Order.

No Neutral Ground

Although the clash of worldviews in America today has been defined as a "culture war," the primary conflict is not between cultures. In Christian America, the many ethnic cultures got along far better than could be expected, melding into the unique American culture.

The warfare for America's future is between two diametrically opposed religions – Christianity, which has undergirded the American people and their government from the beginning vs. religious Humanism, a latecomer, which is subverting Christianity, destroying our time-tested foundations, and promising to sell us out to a one-world secular/socialist system.

Religious Humanism has declared this religious war on American liberty. The battle is joined; and, no American can escape it.

- We have tried to ignore or re-define the religious war; but it will not go away.
- If Christianity loses, America is lost.
- Every future American will live in one or the other of two drastically different worlds – Christian American liberty or Humanist global bondage.

Christianity and Humanism are diametrically opposed worldviews. They cannot be reconciled. The religious war for America's future must be fought to the finish.

For all Americans there is no neutral ground.

The Big "If"

The Bible is, among other things, the ancient history of the Jews. Remember, the Jews handed down to western civilization the Ten Commandments – the capsule of all just ecclesiastical, civil, and criminal law. Also Jesus Christ and Christianity came to us through the Jews.

As well as recording the good deeds of the Jews, their Biblical history is also faithful to record their sins, which we are warned not to repeat. The chronicle of the ancient Jews notes a roller coaster ride of good times and evil – times of God's providential blessing and times of disobedience to the laws of God – followed by chastisement, repentance, and restoration. Tragically, the Jews' moral trend was ever downward, terminating in their destruction as a nation and dispersion as a people. Failure and defeat were never God's plan for His people. Time and time again, He warned them of the consequences of their disobedience to His commands – "the laws of nature and nature's God," as the founders stated it.

Recorded in the biblical chronicles of the ancient kings of Israel, we find one of the most profound and succinct warnings – and coupled with the warning, a promise. During a time of disobedience and chastisement, God spoke to His people and gave certain conditions that must be met before He would intervene in their situation:

If my People,
 which are called by my name,
 shall humble themselves, and pray,
 and seek my face,
 and turn from their wicked ways;
Then will I
 hear from heaven,
 and will forgive their sin,
 and will heal their land.
 -The Bible, 2 Chronicles 7:14

This is a call to repentance, involving confession of – and turning away from – wrong-doing. Contingent upon their obedience is a promise to remove the curse from their land. While this passage from the Hebrew Bible was directed originally to the ancient nation of Israel, we are profoundly impressed with its application to the American people today.

Who Are God's People?

Who are the "my people" of whom God is speaking in this scriptural passage from 2 Chronicles?

In Christian circles, the term, "God's people," is often used in reference to personal salvation – referring to those who have chosen Jesus Christ as their personal Savior. In this regard, we would urge our readers to solemnly consider the words of Jesus, "Enter through the narrow gate. For wide is the gate and broad is the road that leads to destruction, and many enter through it. But small is the gate and narrow the road that leads to life, and only a few find it." (*Matthew 7:13-14, NIV*)

We would urge our readers who have not chosen Christ as their personal Savior and the way to life to read the books of *John* and *Romans* from their Bibles and discuss these eternal matters with a trusted Christian friend or minister.

This book is primarily about God and State, and recognizes God as the "Sovereign of the Universe." In this regard we recognize a broader definition of "God's people."

In the broadest sense all people are "God's people." Although we may have badly marred the Divine image, we are created in the image of God. People belong to God – never to the state. This precept is the bedrock of our civil and religious liberties, affirmed by our Declaration of Independence and our Bill of Rights. Destroy this precept, and you destroy America.

May we suggest there is a sense in which all Americans might be recognized as "God's people." Consider these facts:

- George Washington would agree with this position. We quote, "I am sure that never was a people, who had more reason to acknowledge a Divine interposition in their affairs, than those of the United States; and I should be pained to believe that they have forgotten that agency, which was so often manifested during our Revolution, or that they failed to consider the omnipotence of that God who is alone able to protect them;"
- The vast majority of Americans are descended from centuries of Christian forebears;
- Religious liberty motivated the first European settlers.– persecuted Christians – to brave a treacherous ocean voyage and settle in America;

- The colonial governments which they established were Christianity based;
- America was recognized worldwide as a Christian nation for most of her history;
- The Bible had a profound influence in establishing the United States of America, uniting her founders on "the general principles of Christianity;"
- The great majority of Americans at least give lip-service to the Bible and Christianity;
- Most Americans pledge allegiance to "one nation under God."

Under this definition we continue, for the scope and purpose of this book, to recognize the broader definition of "God's people." In no way, however, are we to be understood to pronounce all people saved and candidates for Heaven. We are dealing with matters of God and State, a temporal institution. We leave the weightier, eternal matters of personal salvation to the Church, the individual, and his Bible.

In this chapter our comments on religion refer to actions of the national body politic. These corporate actions will, of course, spring from decisions and actions of individual citizens.

A Call to Humility

"If my People .. shall humble themselves."
The first step toward healing our land is a call to humility.

Americans today live in a time of in-your-face self-centeredness. This "I-am-God" attitude comes from the doctrines of religious Humanism. Instead of correcting this bane on American society, we make silly TV shows of it and call it comedy. Yet it is safe to say that self-centeredness accounts for the lion's share of our national sickness – crime, family violence, divorce, broken families, abortion, woman and child abuse and abandonment, and on down the line to road rage and incivility in general.

Correcting these evils requires confession of wrongdoing. The old adage – "Honest confession is good for the soul" – is a timeless truth and still valid today. But in the Humanist world of "autonomous" and "situational" ethics, there is no place for honest confession. How could one define "situational confession", or "situational repentance"? Christian humility confesses wrong-doing; Humanist "situational ethics" must find a way to justify it.

Humility is a rare find in Humanist America today; but, there are encouraging signs of renewal. In October, 1997, hundreds of thousands of men – representing the Promise Keepers – gathered in our nation's capitol to publicly humble themselves and pray. In Christian America this call to repentance would have been made by the President, following the precedent set by George Washington – but such is not the character of recent U. S. Presidents.

As the Promise Keepers humbled themselves and prayed for their country, the Presidential helicopter passed overhead. Presumably, President Bill Clinton was observing the scene below – a gathering of those who candidate Clinton had called "fanatics with a message of hate and fear."

As might be expected, the media by the mouth of Andy Roony of CBS, ridiculed the gathering in particular – as well as the whole idea of praying to God for anything.

Nationally as well as personally, we would do well to heed the advice of wise old King Solomon, "Pride goes before destruction, and an haughty spirit before a fall" (Proverbs 16:17).

A Call to Prayer

"If my People . . . pray."
The vast majority of Americans say they sometimes pray. People pray whether they are Christian, unchurched Bible believers, or of other religious persuasions.

"While conscience remains," said founder John Adams, "there is some religion."

Perhaps our prayers are largely confined to our narrow circles of selfish interest. When we encouter personal problems beyond our ability to cope, then (and only then?), we pray. We would do well also to pray daily for the moral health of our society and the political health of our nation.

There is perhaps a dearth of serious, continuous prayer in America today – even among church-going Christians. This lack of prayer in our busy daily lives possibly explains why our society today is caught up in so many problems beyond our ability to cope.

Like the ancient nation of Israel, the American experience also has been much like a roller coaster ride. We experience periods of peace and prosperity, and periods of decline and distress.

In the late 1990s, we are in a period of peace and prosperity accompanied by perhaps the greatest moral and political decline in our nation's history. Subtle though the threat may be, at this time our very moral and political foundations are at risk.

We have, heretofore, recovered from our times of national distress because of our commonly-held Christian worldview, which tends to correct, unite, and elevate us. For some time now, however, we have been dancing to a different piper – to the tune of religious Humanism, which tears apart our national fabric and degrades us.

In the beginning of our nation and at other times of national distress, our Presidents have called for national repentance and prayer and a return to national morality. Except for Ronald Reagan, it has been a very long time since we have had any believable leadership from our Presidents in this regard.

In times of peace and prosperity we are inclined to forget our need for God – as if we have control of all the elements that make our prosperity possible. Our tendency to call on God in times of distress and forget God when the pressure is off, is nothing new.

In 1787, the framers of our Constitution assembled in Philadelphia to write that great document. It was a time of exultation – after winning the war for independence – and they neglected to pray.

The convention was at a stalemate. Some delegates had already left the convention. Agreement on a constitution of government seemed doubtful. Then Benjamin Franklin, who had signed the Declaration of Independence in that same hall, stood in the convention and reminded them of their ingratitude and short memory:

> In the beginning of our Contest with G. Britain, when we were sensible of danger, we had daily prayer in this room for Divine Protection – Our prayers, Sir, were heard, & they were graciously answered. All of us who were engaged in the struggle must have observed frequent instances of a superintending Providence in our favor.
>
> To that kind Providence we owe this happy opportunity of consulting in peace on the means of establishing our future national felicity. And have we now forgotten that powerful Friend? or do we imagine we no longer need his assistance? [1]

These are good questions for America today.

In his speech to the Constitutional Convention, Franklin went on to quote the first part of Psalm 127:1, "Except the Lord build the house, they labor in vain that build it."

As our founding fathers prayed for Divine guidance in building the house (our self-governing Constitutional republic), we would be well advised to pray for its Divine keeping.

The last part of Psalm 127:1 continues, "Except the Lord keep the city, the watchman wakes but in vain."

Will we ever again see strong moral leadership from our Presidents – a national call to humble repentance and prayer for our nation and a return to national morality? Or is America already so infused with the Humanist doctrine of "situational ethics" that confession and repentance are no longer words in the American vocabulary?

Has religious Humanism led America so far from that "kind Providence" who birthed her that she now has nowhere to direct her petitions but to the god of mammon?

Shall we pray?

A Call to Seek God

"If my people . . . seek my face."
This invitation comes from the God of Abraham, Isaac, and Jacob – and, as the Christian New Testament avows– "the God and Father of our Lord Jesus Christ."

We are called to humbly seek God Himself – not something about God or from God. How do we seek God? By studying the Bible and asking God for His Divine help.and guidance

Good clergymen will encourage their congregation to do this, and not to depend solely upon church leaders to do it for them. Good clergymen will thus follow the examples of Jesus, who challenged the Jews to "search the Scriptures." – and St. Paul, who commended the Jews at Berea for searching the Scriptures daily.

We find God when we humbly submit to his Word. The enlightenment of God's Word may come at a church where the Bible is faithfully preached. Or it may come at any other time and place by the work of the Spirit of God.

Seek God's face in the Bible and in prayer and thanksgiving. You will find your life wondrously changed.

A Call to Change.

"If my people . . . turn from their wicked ways."

When we seek God and find our life not conforming to the will of God revealed in the Bible, we are called upon to change our ways.

Nowadays there is too much confession without change, which accomplishes nothing. Confession plus change equals repentance, which accomplishes much.

The Christian community – as well as the individual and the body politic in general – has its sins. It is our studied opinion that, in the realm of God and State, the greatest corporate wickedness of Christians is their abandonment of the government of "God's Country" to those who either ignore God or outrightly reject His sovereignty over the nation. If our analysis is correct, as we firmly believe it is, then American Christendom must quickly turn from this wicked way or abandon their posterity to Humanist tyranny.

"Except the Lord keep the city, the watchman wakes but in vain."

Are Christians praying the Lord to keep the city so they may sleep at their guard posts? Since the great mass of Christians refuse to watch over the city – to participate in the public arena – all the people are abandoned to the mercy of Humanist despots.

Then Will I . . .

"Then will I hear from heaven, and will forgive their sin, and will heal their land."

God makes three promises:

• A Promise to Hear.

"Seek and ye shall find," said Jesus, "knock and it shall be opened unto you."

• A Promise to Forgive.

Seek God in the Bible, and soon you will understand that "God is not willing that any should perish, but that all should come to repentance." Might we claim this promise for our nation as well as for the individual?

• A Promise to Heal.

If we as a people answer the four calls of God, our land will be healed. We have God's word on it.

Faith Without Works is Dead

Perhaps all the books in our nation could not contain all the prayers that have been offered for the safekeeping of our American liberties and all the talk about the ills of our country. Unfortunately, these prayers have been attended by too little Christian action in the public arena.

Perhaps there is some truth in the old adage that "God helps those who help themselves." – when it is in our power, with God's help, to do so. What shall we do then?

In the companion book, *A New Birth of Freedom*, we address the political aspects of this question in greater detail. For a starter we will propose a general course of action.

Critique us severely; but do not take us lightly. This is no political game. At stake is nothing less than a new birth of freedom on the one hand or, on the other, the eventual moral and political collapse of the United States – and our posterity set awash in the socialist New World Order.

First a word on what not to do.

"No More Whining"

We the people of the twentieth century have already tolerated more government intrusion and tyranny than our colonial ancestors, who snatched their firelocks from the wall and put an end to tyranny with musket and bayonet.

Militia groups and their weapons, however, cannot save us today. Our real enemies cannot be reached with firearms. Destroying American property and innocent lives will not restore American liberty but only hasten the destruction of our republic.

Suppose our government should be brought down by terrorism and armed insurrection. Dare we assume that a new government – rising from the ashes of the old – would restore our liberties? All of history's revolutions have produced only one self-sacrificing George Washington to assure that new government is established on "the general principles of Christianity" and the "general principles of English and American liberty."

We cannot institute new government in America superior to the original. We cannot lay superior foundation principles nor write a superior Constitution. It is the despotic abuse of our present Constitution that must be constitutionally corrected.

The proper means of calling government tyrants to task is contained in the Constitution itself. It is as simple as the elective process, the impeachment process, and the amendment process. Admittedly, it is sometimes a slow and frustrating procedure – particularly because of unconstitutional abuses of the elective process and because so many citizens are too lazy to inform themselves and get involved in public affairs.

If the people are virtuous and persistent, however, and if George Washington is correct, "the people will be right at last."

The militias are correct in this: The time for reasoning with tyrants is past. Figuratively speaking, it is time to whet the sword – not to sheath it. George Washington would say, "No more whining."

To rout the Humanist tyrants who have captured our American institutions, metaphorically speaking, we the people must beat our plowshares into swords and prepare to do spiritual, academic, legal, and political battle on several fronts.

Let us consider each of these battlefields to determine how each and all of us might contribute to the healing of our land.

A NEW BIRTH OF FREEDOM

*". . . that this nation, under God, shall have a new birth of freedom –
and that government of the people, by the people, for the people,
shall not perish from the earth." Abraham Lincoln.*

A new birth of freedom in America requires concerted response on
several fronts – religious, civic, economic, and political.

The Religious Response

The Buck Stops Here

"Judgment must begin at the House of God," said St. Peter. Enough
of Christian "whining" and complaining about Humanist mistreatment
of Christians. Whatever Christians suffer in America, we have brought
upon ourselves. Instead of feeling sorry for ourselves, we should rather

be sorrowful that we have shirked our civic responsibilities. And because of this, we have abandoned our country to the tyranny of the Humanist takeover and sellout of America.

Let judgment begin at the House of God. Our land cannot not be healed unless first the Church is renewed. Remember, Christianity, as a worldview, played the major role in creating these United States of America.

- Christianity supplied America's foundations: "The general principles of Christianity" and "the general principles of American and English liberty."
- Christianity supplied the essential structure of our government: "Government of the people, by the people, for the people."
- Christianity, as George Washington stated it, was our government's "indispensable support" until well into the twentieth century.

Let us review the Christian abandonment of our nation's public affairs.

In the late nineteenth and early twentieth centuries, many Church leaders abandoned their Bible-based heritage and – like the ancient Israelites – "went a whoring after other gods."

By the middle of the twentieth century, their Humanist captors no longer referred to them as Christian, but as "liberal religion" and gave them Humanist credentials. These modern-day Iscariots had become more Humanist than Christian. Rejecting the inspiration of the Bible, they invented their own "liberal religion" – with doctrines far-removed from the simple but powerful gospel of Jesus Christ.

Holding high office in their church councils, they passed themselves off as the voice of American Christendom and apostatized great numbers of their followers.

At the same time that "liberal religion" was becoming bedfellows with religious Humanism, Bible-centered Christians abandoned their government en masse and focused on building self-contained Christian comfort zones around their churches.

As a result, Christianity – which had created the American culture and government and for three centuries had been their "indispensable support" – deserted her country to hide in stained-glass security. Religious Humanists seized the opportunity and, virtually unopposed, moved in to fill the vacuum in American institutions, including government. This impostor religion promises to take over our country and sell us out in the next – and possibly our last – century.

Under Church-House Arrest

When American Humanists made their move to capture our country for their destructive religion, they found the public arena abandoned. "Liberal religion" had joined their ranks; and, Bible-centered Christians had withdrawn to Christianized comfort zones. Religious Humanists simply walked in, took office, and commenced to *evaluate, transform, control,* and *direct* American government and other institutions.

Looking back, the Humanist takeover of America appears to have been a well-orchestrated stategy. Early in the process, Humanist lawyers took control of the Supreme Court. Finding Christians, for the most part, already withdrawn into their church houses, the Court proceeded to hold them under church-house arrest.

And there we remain today – confined to our Christianized comfort zones, conducting church as usual, while entrenched religious Humanists gradually dismantle our Christian foundations and the superstructure of our liberties.

American Christendom was once the "indispensable support" of our free, self-governing republic. As the twenty-first century dawns, however, American Christendom has divided and conquered itself – prostituted itself – politically.

This political self-defeat of American Christendom has placed the Christian Coalition – and other associations of Bible-centered Christian activists – in the position of begging entrenched Humanists, for a place at the table in our political process.

When America was great, Christianity moderated at the table in our political process.

Christianity – America's Schoolmaster

Before Horace Mann created public education in 1837, Christianity was almost solely in charge of educating America. At the time, only four out of 1,000 Americans were illiterate – according to then President John Quincy Adams.

John Quincy Adams himself was so well educated at home and by Christian tutors that Congress appointed him to serve in the Court of Catherine the Great in Russia, when he was only 14 years old!

One hundred years later, John Dewey, signer of *Humanist Manifesto I* and first president of the American Humanist Association, made public education "progressive" – in other words, Humanistic. Today, after half a century of Humanistic "progressive" public education, America has 27 million illiterates (about 1 out of 10 Americans) and 30 million more who are "functionally illiterate." American education has plummeted from first place to seventeenth among the developed nations of the world.

In spite of the dismal failure of "progressive" education, American parents today must beg entrenched Humanist "educators" to stop dumbing down their children and indoctrinating them with the Humanist religion in public schools.

When America was good – when America was educated – Christianity was America's schoolmaster.

An Out-of-Joint Statement

A joint effort of 35 religious and legal organizations has produced a pamphlet, dated April, 1995, titled *Religion in the Public Schools: A Joint Statement of Current Law.* This "current law," a collection of dictates of federal judges, is a brazen contradiction of the supreme law of the land – our Constitution.

The Constitution itself is the current law – until changed by Constitutional amendment, the *only* law – regarding the people's religion. The current judge-made "laws" are, therefore, unconstitutional, null and void, and begging for civil disobedience by all freedom loving Americans.

Where, then, is the outcry from American Christendom? With some notable exceptions, the silence on the part of Christian ministers is deafening. And that is not the end of Christian defeatism.

As if seeking to appease entrenched religious Humanists – major Christian denominations, the National Council of Churches, and the National Association of Evangelicals – signed on with the American Humanist Association, Humanist legal organizations, "liberal religion," and a number of non-biblical religions – to endorse the pamphlet, *Religion in the Public Schools: A Joint Statement of Current Law.*

Has American Christendom ceased to stand up for religious liberty guaranteed by our Constitution? Do these Christian leaders not understand that the people have Constitutionally forbidden the government to make any law regarding their religion?

"Congress shall make no law respecting an establishment of religion, or prohibiting the free exercise thereof."

Are these Christian leaders conceding to the government the tyrannical power to deny the people's inalienable rights, endowed by our Creator? Are they surrendering to unelected judicial tyrants law-making powers forbidden to our elected representatives and reserved to the people alone.?

This confused, faint-hearted Christian leadership has so weakened Christianity politically that all Americans today are left at the mercy of entrenched Humanist judges and Humanist legal organizations. The people are expected to beg permission of these despotic impostors as to how, when, and where they may exercise their religious liberty. Never mind that this liberty is guaranteed by our Constitution.

While Christians allow themselves to be held under church-house arrest, Humanist judges release murderers, robbers, rapists, and child molesters when they presume prison conditions to infringe criminals' "rights." These recycled thugs are released into the neighborhoods, unidentified so as to protect their judge-invented "right to privacy."

Thus Christian withdrawal from civic responsibility and pandering for Humanism has left all the people at the mercy of Humanist "justice." And there is no "situational" justice, "needing no theological or ideological sanction."

So, let us have done with "whining" about "Christian rights." Rights for Christians belong on the Cross. Christian responsibility begins when we take up the Cross and follow Christ. Heaven forbid that Christians in America should come to think of themselves as yet another "victim" class. That is not the stuff real Christianity is made of.

Christian rights were not lost, nor were they taken away by force. They were abandoned when Christians retreated into Christianized comfort zones, refusing to occupy places of authority in the public realm. Did not Christ instruct his disciples, "occupy 'til I come?" Are American Christians today "occupying" little more than church pews?

And let us remember: It is not "Christian rights" that are slipping away by Christian neglect of public duty. It is "inalienable rights endowed by the Creator" to all mankind.

Time for Examination

Without hesitation we repeat – Our land cannot be healed unless first the Church is renewed.

The call first goes out to the Church: "Let us humble ourselves, and pray, and seek God's face, and turn from our wicked ways!" Let judgment begin at the House of God.

"Mainline" church members, who hear the call to return to the gospel according to Wesley, Whitefield, Finney, Luther, Mather, Moody, and others – after getting right with God themselves – will need to examine their clergy.

If these Christians are receiving little more at church than a steady diet of "liberal religion" instead of the complete gospel of Jesus Christ, it is time to have a serious talk with their clergy. If their clergy are more Humanist than Christian, it is time to either replace their clergy or move to a different kind of church themselves.

An examination of the National Council of Churches and the World Council of Churches might reveal that church support of these councils is not promoting the gospel of Jesus Christ as much as the Humanist design for the New World Order.

Evangelicals must also examine themselves. Do they flock to theaters and music concerts and lock onto their television sets – and there imbibe values that make them more Humanist than Christian? Do they adore silver screen idols and sports, music, or political superstars more than their Savior? If so, they are called to humble themselves, and pray, and seek God's face, and turn from their wicked ways.

Escapist church members who have abandoned the public arena as well as the Great Commission are likewise called to humble themselves, and pray, and seek God's face, and turn from their wicked ways. Our churches are not to be self-contained religious sanctuaries, where we imbibe more teaching, preaching, fraternizing, and Christian entertainment than we are able to contain.

From the Pulpit to the Pew

There is a positive side to Christian cloistering that we should mention. Real Christian ministers inculcate the basic virtues of the Bible, thus making their adherents peaceable, law-abiding citizens. Nevertheless, cloistered Christians are no deterrent to the Humanist takeover and sellout of our country. Such Christians are more like passive contributors to America's decline.

Neither has withdrawal into our church houses saved our churched families from the ravages of societal decline in America. Should we therefore abandon our church services? Certainly not! "This (church stewardship) we ought to have done, and not left the other (civic stewardship) undone."

Apart from common laziness, Christian withdrawal from public affairs is caused by several sincere interpretations of Scripture:

- A misapplied separatism;
- The inevitability of prophetic events;
- Equating our American government with the early Christian's Roman government.

And let our Christian ministers be ever on guard against that fault in human nature that makes it appealing to pastor "a little flock," – separated unto oneself as much as unto God!

Countless ministers have withdrawn their congregations from the public arena because of misapplied separatism – "come out from among them, and be ye separate." Christians of this persuasion need to understand that this separateness means abstinence from the evil deeds of others – not avoidance of personal contact nor prideful aloofness.

Christians should always look to the lifestyle and teaching of Jesus in all life's involvements. As to the question of separatism, he was "separate from sinners" and, at the same time, rightly accused of being "a friend of publicans and sinners" – in lifestyle, not participating in evil and, at the same time, being everyone's most accessible, most gracious good neighbor.

On earth Jesus, himself, refused to become entangled in matters of civil government. That was not his earthly mission at the time. Neither was it his mission to change fundamental Old Testament principles of civil law, nor to turn civil government over to the ungodly. (*Mathew 5:17-19*)

As to Christian involvement in public affairs, we should evaluate Jesus' charge to his disciples:

> You are the salt of the earth. But if the salt loses its saltiness, how can it be made salty again? It is no longer good for anything, except to be thrown out and trampled by men.
>
> You are the light of the world. A city on a hill cannot be

hidden. Neither do people light a lamp and put it under a bowl. Instead they put it on its stand, and it gives light to everyone in the house. In the same way, let your light shine before men, that they may see your good deeds and praise your Father in heaven. (*Matthew 5:13-16, NIV*)

Do these Scriptures not imply that Jesus would have his disciples highly visible in every place that needs Scriptural enlightenment and godly moderation? And surely no place affords more opportunity – no place has a greater need – for "salt and light" than civil government.

When Christian salt loses its saltiness – refusing, among other things, to take positions of authority and influence in public affairs – can we complain when we are "thrown out and trampled by men?"

Another excuse for Christian withdrawal from civic responsibility is the inevitability of prophetic events concerning the end of the age. Bible scholars, however, have never been able to positively identify America in the end-time prophecies of the Scriptures. Is it possible that our posterity could be saved from the end-time holocaust, as our country has been (with the exception of the Civil War) saved from all world-class calamities for over two centuries?

What did Jesus mean by "occupy 'til I come?". Could he mean for his disciples to occupy every place possible – including civil government – to assure God's will being done – "in earth, as it is in heaven?" In any case, we know this: He did not say "occupy 'til [just before you think] I come!"

Let Humanist cynics rage if they will. God's will in civil government is, in reality, the good government we all pretend to desire.

Under Roman government, Caesar was "god." Early Christians could participate in government only by submitting to civil authorities, praying for them, paying taxes, and suffering government persecution for Christ's sake. The New Testament instructed them to do so. But God has graciously given Americans a better form of government.

Under American government, God is the Sovereign – "one nation under God". The people – including Christians – through their elected representatives *are* the government. American Christians are instructed by the New Testament to submit to civil authorities – our elected representatives, themselves subject to the will of the people – to pray for them, to pay our taxes, and to be faithful stewards of the free, self-governing republic God has given us.

Christian ministers, America cries: Come to the aid of your country! Will you, for God's sake and the people's sake, regularly devote some preaching time and Bible teaching time to "God and Country?" Like your colonial counterparts and the prophets of the Bible – without fear of the judge, the IRS, or partisan spirit in the churches – will you arm yourself with civil knowledge, speak up and take the lead against those in places of public trust who corrupt our people, abuse our Constitution, and pervert our Christian American liberties?

After inculcating Biblical virtues in your adherents, will you train and challenge the true and faithful to participate in offices and professions of public trust? Will you participate with non-sectarian Christian organizations who are active in the public arena?

With leadership and challenge from the pulpit, perhaps rank and file Christians will turn from their neglect of civic stewardship. Perhaps they will become visible in, and give Christian leadership to the institutions that shape our society and direct our government. Perhaps, like their colonial counterparts and the godly statesmen of the Bible, they will take their place in the political and governmental process, and join the fight to save our country from the program and purpose of religious Humanism.

We firmly believe this change in mindset – in the pulpit as well as in the pew – is vitally necessary before we can hope to see our land healed.

Educate for Leadership

One of the remnants of Christian America is Christian Education. Especially to be commended are the home schools, Christian schools, and Christian colleges – both Protestant and Catholic – which have saved countless children from indoctrination with the evil doctrines of religious Humanism in public schools and universities.

Now let our Christian schools quickly get busy preparing some of their brightest students to take a place in the public affairs of our nation. These students should be as inspired, as prepared, and as dedicated to work for God and State as our ministers and missionaries are zealous to work for God and Church.

How can Christian educators prepare young people for responsible positions in our government, educational institutions, and legal professions?

- They should be thoroughly grounded in Bible doctrines, and thoroughly indoctrinated in our true Christian American history, with due respect for our nation's founders and foundations.
- They should be truthfully taught the comparative values and agendas of the major political parties and the political concepts threatening to our liberties.
- They should be indoctrinated with Christian motives for public service, as opposed to ambition for personal fame or fortune.
- Accountability to God and man should be ingrained in them.
- From elementary school days, they should be led in participation in the political process – from student body office, to political campaign assistance, to precinct chairmanship, to officiating elections, to seeking public office.
- Upon graduation from high school they should know the political process thoroughly, having already studied political science and worked in elections and political campaigns for school credit.
- Then they should be encouraged to study Constitutional law and political science in Christian universities, and to seek a place in governmental service and elective office.

When Christian schools add public service to their present curriculum, they will have restored the Christian education system of early America – a two-pronged approach aimed at Christian ministry and Christian public service. Possibly Christian schools are our best hope for filling our public offices with able and righteous men and women. And the Scriptures assure us, "when the righteous are in authority, the people rejoice."

Christian Broadcasting

We are of the opinion that Christian radio and TV networks spend entirely too much time "singing to the choir" – broadcasting programs that appeal to a limited Christian audience with limited tastes. Could not these media perform an additional great service to "God and Country" by devoting some prime broadcast time to an intelligent and objective Christian perspective on societal and political issues that affect all of us?" Is not God involved in all issues that affect all human life – here as well as hereafter?"

Some of these "God and Country" programs might follow a format similar to Pat Robertson's CBN News. Others might be similar to the roundtable discussions and analyses of current events.as seen on network TV. Still others might expose proceedings in Washington and the courts as they relate to the Bible and the Constitution.

The great difference in these Christian programs and personnel and similar programs and personnel on network TV would be the recognition of God in these matters – an element totally lacking in the secular media.

Our appeal to Christian broadcasters is simply our conviction that they are missing a great and needy audience. This audience is made up of millions of good people – both churched and unchurched. They are disillusioned with government and distrustful of the daily dose of newspaper and network news and commentary. They would like to hear the truth, the whole truth, and nothing but the truth on a common sense, common folk level. Christian broadcasters could fill this crying need.

Not for Christians Alone

There are many encouraging signs of Christian renewal in America today.

Early in this decade, many Christian associations were enlightened to the "If my people" promise under study here. Countless Christians believe the promise to heal the land is God's call to renewal – possibly the last call before the total moral and political collapse of our republic. Hopefully, Christians will not confine the renewal within the realm of God and Church, as all twentieth century Christian renewals have been confined.

Unlike their colonial counterparts, most twentieth-century clergy (except the "liberal religion" set), have become almost exclusively occupied with the realm of God and Church. Unlearned and unpracticed in the realm of God and State, they often mislead, or more often, fail to lead at all in this realm.

Consequently, churches may be filled with men and women of talent and sterling character, but mostly unskilled and unchallenged to participate in the realm of God and State. Among other things, genuine renewal of the Church should correct this apathetic condition among Christians – a condition detrimental to our survival as a free, self-governing republic.

Let the clergy fortify themselves with understanding of our Constitution, the supreme law of the land, as well as with the supreme law of God. The government is Constitutionally forbidden to domineer the Church; and, it cannot do so as long as the Church presents a united front. No more faltering in the face of Humanist legal organizations, Humanist judges, and the Internal Revenue Service, sometimes acting as the strong-arm for the Humanist agenda. Let God arise and his enemies be scattered!

The promise is to heal the land, in the realm of God and State – we the people, the whole body politic. The promise is not for Christians alone. Christians are a vital part – but only a part – of the body politic. So let Christian renewal overflow into the whole body politic.

Religious Humanists are so entrenched that it will take all the strength of all God-fearing, Bible-believing Americans – Catholic, Protestant, Jewish, and unchurched – to rescue our country from the *program* and *purpose* of religious Humanism.

And what are "we the people" – the whole body politic – expected to do?

The Scriptures tell us, "God is no respecter of persons." The call is the same to all: We must humble ourselves, and pray, and seek God's face, and turn from our wicked ways.

Divided we Fall

Christians cannot win the war for America's future by merely going to church and singing "Onward Christian Soldiers."

- They cannot be single-issue protestors.
- They must move from reaction to positive political involvement.
- Their political involvement must be Christian – not Party.
- They must lay aside sectarian differences and unite as their forefathers did under "the general principles of Christianity" against a common enemy of the American people – religious Humanism.
- They must recognize Humanism as a foe that is economic and political as well as religious and join with economic and political conservatives and participate, as they once did, in all the public affairs of their country.

Unchurched Bible-believers might re-consider their abandonment of church. In spite of the imperfections of the human side of this institution, much is to be gained there – inspiration, encouragement, exhortation in the Word of God, connection with our Christian past, Biblical interpretation of current events.

Economic and political conservatives cannot win their economic causes without coming to terms with the religious war for the soul of America.

- They must recognize that our private property, free enterprise economic system and our free self-governing republic comes to us from the Bible through our Christian ancestors.
- They must join Bible-centered Christians against a common foe – Humanism – a foe that is religious, economic, and political. One cannot be a Humanist religiously and a conservative economically or politically.
- They must understand that if America is lost to religious Humanism, our economic and political system collapses with her.

The Civic Response

Be Wisely Informed

Only rightly informed people can be self-governing and reasonably content with their government. Much of our political waywardness today is due to deceptive politicians and misinformation from various sources.

Television, the easy road to information, misleads politically at least as often as it rightly informs. This is because all network media is politically slanted toward liberalism – actually Humanism. This political bias results from the fact that network media is controlled by religious Humanism. This is not to imply that all who work in the media are religious Humanists but only to say where the control and bias lies.

Reliable alternate sources of information are available. Some special television reports, such as *20/20*, presently provide valuable supplements to the news and with limited bias. *CBN News*, the first half hour of the *700 Club* TV broadcast, reports on issues and provides information often ignored or slanted by the major news networks. The *700 Club* broadcast is listed in the TV Guide in areas where the broadcast is available.

Conservative talk radio – a good public forum for discussion of the issues – has become a popular, alternate source of information. Humanists have talk shows, too, so the listener must be on the alert.

A number of reliable periodicals are available; and every home should have a library of reliable and informative books. At the end of this chapter, a list of reliable books and periodicals is provided.

Also, the recommended reading list at the end of each chapter lists excellent resources that educate the concerned citizen on many important issues. Good selections can be purchased regularly from the Conservative Book Club at discount prices.

A number of concerned citizens organizations – such as Christian Coalition, Focus on the Family, Eagle Forum, American Family Association, Concerned Women of America, and others – monitor Congress and State Legislatures and make their findings available. Individuals and public affairs committees may contact these organizations for ongoing information. Some of these organizations are listed at the end of this chapter.

Study Chapters 12 through 15 of this book until you can recognize religious Humanism at work in the institutions that affect your life. Then get involved and help cleanse our institutions of this despotic worldview, destructive to our liberties.

Become Vitally Involved

A head full of good information will accomplish little if it is merely kept there. The Humanist enemies of our liberties are firmly entrenched and determined. To rout them will take commitment for the long haul.

It is truly maddening when we realize that we can no longer send our own children to public school, fully confident that they will receive necessary academic education and not be indoctrinated against their faith in God, their Bible, their parents, their American heritage, and their moral upbringing. But such is the sorry state of public education under the *control* and *direction* of religious Humanism.

Parents of public school children have only two choices: Either turn over your children unreservedly to the public school – where they will likely receive large doses of Humanist values and ideals – or get vitally involved in your children's education.

How can you become vitally involved?

- Elect reliable members to your school board, attend school board meetings, and monitor its programs.
- Join citizen associations that monitor your state board of of edu-

cation concerning policies, curriculum, federal aid and regulation, etc.

- Get acquainted with your children's teachers, principals, and administrators, their character and personal value system, and their teaching methods and curriculum.
- Monitor your children's progress in values, goals, and ideals, as well as academics.

This is a big assignment after you have done your day's work, paid your school taxes, and met your other responsibilities. But, nowadays it is entirely possible that, while you are working to provide for your family and pay your taxes, your public school is dumbing down your children with Humanist nonsense and undermining your parental authority, your religion, your moral values, and your political and social ideals. Just the same, expect to meet Goals 2000 public relations personnel – at the school board and the schoolhouse – assuring you that everything is okay.

Every parent needs (and certainly deserves) the relief of leaving the kids at school in complete confidence. How wicked a school system that betrays that trust! Yet that is all too often the condition of public education in America today.

Parents and Teachers, Arise!

Sixty-two percent of public school teachers and administrators take their kids to private school and leave them there in confidence – a loud and clear statement of their lack of confidence in public education.

Some of the nation's poorest kids are given school vouchers so they can attend the school of their choice and escape failed public schools. Does not equality under the law demand that all have the same right to school choice?

Parents of more than a millions school children are escaping failed public schools by educating their children at home. Private Christian schools remain an option to those who can afford the tuition.

All parents who find their children being poorly educated or indoctrinated against their religion and moral values should make every effort to home school or place their children in private school. Unfortunately this will be impossible for some – such as single mothers and others unable to pay the tuition – and difficult for many more.

It may be necessary for some parents to donate time to the private school to help pay the tuition. Hopefully, in time, we together can break the despotic yoke of the education establishment and end taxation without representation – paying once for private education, then paying taxes for the public school your child is not attending.

Christian public educators, why assist the federal government and the NEA in strangling quality education in America? Why not get out of the public system, organize private school associations, give America a better education at a better price, and, in the process, pay yourselves a better salary? Yes, you can do it, if you will also help us shut down the U. S. Department of Education and stop taxation without representation for private school students.

We need to expel the federal government and the National Education Association – not God – from school.

The Economic Response

Go on the Offensive

Parents of America, Hollywood doesn't care about you, your children, your religion, or your moral values. They are on a Humanist mission to reduce Americans morally to the lowest common denominator. As religious zealots, they will carry out that mission, even when their blasphemous movies are box office flops and TV ratings show their morally corrupt and religiously repulsive shows to be unpopular.

Repulsive TV shows cannot last long without corporate sponsors. No doubt there are Humanist zealots on corporate boards who will sponsor these shows even if they lose money doing so. By and large, however, corporate executives respond to the language of money, and only to the language of money. They will cease to sponsor shows if they know their advertising dollars are not paying off in sales of their products. And that's where you have something to say about TV programming.

Stop buying products advertised on repulsive TV shows and boycott all products sold by the sponsoring company, then send the corporate director a letter announcing your action. When enough people do this, collectively they will have an impact on the corporate income statement, and their voice will be heard.

You will then have the satisfaction of knowing you did your duty to God and Country, regardless of what others do and regardless of what media cynics say. On the positive side, buy the products of companies that sponsor decent shows and advise the sponsors and the TV networks of your response.

Because of corporate conglomerates, it is sometimes difficult to identify the name and address of the sponsoring parent company and all its products. But it can be done. Get in touch with the American Family Association for help in this. Their address is at the end of this chapter.

Economic responses, admittedly, are inconvenient; and we should not have to endure them. But we are forced to take action against Hollywood and their irresponsible corporate sponsors or witness the moral collapse of American society. And what is a little inconvenience, if by enduring it, we can save our country from ruin?

Informing ourselves and purchasing Brand B, when we might otherwise purchase Brand A is a small sacrifice compared to the sacrifice of our colonial ancestors in giving us this great land.

The Political Response

Don't Be a "Yellow Dog"

All who blindly vote a straight party ticket, never bothering to study the issues – or the candidates' character and their stand on the issues – are politically lazy and servile. Politically, you are pawns in the hands of party operatives. You are written off by all candidates as "yellow dog Democrats" or "yellow dog Republicans," unworthy of consideration.

Smooth politicians of all political persuasions routinely pass themselves off as either Democrats or Republicans, depending upon which way the political winds are blowing at the moment. Political parties change direction and leadership. Papa's party is not necessarily the same today as it was yesterday.

For voters to be beneficial to ourselves or our country, we must be aware of the trends, the values, and the agendas of political parties, party leaders, and candidates, as they really are today.

For a starter, we need to severely scrutinize the commonly repeated myths concerning the two major political parties.

One such myth, as an example, assures us that the Democratic Party is the party of hard-working, common folk, while the Republicans are fat cats, concerned only with making the rich richer. Actually, both parties have a range of adherents from the poorest to the richest.

We need to concern ourselves with party values and agendas as they affect the liberty and security of our children and grandchildren.

If we want good government, we must put away long-standing political myths and inform ourselves truthfully and objectively regarding the values and direction of the two parties as they stand today.

Be Part of the Process

Study Chapters 12 through 15 of this book until you can recognize the level of Humanist *transformation*, *control*, and *direction* in the political parties. Then give your support to the party less controlled by the Humanist worldview. Only from inside can you assist your party in ridding itself of that destructive worldview and help it become the true party of Constitutional government.

It is our studied opinion that both major political parties are aiding the Humanist agenda to some extent as we prepare to enter the twenty-first century – the Democrats more agressively than the Republicans. Therefore, the Republican party is, we believe, more likely to improve and move the country back onto the right track.

For our part, we are persuaded that a better plan could be devised, precluding the interference of political parties in elections and governmental processes. But such a plan is not in sight. The present system, faulty as it is, is the only system we have for electing candidates to office and conducting government business. Therefore, we believe, until a better system can be devised, our best course is to choose one of the two major parties and get involved in the process.

For more information, phone the county headquarters of your chosen party, and ask for the name and phone number of your precinct chairman. Call your precinct chairman, offer your help, and expect your precinct chairman to introduce you to the process. With a little experience you may want to seek the position of precinct chairman or some other office of public trust.

Those who desire a Christian introduction and training in the political process should contact Christian Coalition in your county or state or – if that address is unavailable – at the national address at the end of this chapter.

Beware the Untouchable Rulers

All power of the federal government is in the hands of 545 persons:

• One President;
• Nine Supreme Court Justices;
• 100 Senators; and
• 435 Representatives

Since local and state governments have been reduced to little more than subdivisions of the federal government, we can say that the 260 million Americans are ruled by these 545 persons.

Nine of our ruling elite, the Supreme Court Justices, are appointed for life by the President. They are virtually untouchable by the will of the people, regardless of how they exercise the power entrusted to them.

At any given time, the Court will be composed of both Democratic and Republican appointees. Since federal judges hold office for life and the people cannot dismiss them, the judges have little to restrain them from tyranny except the restraint they place upon themselves. And judicial restraint has been conspiciously lacking for the last half century.

The appointment of life-tenured federal judges is the most awesome power and the most sacred trust vested in the President. This is the most critical reason we should elevate no one to the Presidency except a person of proven impeccable character, who is dedicated to strict adherence to government by the common-sense, plain language of our Constitution, and who is clear of all adherence to the Humanist religion and agenda.

Every four years we make much ado about electing a President, as if all our fortunes depended upon our selection. Presidents come and Presidents go. They are Constitutionally limited to eight years in office. Up against a Congress jealous of the sanctity of the Constitution, Presidents have little chance of becoming despots. But, when they appoint federal judges during their term of office, their Presidency, for good or evil, will live long after they are practically forgotten.

Hold Congress Accountable

Responsibility for the kind of government we have rests squarely upon the shoulders of our U. S. Senators and Representatives – and ultimately upon we the people; for we decide who will represent us in Congress. Good government, therefore, requires that we carefully elect persons of talent and sound character as our U. S. Senators and Representatives and then watchfully hold them accountable for the stewardship of our trust.

In the beginning of our nation the people created the Congress and there was only the Congress. The President was President of Congress, elected by the Congress. Congress wrote and ratified the Constitution, with George Washington as President of Congress.

Congress, therefore, is the creator of the Constitution, the Supreme Court, the office of President of the United States, and all the laws and agencies of the federal government. Congress, as creator of the Constitution, has the prime responsibility to protect its authority and limitations as the final word of law, and to initiate the process for amending it.

Congress, with 100 Senators and 435 Representatives, is the most numerous and most representative branch of federal government. Two thirds of Congress – 67 Senators and 290 Representatives – have the power to pass or repeal any law without the President's signature, or to overturn any decision of the Supreme Court. This majority has the power to impeach any President, federal judge, or head of any federal agency that proves a threat to Constitutional government.

Congress is the law-making branch – the *only* law-making branch – of the federal government. Any assumed law originated by the President or the Supreme Court is null and void. Such a law does not spring from the people. Such a law is tyranny.

Any Congress that allows Executive ordered or Court decreed "law" to be imposed on the people has abdicated to the Executive and/or the Judicial branch. Members of that Congress who tolerate such "laws" should be summarily replaced at the next election. It is to be understood, of course, that Executive orders and Court decisions consistent with the common-sense, plain language of the Constitution have been pre-approved by Congress when creating the Constitution. It is to be further understood that such orders and decrees are still subject to Congressional review for approval or rejection by Congressional action.

In recognizing that primary power has been vested in the Congress, we need to ever keep in mind that Congress is the creation of the people – and the real power finally lies with us. This is true of the present composition of Congress as well as it was true of the original Continental Congress.

Congress is the most accountable branch. U. S. Representatives must give account to their constituents every two years at the ballot box; and, Senators must give account every six years.

Stop Party Rule

Congress makes its own election laws and rules of operation. One such rule of operation gives "control of Congress" to the political party with the most members in Congress. We cannot explain the logic behind a rule that gives control of Congress to any political party; but, we suspect this rule with all its implications is detrimental to the conduct of Congress in the best interest of all the people. The Constitution makes no provision for political parties in the conduct of government business.

For 40 years prior to 1994, the Democratic Party had control of Congress. In 1994, apparently fed up with the way their Congress was conducting their government's business, the people elected 72 Republicans to Congress. This election turned control of Congress over to Republicans for the first time in 40 years.

In a flurry of activity, named "Contract with America," some beneficial changes have been made. In our opinion, however, serious federal government violations and corruptions of our Constitution have not yet been addressed.

Rare are the persons in federal office who are willing to return the federal government back to its Tenth Amendment bounds, and return confiscated power back to the states respectively or to the people.

Eliminate Professional Legislators

Those who aspire to serve in Congress need to keep in mind that, in that capacity, they are mere expressions of the will of the people – and that they are presumed to be of such wisdom and integrity as to be worthy of the people's trust.

Congress has become altogether too professional, and its membership self-perpetuating. The founders had the idea that citizen legislators would serve for a short time and return to their private lives. Congressmen today have different ideas; so they resist all efforts to limit their terms. The time for term limits imposed by law has probably come.

Professional legislators weaken America's representative form of government. How? Because of money-driven elections, their self-endowed advantages of incumbency, and their intense desire for re-election:

- They are vulnerable to the corruptions of campaign money and party arm-twisting;
- They falter before high-dollar lobbyists and popular Presidents who might threaten their re-election;
- They bow to the will of more powerful politicians and to their party's "whips" in Congress;
- They perpetuate a ruling elite.

Perhaps 72 new members should be elected to Congress every two years until Congress is again in the hands of citizen legislators.

If we elect corruptible persons to Congress, can we expect anything from them but corrupted government? Responsibility for corrupt government rests finally upon we the people.

Some have oversimplified the procedure for ridding Congress of corrupt members. They assume incumbency alone to be reason enough to "throw the rascals out." This attitude is just another example of voter laziness. Good government requires that we know the character and voting record of those who represent us.

Thanks to the work of conservative and Christian activist organizations – Concerned Women of America, Focus on the Family, American Family Association, Christian Coalition, and others – it is now possible to cut through political rhetoric and get a better understanding of the characters who represent us in public office.

These organizations question candidates and publish their responses to questions pertinent to their qualification for office. They also publish the voting record of members of Congress. At election time these Congressional scorecards and candidate responses are available at cooperating churches and businesses. Or they can be obtained by contacting one of the above named organizations.

"Fire, fellow soldiers, for God's sake, Fire!"

This writer now wishes to confess that he is a mere amateur, viewing Congress from the outside. For an insider's view of the inner workings of Congress – and for an appeal to action – we defer to a higher authority, the "Father of our Country."

George Washington: By one who wishes the prosperity of America most devoutly and sees or thinks he sees it, on the brink of ruin, you are beseeched in endeavouring to rescue your Country, by, (let me add) sending your ablest and best Men to Congress; these characters must not slumber, nor sleep at home, in such times of pressing danger; they must not content themselves in the enjoyment of places of honor or profit in their own Country, while the common interests of America are mouldering and sinking into irretrievable (if remedy is not soon applied) ruin, in which theirs also must ultimately be involved.

If I was to be called upon to draw A picture of the times, and of men; from what I have seen, heard, and in part know I should in one word say idleness, dissipation, and extravagance seem to have laid fast hold of most of them. That Speculation, peculation, and an insatiable thirst for riches seems to have got the better of every other consideration and almost of every order of Men.

That party disputes and personal quarrels are the great business of the day whilst the momentous concerns of an empire, a great and accumulated debt; ruined finances, depreciated money . . . are but secondary considerations and postponed from day to day, week to week as if our affairs wore the most promising aspect; after drawing this picture, which from my Soul I believe to be a true one I need not repeat to you that I am alarmed and wish to see my Countrymen roused. . . .

Where is Mason, Wythe, Jefferson, Nicholas, Pendleton, Nelson, and another I could name. . . . Providence has heretofore taken us up when all other means and hope seemed to be departing from us, in this I will confide. [1]

The Liberator: It seems that some things never change in Congress, Mr. President.

With all my soul, sir, I believe, if we are to see a new birth of freedom in America, a reformed Congress must reform our federal government.

And (I might add) the 104th Congress could not lay down party disputes and personal quarrels long enough to restore our religious liberty, to balance the federal budget, to outlaw the killing of babies partially born, or to attend other matters critical to our posterity – their safety, their financial security, and their liberties.

It seems to me, sir, that the religious despots, the wastrels, and the abortionists are the first to be replaced in Congress. But where are the Jeffersons, the Masons, the Madisons, the Wythes. Where are the Reverends Witherspoon and Sherman. Where is self-sacrificing Washington, who alone can command the respect of the people?

Where are the Mainliners who still believe the gospel according to Edwards, Mather, Luther, Whitefield, Wesley? Where are the Fundamentalists, the Evangelicals, the Pentecostals? Where are the Catholics, the Charismatics? Where are the patriot parsons to fire the pulpits of America.

Where is black Christendom? Marching on Washington behind a Muslim rabble-rouser? Do they not understand that their spiritual roots are not in Mecca, nor in Africa, but in the little Christian churches on the plantations of America? There is the source of their liberty. There is the hope of their future.

Will they surrender this their hour to a Muslim racist or give it up to welfare slavery? Or will they take their well-earned place in the American parade, and march on Washington with the Promise Keepers of America?

Where are the Israelites in whom is no guile? Where are the armies of David?

No more retreating to our secluded neighborhoods and our religious comfort zones. Let us put on the whole armor of God, and go up together against the enemies of our liberties and repossess our American birthright!

If our countrymen can be roused, Mr. President, to humble ourselves, and pray, and seek God's face, and turn from our wicked ways, I believe kind Providence can be persuaded to take us up again and heal our land. In this, I too will confide.

Some Sources of Reliable Books and Periodicals

General Topics

Insight on the News
3600 New York Avenue
Washington, DC 20002

World
P. O. Box 2330
Asheville, NC 28002

National Review
P. O. Box 96639
Washington, DC 20090-6639

Reader's Digest
Pleasantville, NY 10570

The Limbaugh Letter
P. O. Box 420234
Palm Coast, FL 32142-0234

Phyllis Schlafly Report
P. O. Box 618
Alton, IL 62002

Media Bypass
P. O. Box 5326
Evansville, IN 47716

Common Cause
2030 M Street, NW
Washington, DC 20036

The Heritage Foundation
214 Massachusetts Ave., NE
Washington, DC 20002-4999

Family Research Council
700 13th St., NW Suite 500
Washington, DC 20005

Special Topics

Focus on the Family
102420 N. Cascade Ave.
Colorado Springs, CO 80903

Family Issues

Education Reporter
7800 Bonhomme Avenue
St. Louis, MO 63105

Emphasis on Education

American Family Association
P. O. Drawer 2440
Tupelo, MS 38003

Watchdog on Hollywood,
Media, and Advertisers.
Political Action

Christian Coalition
P. O. Box 1990
Chesapeake, VA 23320

Christian Political Action
and Information.
Non-Sectarian, Non-Partisan

National Minority Politics
5757 Westheimer Rd. Suite 3-296
Houston, TX 77057-9764

Political viewpoint from Conservative Black America. Good
reading for all Americans.

Citizens Against Government Waste
1301 Connecticut Ave., NW Ste. 400
Washington, DC 20036

Watchdog on Government
Spending.

Conservative Book Club
One Massachuetts Ave. NW
Suite 600
Washington, DC 20001

Conservative Books of
Interest to Mainstream
Americans.
All Topics, Discount Prices.

Appendix A

A TRIBUTE TO THE FATHER OF OUR COUNTRY

George Washington's Funeral Oration
Delivered by Major Henry Lee December 26, 1799
By Resolution of the Congress of the United States

In obedience to your will, I rise, your humble organ, with the hope of executing a part of the system of public mourning which you have been pleased to adopt, commemorative of the death of the most illustrious and most beloved personage this country has ever produced; and which, while it transmits to posterity your sense of the awful event, faintly represents your knowledge of the consummate excellence you so cordially honor.

Desperate indeed is any attempt on earth to meet correspondingly this dispensation of Heaven; for, while with pious resignation we submit to the will of an all – gracious Providence, we can never cease lamenting, in our finite view of Omnipotent Wisdom, the heart – rendering privation for which our nation weeps.

When the civilized world shakes to its centre; when every moment gives birth to strange and momentous changes; when our peaceful quarter of the globe, exempt as it happily has been from any share in the slaughter of the human race, may yet be compelled to abandon her pacific policy, and to risk the doleful casualties of war: What limit is there to the extent of our loss? None within the reach of my words to express; none which your feelings will not disvow.

The founder of our federate republic – our bulwark in war, our guide in peace, is no more! Oh that this were but questionable! Hope, the comforter of the wretched, would pour into our agonizing hearts its balmy dew. But, alas! there if no hope for us; our Washington is removed forever!

Possessing the stoutest frame, and purest mind, he had passed nearly to his sixty-eighth year, in the enjoyment of high health, when, habituated by his care of us to neglect himself, a slight cold, disregarded, became inconvenient on Friday, oppressive on Saturday, and, defying every medical interposition, before the morning of Sunday, put an end to the best of men.

An end did I say? – his fame survives! – bounded only by the limits of the earth, and by the extent of the human mind. He survives in our hearts, in the growing knowledge of our children, in the affections of the good throughout the world; and when our monuments shall be done away; when the nations now existing shall be no more; when even our young and far-spreading empire shall have perished, still will our Washington's glory unfaded shine, and die not, until love of virtue cease on earth, or earth itself sinks into chaos.

How, my fellow-citizens, shall I single to your grateful hearts his pre-eminent worth! Where shall I begin in opening to your view a character throughout sublime? Shall I speak of his warlike achievements, all springing from obedience to his country's will – all directed to his country's good?

Will you go with me to the banks of the Monongahela, to see your youthful Washington, supporting, in the dismal hour of Indian victory, the ill-fated Braddock, and saving, by his judgment and by his valor, the remains of a defeated army, pressed by the conquering savage foe? Or, when oppressed America, nobly resolving to risk her all in defense of her violated rights, he was elevated by the unanimous voice of Congress to the command of her armies:

Will you follow him to the high grounds of Boston, where to an undisciplined, courageous, and virtuous yeomanry, his presence gave the stability of system, and infused the invincibility of a country; or shall I carry you to the painful scenes of Long Island, York Island and New Jersey, when, combating superior and gallant armies, aided by powerful fleets, and led by chiefs high in the roll of fame, he stood, the bulwark of our safety; undismayed by disaster; unchanged by change of fortune.

Or will you view him in the precarious fields of Trenton, where deep gloom unnerving every arm, reigned triumphant through our thinned, worn down, unaided ranks; himself unmoved. Dreadful was the night. It was about this time of winter – the storm raged – the Delaware rolling furiously with floating ice, forbade the approach of man. Washington, self-collected, viewed the tremendous scene – whose country called; unappalled by surrounding dangers, he passed to the hostile shore; he fought; he conquered. The morning sun cheered the American world. Our country rose on the event; and her dauntless chief, pursuing his blow, completed in the lawns of Princeton, what his vast soul had conceived on the shores of the Delaware.

Thence to the strong grounds of Morristown he led his small but gallant band; and through the eventful winter, by high efforts of his genius, whose matchless force was measurable only by the growth of difficulties, he held in check formidable hostile legions; conducted by a chief experienced in the art of war, and famed for his valor on the ever memorable heights of Abraham, where fell Wolfe, Montcalm, and since our much lamented Montgomery – all covered with glory. In this fortunate interval, produced by his masterly conduct, our fathers, ourselves, animated by his resistless example, rallied around our country's standard, and continued to follow her beloved chief through the various and trying scenes to which the destinies of our union led.

Who is there that has forgotton the vales of Brandywine – the field of Germantown – or the plains of Monmouth? Everywhere present, wants of every kind obstructing, numerous and valiant armies encountering, himself a host, he assuaged our sufferings, limited our privations, and upheld our tottering republic. Shall I display to you the spread of the fire of his soul, by rehearsing the praises of the Hero of Saratoga, and his much loved compeer of the Carolinas? No; our Washington wears no borrowed glory; to Gates – to Greene, he gave without reserve the applause due to their eminent merit; and long may the chiefs of Saratoga, and of Eutaws, receive the grateful respect of a grateful people.

Moving in his own orbit, he imparted heat and light to his most distant satellites; and combining the physical and moral force of all within his sphere, with irresistible weight he took his course, commiserating folly, disdaining vice, dismaying treason, and invigorating despondency; until the auspicious hour arrived, when, united with the intrepid forces of a potent and magnanimous ally, he brought to submission the since conqueror of India; thus finishing his long career of military glory with a lustre corresponding to his great name, and in his last act of war affixing the seal of fate to our nation's birth.

To the horrid din of battle sweet peace succeeded, and our virtuous chief, mindful only of the common good, in a moment tempting personal aggrandizement, hushed the discontents of growing sedition; and, surrendering his power into the hands from which he had received it, converted his sword into a plowshare, teaching an admiring world that to be truly great you must be truly good.

Was I to stop here, the picture would be incomplete and the task imposed unfinished. Great was our Washington in war, and as much as did that greatness contribute to produce the American republic, it is not in war alone his pre-eminence stands conspicuous. His various talents combining all the capacities of a statesman with those of a soldier, fitted him alike to guide the councils and the armies of our nation. Scarcely had he rested from his martial toils, while his invaluable parental advice was still sounding in our ears, when he who had been our shield and our sword, was called forth to act a less splended but more important part.

Possessing a clear and penetrating mind, a strong and sound judgement, calmness and temper for deliberation, with invincible firmness, and perseverance and resolutions maturely formed, drawing information from all, acting from himself, with incorruptible integrity and unvarying patriotism: his own superiority and the public confidence alike marked him as the man designed by Heaven to lead in the great political as well as military events which have distinguished the ara of his life.

The finger of an overruling providence, pointing at Washington, was neither mistaken nor unobserved; when, to realize the vast hopes to which our revolution had given birth, a change of political system became indispensable.

How novel, how grand the spectacle! Independent states stretched over an immense territory, and known only by common difficulty, clinging to their union as the rock of their safety, deciding by frank comparison of their relative condition, to rear on that rock, under the guidance of reason, a common government, through whose commanding protection, liberty and order, with their long train of blessings, should be safe to themselves, and the sure inheritance of their posterity.

This arduous task devolved on citizens selected by the people, from knowledge of their wisdom and confidence in their virtue. In this august assembly of sages and patriots, Washington of course was found; and, as if acknowledged to be most wise, where all were wise, with one voice he was declared their chief. How well he merited this rare distinction, how faithful were the labors of himself and his compatriots, the work of their hands and our union, strength and prosperity, the fruits of that work, best attest.

But to have essentially aided in presenting to his country this consummation of her hopes, neither satisfied the claims of his fellow-citizens on his talents, nor those duties which the possession of those talents imposed. Heaven had not infused into his mind such an uncommon share of its ethereal spirit to remain unemployed, nor bestowed on him his genious unaccompanied with the corresponding duty of devoting it to the common good.

To have framed a constitution, was showing only, without realizing, the general happiness. This great work remained to be done; and America, steadfast in her preference, with one voice summoned her beloved Washington, unpracticed as he was in the duties of civil administration, to execute this last act in the completion of the national felicity. Obedient to her call he assumed the high office with that self-distrust pecular to his inate modesty, the constant attendant of pre-eminent virtue. What was the burst of joy through our anxious land on this exhilarating event is known to us all.

The aged, the young, the brave, the fair rivaled each other in demonstrations of their gratitude; and this high-wrought, delightful scene was heightened in its effect, by the singular contest between the zeal of the bestowers and the avoidance of the receiver of the honors bestowed. Commencing his administration, what heart is not charmed with the recollection of the pure and wise principles announced by himself, as the basis of his political life.

He best understood the indissoluble union between virtue and happiness, between duty and advantage, between the genuine maximums of an honest and magnanimous policy, and the solid rewards of public prosperity and individual felicity; watching with an equal and comprehensive eye over this great assemblage of communities and interests, he laid the foundations of our national policy in the unerring, immutable principles of morality, based on religion, exemplifying the pre-eminence of a free government; by all the attributes which win the affections of its citizens, or command the respect of the world.

"O fortunatos nimium, sua si bona norint!"

Leading through the complicated difficulties produced by previous obligations and conflicting interests, seconded by succeeding houses of Congress, enlightened and patriotic, he surmounted all original obstructions, and brightened the path of our national felicity.

The presidential term expiring, his solicitude to exchange exaltation for humility returned with a force increased with increase of age; and he had prepared his farewell address to his countrymen, proclaiming his intentions, when the united interposition of all around him, enforced by the eventful prospects of the epoch, produced a further sacrifice of inclination to duty.

The election of President followed, and Washington, by unanimous vote of the nation, was called to resume the Chief Magistry. What a wonderful fixture of confidence! Which attracts most our admiration, a people so correct, or a citizen combining an assemblage of talents forbidding rivalry, and stifling even envy itself? Such a nation ought to be happy, such a chief must be forever revered.

War, long menaced by the Indian tribes, now broke out; and the terrible conflict, deluging Europe with blood, began to shed its baneful influence over our happy land. To the first, outstreching his invincible arm, under the orders of the gallant Wayne, the American eagle soared triumphant through distant forests. Peace followed victory; and the melioration of the condition of the enemy followed peace. Godlike virtue, which uplifts even the enemy followed.

To the second he opposed himself. New and delicate was the conjuncture, and great was the stake. Soon did his penetrating mind discern and seize the only course, continuing to us all the felicity enjoyed. He issued his proclamation of neutrality. This index to his whole subsequent conduct was sanctioned by the approbation of both houses of Congress, and the approving voice of the people.

To this sublime policy he invioably adhered, unmoved by foreign intrusion, unshaken by domestic turbulence.

Justum et tenacem propositi virum,
Non civium ardor prava jubentium,
Non vultus instantis tyranni,
Mente quatit folida.

Maintaining his pacific system at the expense of no duty, America, faithful to herself, and sustained in her honor, continued to enjoy the delights of peace, while afflicted Europe mourns in every quarter under the accumulated miseries of an unexampled war; miseries in which our happy country must have shared, had not our preeminent Washington been as firm in council as he was brave in the field.

Pursuing steadfastly his course, he held safe the public happiness, preventing foreign wars, and quelling internal discord, til the revolving period of a third election approached, when he executed his interrupted but inextinquishable desire of returning to the humble walks of private life.

The promulgation of his fixed resolution stopped the anxious wishes of affectionate people, from adding a third unanimous testimonial of their unabated confidence in the man so long enthroned in their hearts. When before was affection like this exhibited on the earth? Turn over the records of ancient Greece! Review the anals of mighty Rome! Examine the volume of modern Europe; you search in vain. America and her Washington only afford the dignified exemplification.

The illustrious personage called by the national voice in succession to the arduous office of guiding a free people, had new difficulties to encounter. The amicable effort of settling difficulties with France, begun by Washington, and pursued by his successor in virtue as in station, proving abortive, America took measures of self-defence. No sooner was the public mind roused by a prospect of danger, than every eye was turned to the friend of all, though secluded from public view, and gray in public service the virtuous veteran following his plow, received the unexpected summons with mingled emotions of indignation at the unmerited ill-treatment of his country, and of a determination once more to risk all in her defense.

The annunciation of these feelings, in his affecting letter to the President, accepting the command of the army, concludes his official conduct.

First in war, first in peace, and first in the hearts of his countrymen, he was second to none in the humble and endearing scenes of private life: pious, just, humane, temperate, and sincere, uniform, dignified, and commanding, his example was as edifying to all around him as were the effects of that example lasting.

To his equals he was condescending; to his inferiors kind; and to the dear object of his affections exemplarily tender. Correct throughout, vice shuddered in his presence, and virtue always felt his fostering hand; the purity of his character gave effulgence to his public virtues.

His last scene comported with the whole tenor of his life; although in extreme pain, not a sigh, not a groan escaped him; and with undisturbed serenity he closed his well-spent life. Such was the man America had lost. Such was the man for whom our nation mourns! Methinks I see his august image, and hear, falling from his venerable lips, these deep-sinking words:

"Cease, sons of America, lamenting our seperation: Go on, and confirm by your wisdom the fruits of our joint councils, joint efforts, and common dangers. Reverence religion: diffuse knowledge throughout your land; patronize the arts and sciences; let liberty and order be inseparable companions; control party-spirit, the bane of free government; observe good faith to, and cultivate peace with all nations; shut up every avenue to foreign influence; rely on yourselves only; be American in thought and deed. Thus will you give immortality to that union which was the constant object of my terrestrial labors. Thus will you preserve undisturbed to the latest posterity the felicity of a people to me most dear; and thus will you supply [if my happiness is now aught to you] the only vacancy in the round of pure bliss high Heaven bestows."

Appendix B

THE CONSTITUTION OF THE UNITED STATES OF AMERICA

We *the People* of the United States, in order to form a more perfect Union, establish Justice, insure domestic Tranquility, provide for the common defense, promote the general Welfare, and to secure the Blessings of Liberty to ourselves and our Posterity, do ordain and establish this Constitution for the United States of America.

Article I

Section 1. All legislative Powers herein granted shall be vested in a Congress of the United States, which shall consist of a Senate and House of Representatives.

Section 2. The House of Representatives shall be composed of Members chosen every second Year by the People of the several States, and the Electors in each State shall have the Qualifications requisite for Electors of the most numerous Branch of the State Legislature.

No Person shall be a Representative who shall not have attained to the Age of twenty-five Years, and been seven Years a Citizen of the United States, and who shall not, when elected, be an Inhabitant of that State in which he shall be chosen.

Representatives and direct Taxes shall be apportioned among the several States which may be included within this Union, according to their respective Numbers, which shall be determined by adding to the whole Number of free Persons, including those bound to Service for a Term of Years, and excluding Indians not taxed, three-fifths of all other Persons. The actual Enumeration shall be made within three Years after the first Meeting of the Congress of the United States, and within every subsequent Term of ten Years, in such Manner as they shall by Law direct. The Number of Representatives shall not exceed one for every thirty Thousand, but each State shall have at Least on Representative; and until such enumeration shall be made, the State of New Hampshire shall be entitled to choose three, Massachusetts eight, Rhode Island and Providence Plantations one, Connecticut five, New York six, New Jersey four, Pennsylvania eight, Delaware one, Maryland six, Virginia ten, North Carolina five, South Carolina five, and Georgia three.

When vacancies happen in the Representation from any State, the Executive Authority thereof shall issue Writs of Election to fill such Vacancies.

The House of Representatives shall choose their Speaker and other Officers; and shall have the sole Power of Impeachment.

Section 3. The Senate of the United States shall be composed of two Senators from each State, chosen by the Legislature thereof, for six Years; and each Senator shall have one Vote.

Immediately after they shall be assembled in Consequence of the first Election, they shall be divided as equally as may be into three Classes. The Seats of the Senators of the first Class shall be vacated at the Expiration of the second Year, of the second Class at the Expiration of the fourth Year, and of the third class at the Expiration of the sixth Year, so that one-third may be chosen every second Year; and if Vacancies happen by Resignation, or otherwise, during the Recess of the Legislature of any State, the Executive thereof may make temporary Appointment until the next Meeting of the Legislature, which shall then fill such Vacancies.

No Person shall be a Senator who shall not have attained to the Age of thirty Years, and been nine Years a Citizen of the United States, and who shall not, when elected, be an Inhabitant of that State for which he shall be chosen.

The Vice President of the United States shall be President of the Senate but shall have no Vote, unless they be equally divided.

The Senate shall choose their other Officers, and also a President pro tempore, in the Absence of the Vice President or when he shall exercise the Office of President of the United States.

The Senate shall have the sole Power to try all Impeachments. When sitting for that Purpose, they shall be on Oath or Affirmation. When the President of the United States is tried, the Chief Justice shall preside. And no Person shall be convicted without the Concurrence of two-thirds of the Members present.

Judgments in Cases of Impeachment shall not extend further than to removal from Office, and Disqualification to hold and enjoy any Office of honor, Trust, or Profit under the United States; but the Party convicted shall nevertheless be liable and subject to Indictment, Trial, Judgment, and Punishment, according to Law.

Section 4. The Times, Places, and Manner of holding Elections for Senators and Representatives shall be prescribed in each State by the Legislature thereof; but the Congress may at any time by Law make or alter such Regulations, except as to the places of choosing Senators.

The Congress shall assemble at least once in every Year, and such Meeting shall be on the first Monday in December, unless they shall by Law appoint a different Day.

Section 5. Each House shall be the Judge of the Elections, Returns, and Qualifications of its Members, and a Majority of each shall constitute a Quorum to do Business; but a smaller Number may adjourn from day to day, and may be authorized to compel the Attendance of absent Members, in such Manner, and under such Penalties as each House may provide.

Each House may determine the Rules of its Proceedings, punish its Members for disorderly Behavior, and, with Concurrence of two-thirds, expel a Member.

Each House shall keep a Journal of its Proceedings, and from time to time publish the same, excepting such Parts as may in their Judgment require Secrecy; and the Yeas and Nays of the Members of either House on any question shall, at the Desire of one-fifth of those Present, be entered on the Journal.

Neither House, during the Session of Congress, shall, without the Consent of the other, adjourn for more than three days, nor to any other Place than that in which the two Houses shall be sitting.

Section 6. The Senators and Representatives shall receive a Compensation for their Services, to be ascertained by Law, and paid out of the Treasury of the United States. They shall in all Cases, except Treason, Felony, and Breach of the Peace, be privileged from Arrest during their Attendance at the Session of their respective Houses, and in going to and returning from the same; and for any Speech or Debate in either House, they shall not be questioned in any other Place.

No Senator or Representative shall, during the Time for which he was elected, be appointed to any civil Office under the Authority of the United States, which shall have been created, or the Emoluments whereof shall have been increased during such time; and no Person holding any Office under the United States shall be a Member of either House during his Continuance in Office.

Section 7. All Bills for raising Revenue shall originate in the House of Representatives; but the Senate may propose or concur with Amendments as on other Bills.

Every Bill which shall have passed the House of Representatives and the Senate shall, before it become a Law, be presented to the President of the United States. If he approve, he shall sign it, but, if not, he shall return it, with his Objections to that House in which it shall have originated, who shall enter the Objections at large on their Journal, and proceed to reconsider it. If after such Reconsideration two-thirds of that House shall agree to pass the Bill, it shall be sent, together with the Objections, to the other House, by which it shall likewise be reconsidered, and if approved by two-thirds of that House, it shall become a Law. But in all such Cases the Votes of both Houses shall be determined by yeas and Nays, and the Names of the Persons voting for and against the Bill shall be entered on the Journal of each House respectively.

If any Bill shall not be returned by the President within ten Days (Sundays excepted) after it shall have been presented to him, the Same shall be law, in like Manner as if he had signed it, unless the Congress by their Adjournment prevent its Return, in which Case it shall not be a Law.

Every Order, Resolution, or Vote to which the Concurrence of the Senate and House of Representatives may be necessary (except on a question of Adjournment) shall be presented to the President of the United States and, before the Same shall take Effect, shall be approved by him, or, being disapproved by him, shall be repassed by two-thirds of the Senate and House of Representatives, according to the Rules and Limitations prescribed in the Case of a Bill.

Section 8. The Congress shall have Power

To lay and collect Taxes, Duties, Imposts and Excises, to pay the Debts and provide for the common Defense and general Welfare of the United States; but all Duties, Imposts, and Excises shall be uniform throughout the United States;

To borrow Money on the credit of the United States;

To regulate Commerce with foreign Nations, and among the several States and with the Indian Tribes;

To establish a uniform Rule of Naturalization, and uniform Laws on the subject of Bankruptcies throughout the United States;

To coin Money, regulate the Value thereof, and of foreign Coin, and fix the Standard of Weights and Measures;

To provide for the Punishment of counterfeiting the Securities and current Coin of the United States;

To establish Post Offices and post Roads;

To promote the progress of Science and useful Arts, by securing for limited Times to Authors and Inventors the exclusive right to their respective Writings and Discoveries;

To constitute Tribunals inferior to the Supreme Court;

To define and punish Piracies and Felonies committed on high Seas, and Offences against the Law of Nations;

To declare War, grant Letters of Marque and Reprisal, and make Rules concerning Captures on Land and Water;

To raise and support Armies, but no Appropriation of Money to that Use shall be for a longer Term than two Years;

To provide and maintain a Navy;

To make Rules for the Government and Regulation of the land and naval Forces;

To provide for calling forth the Militia to execute the Laws of the Union, suppress Insurrections and repel Invasions;

To provide for organizing, arming, and disciplining the Militia, and for governing such Part of them as may be employed in the Service of the United States, reserving to the States, respectively, the Appointment of the Officers, and the Authority of training the Militia according to the Discipline prescribed by Congress.

To exercise exclusive Legislation in all Cases whatsoever, over such District (not exceeding ten Miles square) as may, by Cession of particular States, and the Acceptance of Congress, become the Seat of the Government of the United States, and to excerise like Authority over all Places purchased by the Consent of the Legislature of the State in which the Same shall be, for the Erection of Forts, Magazines, Arsenals, Dock-Yards, and other needful Buildings and

To make all Laws which shall be necessary and proper for carrying into Execution the foregoing Powers, and all other Powers vested by this Constitution in the Government of the United States, or in any Department or Officer thereof.

Section 9. The Migration or Importation of such Persons as any of the States now existing shall think proper to admit shall not be prohibited by the Congress prior to the Year one thousand eight hundred and eight, but a Tax or Duty may be imposed on such Importation, not exceeding ten dollars for each Person.

The Privilege of the Writ of Habeas Corpus shall not be suspended, unless when in Cases of Rebellion or Invasion the public Safety may require it.

No Bill of Attainder or ex post facto Law shall be passed.

No Capitation, or other direct, Tax shall be laid, unless in Proportion to the Census or Enumeration herein before directed to be taken.

No Tax or Duty shall be laid on Articles exported from any State.

No Preference shall be given by any Regulation of Commerce or Revenue to the Ports of one State over those of another; nor shall Vessels bound to, or from, one State, be obligated to enter, clear, or pay Duties in another.

No Money shall be drawn from the Treasury, but in Consequence of Appropriations made by Law; and a regular Statement and Account of the Receipts and Expenditures of all public Money shall be published from time to time.

No Title of Nobility shall be granted by the United States. And no Person holding any Office of Profit or Trust under them, shall, without the Consent of the Congress, accept of any present, Emolument, Office, or Title, of any kind whatever, from any King, Prince, or foreign State.

Section 10. No State shall enter into any Treaty, Alliance, or Confederation; grant Letters of Marque and Reprisal; coin Money; emit Bills of Credit; make any Thing but gold and silver Coin a Tender in Payment of Debts; pass any Bill of Attainder, ex post facto Law, or Law impairing the Obligation of Contracts, or grant any Title of Nobility.

No State shall, without the consent of the Congress, lay any Imposts or Duties on Imports or Exports, except what may be absolutely necessary for executing its inspection Laws; and the net Produce of all Duties and Imposts, laid by any State on Imports or Exports shall be for the Use of the Treasury of the United States; and all such Laws shall be subject to the Revision and Control of the Congress.

No State shall, without the Consent of Congress, lay any Duty of Tonage, keep Troops, or Ships of War in time of Peace, enter into any Agreement or Compact with another State, or with a foreign Power, or engage in War, unless actually invaded, or in such imminent Danger as will not admit of Delay.

Article II

Section 1. The executive Power shall be vested in a President of the United States of America. He shall hold his Office during the Term of four Years, and, together with the Vice-President, chosen for the same Term, be elected as follows:

Each State shall appoint, in such Manner as the Legislature thereof may direct, a Number of Electors, equal to the whole Number of Senators and Representatives to which the State may be entitled in the Congress; but no Senator or Representative, or Person holding an Office of Trust or Profit under the United States, shall be appointed an Elector.

The Electors shall meet in their respective States, and vote by Ballot for two Persons, of whom one at least shall not be an Inhabitant of the same State with themselves. And they shall make a List of all the Persons voted for, and of the Number of Votes for each; which List they shall sign and certify, and transmit sealed to the Seat of the Government of the United States, directed to the President of the Senate. The President of the Senate shall, in the Presence of the Senate and House of Representatives, open all the Certificates, and the Votes shall then be counted.

The Person having the greatest Number of Votes shall be the President, if such Number be a Majority of the whole Number of Electors appointed; and if there be more than one who have such Majority, and have an equal Number of Votes, then the House of Representatives shall immediately choose by Ballot one of them for President; and if no Person have a Majority, then from the five highest on the List the said House shall in like Manner choose the President. But in choosing the President, the Votes shall be taken by States, the Representation from each State having one Vote; a Quorum for this Purpose shall consist of a Member or Members from two-thirds of the States, and a Majority of all the States shall be necessary to a Choice. In every Case, after the Choice of the President, the Person having the greatest Number of Votes of the Electors shall be the Vice-President But if there should remain two or more who have equal Votes, the Senate shall choose from them by Ballot the Vice-President.

The Congress may determine the Time of choosing the Electors, and the Day on which they shall give their Votes; which Day shall be the same throughout the United States.

No Person except a natural-born Citizen, or a Citizen of the United States, at the time of the Adoption of this Constitution, shall be eligible to the Office of President; neither shall any Person be eligible to that Office who shall not have attained to the Age of thirty-five Years, and been fourteen Years a resident within the United States.

In Case of the Removal of the President from Office, or of his Death, Resignation, or Inability to discharge the Powers and Duties of the said Office, the same shall devolve on the Vice-President, and the Congress may by law provide for the Case of Removal, Death, Resignation, or Inability, both of the President and Vice-President, declaring what Officer shall then act as President and such Officer shall act accordingly, until the Disability be removed, or a President shall be elected.

The President shall, at stated Times, receive for his Services, a Compensation, which shall neither be increased nor diminished during the Period for which he shall have been elected, and he shall not receive within that Period any other Emolument from the United States, or any of them.

Before he enter on the Execution of his Office, he shall take the following Oath or Affirmation:—

"I do solemnly swear (or affirm) that I will faithfully

"execute the Office of the President of the United States, and

"will to the best of my Ability, preserve, protect, and

"defend the Constitution of the United States.

Section 2. The President shall be Commander-in-Chief of the Army and Navy of the United States, and of the Militia of the several States, when called into the actual Service of the United States; he may require the Opinion, in writing, of the principal Officer in each of the executive Departments, upon any Subject relating to the Duties of their respective Offices, and he shall have Power to grant Reprieves and Pardons for Offenses against the United States, except in Cases of Impeachment.

He shall have Power, by and with the Advice and Consent of the Senate, to make Treaties, provided two-thirds of the Senators present concur; and he shall nominate, and by and with the Advice and Consent of the Senate, shall appoint Ambassadors, other public Ministers and Consuls, Judges of the supreme Court, and all other Officers of the United States, whose Appointments are not herein otherwise provided for, and which shall be established by Law; but the Congress may by Law vest the Appointment of such inferior Officers, as they think proper, in the President alone, in the Courts of Law, or in the Heads of Departments.

The President shall have Power to fill up all Vacancies that may happen during the Recess of the Senate, by granting Commissions which shall expire at the End of their next Session.

Section 3. He shall from time to time give to the Congress Information of the State of the Union, and recommend to their Consideration such Measures as he shall judge necessary and expedient; he may, on extraordinary Occasions, convene both Houses, or either of them, and in Case of Disagreement between them, with Respect to the Time of Adjournment, he may adjourn them to such Time as he shall think proper; he shall receive Ambassadors and other public Ministers; he shall take Care that the Laws be faithfully executed, and shall Commission all the officers of the United States.

Section 4. The President, Vice-President, and all civil Officers of the United States shall be removed from Office on Impeachment for, and Conviction of, Treason, Bribery, or other high Crimes and Misdemeanors.

Article III

Section 1. The judicial Power of the United States shall be vested in one supreme Court, and in such inferior Courts as the Congress may from time to time ordain and establish. The Judges, both of the supreme and inferior Courts, shall hold their Offices during good Behavior, and shall at stated Times, receive for their Services, a Compensation, which shall not be diminished during their Continuance in Office.

Section 2. The judicial Power shall extend to all Cases, in Law and Equity, arising under this Constitution, the Laws of the United States, and Treaties made, or which shall be made, under their Authority;—to all Cases affecting Ambassadors, other public Ministers and Consuls;—to all Cases of admiralty and maritime Jurisdiction;—to Controversies to which the United States shall be a Party;—to Controversies between two or more States;—between a State and Citizens of another State;—between Citizens of different States;—between Citizens of the same State claiming Lands under Grants of different States, and between a State, or the Citizens thereof, and foreign States, Citizens, or Subjects.

In all Cases affecting Ambassadors, other public Ministers and Consuls, and those in which a State shall be Party, the supreme Court shall have original Jurisdiction. In all the other Cases before mentioned, the supreme Court shall have appellate Jurisdiction, both as to Law and Fact, with such Exceptions, and under such Regulations as the Congress shall make.

The Trial of all Crimes, except in Cases of Impeachment, shall be by Jury; and such Trial shall be held in the State where the said Crimes shall have been committed; but when not committed within any State, the Trial shall be at such Place or Places as the Congress may by Law have directed.

Section 3. Treason against the United States shall consist only in levying War against them, or in adhering to their Enemies, giving them Aid and Comfort. No Person shall be convicted of Treason unless on the Testimony of two Witnesses to the same overt Act, or on Confession in open Court.

The Congress shall have Power to declare the Punishment of Treason, but no Attainder of Treason shall work Corruption of Blood, or Forfeiture except during the Life of the Person attained.

Article IV

Section 1. Full Faith and Credit shall be given in each State to the public Acts, Records, and judicial Proceedings of every other State. And the Congress may by general Laws prescribe the Manner in which such Acts, Records, and Proceedings shall be proved, and the Effect thereof.

Section 2. The Citizens of each State shall be entitled to all Priviledges and Immunities of Citizens in the several States.

A Person charged in any State with Treason, Felony, or other Crime, who shall flee from Justice, and be found in another State, shall, on Demand of the executive Authority of the State from which he fled, be delivered up, to be removed, to the State having Jurisdiction of the Crime.

No Person held to Service or Labor in one State, under the Laws therof, escaping into another, shall, in Consequence of any Law or Regulation therein, be discharged from such Service or Labor, but shall be delivered up on Claim of the Party to whom such Service or Labor may be due.

Section 3. New States may be admitted by Congress into this Union; but no new State shall be formed or erected within the Jurisdiction of any other State; nor any State be formed by the Junction of two or more States, or Part of States, without the Consent of the Legislatures of the States concerned as well as of the Congress.

The Congress shall have Power to dispose of and make all needful Rules and Regulations respecting the Territory or other Property belonging to the United States; and nothing in this Constitution shall be so construed as to Prejudice any Claims of the United States, or of any particular State.

Section 4. The United States shall guarantee to every State in this Union a Republican Form of Government, and shall protect each of them against Invasion; and on Application of the Legislature, or of the Executive (when the Legislature cannot be convened), against domestic Violence.

Article V

The Congress, whenever two-thirds of both Houses shall deem it necessary, shall propose Amendments to this Constitution, or, on the Application of the Legislatures of two-thirds of the several States, shall call a Convention for proposing Amendments, which, in either Case, shall be valid to all Intents and Purposes, as Part of this Constitution, when ratified by the Legislatures of three-fourths of the several States, or by Conventions in three-fourths thereof, as the one or the other Mode of Ratification may be proposed by the Congress; Provided that no Amendment which may be made prior to the Year one thousand eight hundred and eight shall in any Manner affect the first and fourth Clauses in the Ninth Section of the First Article; and that no State, without its Consent shall be deprived of its equal Suffrage in the Senate.

Article VI

All Debts contracted and Engagements entered into, before the Adoption of this Constitution, shall be as valid against the United States under this Constitution, as under the Confederation.

This Constitution, and the Laws of the United States which shall be made in Pursuance thereof, and all Treaties made, or which shall be made, under the authority of the United States, shall be the supreme Law of the Land; and the Judges in every State shall be bound thereby, any Thing in the Constitution or Laws of any State to the Contrary not withstanding.

The Senators and Representatives before mentioned, and the Members of the several State Legislatures, and all executive and judicial Officers, both of the United States and of the several States, shall be bound, by Oath or Affirmation, to support this Constitution; but no religious Test shall ever be required as a Qualification to any Office or public Trust under the United States.

Article VII

The Ratification of the Conventions of nine States shall be sufficient for the Establishment of the Constitution between the States so ratifying the Same.

Done in Convention by the Unanimous Consent of the States present, the Seventeenth Day of September, in the Year of our Lord one thousand seven hundred and Eighty seven and of the Independence of the United States of America the twelfth. In witness whereof we have hereunto subscribed our Names.

George Washington– President and Deputy from Virginia

Articles
In addition to, and amendments of,

The Constitution of the
United States of America

Proposed by Congress, and ratified by the Legislatures of the several States, pursuant to the fifth article of the original Constitution.

The Bill of Rights (1791)

Article I

Congress shall make no law respecting an establishment of religion, or prohibiting the free exercise thereof; or abridging the freedom of speech or of the press; or the right of the people to peaceably assemble, and to petition the Government for redress of grievances.

Article II

A well-regulated Militia being necessary to the security of a free State, the right of the people to keep and bear Arms shall not be infringed.

Article III

No Soldier shall, in the time of peace, be quartered in any house, without the consent of the Owner, nor in time of war, but in a manner to be prescribed by law.

Article IV

The right of the people to be secure in their persons, houses, papers, and effects against unreasonable searches and seizures shall not be violated, and no Warrants shall issue, but upon probable cause, supported by Oath or affirmation, and particularly describing the place to be searched, and the persons or things to be seized.

Article V

No person shall be held to answer for a capital or otherwise infamous crime, unless on a presentment or indictment of a Grand Jury, except in cases arising in the land or naval forces, or in the Militia, when actual service in time of War or public danger; nor shall any person be subject for the same offense to be twice put in jeopardy of life or limb; nor shall be compelled in any Criminal Case to be a witness against himself, nor be deprived of life, liberty, or property, without due process of law; nor shall private property be taken for public use, without just compensation.

Article VII

In all criminal prosecutions, the accused shall enjoy the right to a speedy and public trial, by an impartial jury of the State and district wherein the crime shall have been committed, which district shall have been previously ascertained by law, and to be informed of the nature and cause of the accusation; to be confronted with the witnesses against him; to have Compulsory process for obtaining Witnesses in his favor, and to have the Assistance of Counsel for his defense.

Article VII

In Suits at common law, where the value in controversy shall exceed twenty dollars the right of trial by jury, shall be preserved, and no fact tried by a jury, shall be otherwise re-examined in any Court of the United States, than according to the rules of the common law.

Article VIII
Excessive bail shall not be required, nor excessive fines imposed, nor cruel and unusual punishments inflicted.

Article IX
The enumeration in the Constitution, of certain rights, shall not be construed to deny or disparage others retained by the people.

Article X
The powers not delegated to the United States by the Constitution, nor prohibited by it to the States, are reserved to the states respectively, or to the people.

Early Amendments

Article XI (1804)
The Judicial power of the United States shall not be construed to extend to any suit in law or equity, commenced or prosecuted against one of the United States by Citizens of another State, or by Citizens or Subjects of any Foreign State.

Article XII (1804)
The Electors shall meet in their respective states, and vote by ballot for President and Vice-President, one of whom, at least, shall not be an inhabitant of the same state with themselves; they shall name in their ballots the person voted for as President, and in distinct ballots the person voted for as Vice-President, and they shall make distinct lists of all persons voted for as President, and of all persons voted for as Vice-President, and of the number of votes for each, which lists they shall sign and certify, and transmit sealed to the seat of government of the United States directed to the President of the Senate;–The President of the Senate shall, in the presence of the Senate and House of Representatives, open all the certificates and the votes shall then be counted;–The person having the greatest number of votes for President, shall be the President, if such number be a majority of the whole number of Electors appointed; and if no person have such majority, then from the persons having the highest numbers not exceeding three on the list of those voted for as President, the House of Representatives shall choose immediately, by ballot, the President. But in choosing the President, the votes shall be taken by states, the representation from each state having one vote; a quorum for this purpose shall consist of a member or members from two-thirds of the states, and a majority of all the states shall be necessary to a choice. And if the House of Representatives shall not choose a President whenever the right of choice shall devolve upon them, before the fourth day of March next following, then the Vice-President shall act as President, as in the case of the death or other constitutional disability of the President. The person having the greatest number of votes as Vice-President shall be the Vice-President, if such number be a majority of the whole number of Electors appointed, and if no person have a majority, then from the two highest numbers on the list, the Senate shall choose the Vice-President; a quorum for the purpose shall consist of two-thirds of the whole number of Senators, and a majority of the whole number shall be necessary to a choice. But no person constitutionally ineligible to the office of President shall be eligible to that of Vice-President of the United States.

Civil War Amendments

Article XIII (1865)
Section 1. Neither slavery nor involuntary servitude, except as a punishment for crime whereof the party shall have been duly convicted, shall exist within the United

States, or any place subject to their jurisdiction.

Section 2. Congress shall have power to enforce this article by appropriate legislation.

Article XIV (1868)

Section 1. All persons born or naturalized in the United States, and subject to the jurisdiction thereof, are citizens of the United States and of the state wherein they reside. No state shall make or enforce any law which shall abridge the privileges or immunities of citizens of the United States; nor shall any state deprive any person of life, liberty, or property, without due process of law; nor deny to any person within its jurisdiction the equal protection of the laws.

Section 2. Representatives shall be apportioned among the several states according to their respective numbers, counting the whole number of persons in each state, excluding Indians not taxed. But when the right to vote at any election for the choice of electors for President and Vice-President of the United States, Representatives in Congress, the executive and judicial officers of a state, or the members of the legislature thereof, is denied to any of the male inhabitants of such state, being twenty-on years of age, and citizens of the United States, or in any way abridged, except for participation in rebellion, or other crime, the basis of representation therein shall be reduced in the proportion which the number of such male citizens shall bear to the whole number of male citizens twenty-five years of age in such state.

Section 3. No person shall be a Senator or Representative in Congress, or elector of President and Vice-President, or hold any office, civil or military, under the United States, or under any state, who, having previously taken an oath, as a member of Congress or as an executive or judicial officer of any state, to support the Constitution of the United States, shall have engaged in insurrection or rebellion against the same, or given aid or comfort to the enemies thereof. But Congress may, by vote of two-thirds of each House, remove such disability.

Section 4. The validity of the public debt of the United States, authorized by law, including debts incurred for payment of pensions and bounties for services in suppressing insurrection or rebellion, shall not be questioned. But neither the United States nor any state shall assume or pay any debt or obligation incurred in aid of insurrection or rebellion against the United States, or any claim for the loss or emancipation of any slave; but all such debts, obligations, and claims shall be held illegal and void.

Section 5. The Congress shall have power to enforce, by appropriate legislation, the provisions of this article.

Article XV (1870)

Section 1. The right of citizens of the United States to vote shall not be denied or abridged by the United States or by any state on account of race, color, or previous condition of servitude.

Section 2. The Congress shall have power to enforce this article by appropriate legislation.

Twentieth Century Amendments

Article XVI (1913)

The Congress shall have power to lay and collect taxes on incomes, from whatever source derived, without apportionment among the several states, and without regard to any census or enumeration.

Article XVII (1913)

Section 1. The Senate of the United States shall be composed of two Senators from each state, elected by the people thereof, for six years; and each Senator shall have one vote. The electors in each state shall have the qualifications requisite for electors of the most numerous branch of the state legislatures.

Section 2. When vacancies happen in the representation of any state in the Senate, the executive authority of such state shall issue writs of election to fill such vacancies: Provided, That the legislature of any state may empower the executive thereof to make temporary appointments until the people fill the vacancies by election as the legislature may direct.

Section 3. This amendment shall not be so construed as to affect the election or term of any Senator chosen before it becomes valid as part of the Constitution.

Article XVIII(1919)

Section 1. After one year from the ratification of this article the manufacture, sale, or transportation of intoxicating liquors within, the importation thereof into, or the exportation thereof from the United States and all territory subject to the jurisdiction thereof for beverage purposes is hereby prohibited.

Section 2. The Congress and the several states shall have concurrent power to enforce this article by appropriate legislation.

Section 3. This article shall be inoperative unless it shall have been ratified as an amendment to the Constitution by the legislatures of the several states, as provided in the Constitution, within seven years from the date of the submission hereof to the states by the Congress.

Article XIX (1920)

Section 1. The right of citizens of the United States to vote shall not be denied or abridged by the United States or by any state on account of sex.

Section 2. Congress shall have power to enforce this article by appropriate legislation.

Article XX (1933)

Section 1. The terms of the President and Vice-President shall end at noon on the twentieth day of January, and the terms of Senators and Representatives at noon on the third day of January, of the years in which such terms would have ended if this article had not been ratified; and the terms of their successors shall then begin.

Section 2. The Congress shall assemble at least once in every year, and such meeting shall begin at noon on the third day of January, unless they shall by law appoint a different day.

Section 3. If, at the time fixed for the beginning of the term of the President, the President-elect shall have died, the Vice-President-elect shall become President. If a President shall not have been chosen before the time fixed for the beginning of his term, or if the President-elect shall have failed to qualify, then the Vice-President-elect shall act as President until a President shall have been qualified; and the Congress may by law provide for the case wherein neither a President-elect nor a Vice-President-elect shall have qualified, declaring who shall then act as President, or the manner in which one who is to act shall be selected, and such person shall act accordingly until a President or Vice-President shall have qualified.

Section 4. The Congress may by law provide for the case of the death of any of the persons from whom the House of Representatives may choose a President whenever the right of choice shall have devolved upon them, and for the case of the death of any of the persons from whom the Senate may choose a Vice-President whenever the right of choice shall have devolved upon them.

Section 5. Sections 1 and 2 shall take effect on the fifteenth day of October following the ratification of this article.

Section 6. This article shall be inoperative unless it shall have been ratified as an amendment to the Constitution by the legislatures of three-fourths of the several states within seven years from the date of its submission.

Article XXI (1933)

Section 1. The eighteenth article of amendment to the Constitution of the United States is hereby repealed.

Section 2. The transportation or importation into any state, territory. or possession of the United States for delivery or use therein of intoxicating liquors, in violation of the laws thereof, is hereby prohibited.

Section 3. This article shall be inoperative unless it shall gave been ratified as an amendment to the Constitution by conventions in the several states, as provided in the Constitution, within seven years from the date of the submission hereof to the states by the Congress.

Article XXII (1951)

Section 1. No person shall be elected to the office of the President more than twice, and no person who has held the office of President, or acted as President, for more than two years of a term to which some other person was elected President shall be elected to the office of the President more than once. But this Article shall not apply to any person holding office of President when this Article was proposed by the Congress, and shall not prevent any person who may be holding the office of President, or acting as President, during the term within which this Article becomes operative from holding the office of President, or acting as President during the remainder of such term.

Section 2. This Article shall be inoperative unless it shall have been ratified as an amendment to the Constitution by legislatures of three-fourths of the several States within seven years from the date of its submission to the States by the Congress.

Article XXIII (1961)

Section 1. The District constituting the seat of Government of the United Stares shall appoint to such manner as the Congress may direct:

A number of electors of President and Vice-President equal to the whole number of Senators and Representatives in Congress to which the District would be entitled if it were a State, but in no event more than the least populous state; they shall be in addition to those appointed by the states, but they shall be considered, for the purpose of election of President and Vice-President, to be electors appointed by a state; and they shall meet in the District and perform such duties as provided by the twelfth article of amendment.

Section 2. The Congress shall have power to enforce this article by appropriate legislation.

Article XXIV 1964)

Section 1. The right of citizens of the United States to vote in any primary or other election for President or Vice-President, for electors for President or Vice-President, or for Senator or Representative in Congress, shall not be denied or abridged by the United States or any State by reason of failure to pay any poll tax or other tax.

Section 2. The Congress shall have power to enforce this article by appropriate legislation.

Article XXV (1976)

Section 1. In case of the removal of the President from office or of his death or resignation, the Vice-President shall become President.

Section 2. Whenever there is a vacancy in the office of the Vice-President, the President shall nominate a Vice-President who shall take office upon confirmation by a majority vote of both Houses of Congress.

Section 3. Whenever the President transmits to the President pro tempore of the senate and the Speaker of the House of Representatives his written declaration that he is unable to discharge the powers and duties of his office, and until he transmits to them a written declaration to the contrary, such powers and duties shall be discharged by the Vice-President as Acting President.

Section 4. Whenever the Vice-President and a majority of either the principal officers of the executive departments or of such other body as Congress may by law provide, transmit to the President pro tempore of the Senate and the Speaker of the House of Representatives their written declaration that the President is unable to discharge the powers and duties of his office, the Vice-President shall immediately assume the powers and duties of the office as Acting President.

Thereafter, when the President transmits to the President pro tempore of the Senate and the Speaker of the House of Representatives his written declaration that no inability exists, he shall resume the powers and duties of his office unless the Vice-President and a majority of either the principal officers of the executive department or of such other body as Congress may by law provide, transmit within four days to the President pro tempore of the Senate and the Speaker of the House of Representatives their written declaration and the President is unable to discharge the powers and duties of his office. Thereupon Congress shall decide the issue, assembling within forty-eight hours for that purpose if not in session. If the Congress, within twenty-one days after receipt of the latter written declaration, or, if Congress is not in session, within twenty-one days after Congress is required to assemble, determines by two-thirds vote of both houses that the President is unable to discharge the powers and duties of his office, the Vice-President; shall continue to discharge the same as acting President; otherwise, the President shall resume the powers and duties of his office.

Article XXVI (1971)

Section 1. The right of citizens of the United States, who are eighteen years of age or older, to vote shall not be denied or abridged by the United States or by any State an account of age.

Section 2. The Congress shall have power to enforce this article.

ENDNOTES

Chapter 3
The Absolute Owners and Movers

1. Federer, William, J., *America's God and Country*, (Coppell, TX: Fame Publishing, Inc., 1994), page 706

2. Halley, Henry, H., *Bible Handbook*, (Grand Rapids, MI: Zondervan Publishing House, 1965), page 22.

3. Cappon, Lester J., Editor, *The Adams-Jefferson Letters*, (Chapel Hill, NC: University of North Carolina Press, 1959), page 412.

4. Federer, Ibid., page 12.

5. DeMar, Gary, *The Untold Story*, (Atlanta, GA: American Vision Publishers, Inc., 1993), page 59.

6. Ibid.

7. Ibid., pages 59-60

8. Ibid., page 60

9. Ibid.

10. Ibid.

11. Ibid.

12. Ibid., pages 60-61

13 Federer,Ibid., pages 236-237

14 Ibid., page 528.

Chapter 4
A More Perfect Union

1. Madison, James, *Notes of Debates in the Federal Convention of 1787*, (New York: W.W. Norton & Co., 1987), pages 209-210.
2. Federer, William, J., *America's God and Country*, (Coppell, TX: Fame Publishing, Inc., 1994), pages 151-152.
3. Madison, Ibid, page 210.
4 Ibid., pages 210-211.
5 Hickey, W., The *Constitution*, (Philadelphia: T. K. & P. G. Collins, 1853), page xxviii
6. Mayo, Bernard, Jefferson Himself, (Charlottesville, VA: The University Press of Virginia, 1970), page 239.
7. Hickey, Ibid., page iii
8. Ibid., page x

Chapter 6
In Their Own Words

1. Adams, John, *Diary and Autobiography of John Adams*, (Cambridge, MA: The Belknap Press, 1961), page 234
2. Smyth, Albert Henry, Editor, *The Writings of Benjamin Franklin*, (New York: Haskell House Publishers, Ltd., 1970), v. IX, page 520-521
3. Ibid., page 521-522
4. Federer, William, J., *America's God and Country*, (Coppell, TX: Fame Publishing, Inc., 1994), page 490
5. Smyth, Ibid., page 522
6. Franklin, Benjamin, *The Autobiography of Benjamin Franklin* (Reading, PA: The Spencer Press, 1936), page 76
7. Ibid., page 78.
8. Ibid., page 77
9. Cappon, Lester J., Editor, *The Adams-Jefferson Letters*, (Chapel Hill, NC: University of North Carolina Press, 1959), page 339
10. Ibid.
11. Federer, Ibid. page 247
12. Cappon,Ibid., page 339
13. Mayo, Bernard, *Jefferson Himself*, (Charlottesville, VA: The University Press of Virginia, 1970), page 231
14. Barton, David, *The Myth of Separation*, (Aledo, TX: Wallbuilder Press, 1992), page 98.
15. Federer, Ibid., page 24.
16. Madison, James, *Notes of Debates in the Federal Convention of 1787*, (New York: W.W. Norton & Co., 1987), page 17.
17. Ibid., page 19.
18. Cappon, Ibid., page 339-340.
19. Ibid., page 340.
20. Federer, Ibid., page 423.
21. Ibid., page 512.
22. Ibid., page 24.

23. Barton, Ibid., page 120.
24. Federer, Ibid., page 8.
25. Ibid., page 543.
26. Ibid.
27. Ibid.
28. Madison, Ibid., page 209.
29. Cappon, Ibid., page 340.

Chapter 7
A Nation Thoroughly Corrupted?

1. Cappon, Lester J., Editor, *The Adams-Jefferson Letters*, (Chapel Hill, NC: University of North Carolina Press, 1959), page 551
2. Federer, William, J., *America's God and Country*, (Coppell, TX: Fame Publishing, Inc., 1994), page 26
3. Barton, David, *The Myth of Separation*, (Aledo, TX: Wallbuilder Press, 1992), pages 121, 130
4. Federer, Ibid., pages 543
5. Ibid., page 443
6. Ibid., pages 10-11
7. Ibid., pages 697
8. Barton, Ibid., pages 64, 151
9. Ibid., pages 48, 50
10. Ibid., page 177
11. Ibid., page 207
12. Federer, Ibid., page 412
13. Ibid., page 330
14 Cappon, Ibid., page 279
15. Barton, Ibid., page 177
16. Mayo, Bernard, *Jefferson Himself*, (Charlottesville, VA: The University Press of Virginia, 1970), page 339
17. Cappon, Ibid., page 279
18. Federer, Ibid., page 325
19. Ibid., page 328
20. Ibid., page 327
21. Ibid., page 8
22. Ibid.
23. Mayo, Ibid., page 64
24. Ibid., pages 91-92
25. Ibid., pages 35, 91, 332

Chapter 8
Meet the Commander-in-Chief

1. Barton, David, *The Bulletproof George Washington*, (Aledo, TX: Wallbuilders Press, 1990), page 49
2. Ibid., pages 50-51
3. Federer, William, J., *America's God and Country*, (Coppell, TX: Fame Publishing, Inc., 1994), page 249

4. Bancroft, George, *History of the United States*, (Boston: Little Brown, and Company, 1858) Volume VII, page 403

5. Federer, Ibid., pages 640-641

6. Ibid.

7. Hickey, W., *The Constitution*, (Philadelphia: T. K. & P. G. Collins, 1853), page 206

8. Ibid., page 256

9. Ibid., pages 393-403

10 Ibid. pages 208-209

11. Ibid., page 209

12. Musto, David F., *George Washington and the Temptations of Political Life*, (Washington, DC 1982), page 13

13. Federer, Ibid., page 703

Chapter 9
George Washington Speaks

1. Washington, George, *Rules of Civility and Decent Behaviour in Company and Conversation*, (Mount Vernon, VA: The Mount Vernon Ladies Association, 1989), page 31

2. Allen, W. B. *George Washington*, (Indianapolis, IN: Liberty Fund, Inc., 1988), page 539

3. Ibid.

4. Ibid. page 282

5. Federer, William, J., *America's God and Country*, (Coppell, TX: Fame Publishing, Inc., 1994), page 417

6. Ibid., page 636

7. Ibid., page 641

8. Ibid., page 640

9. Allen, Ibid., page 267

10. Ibid., page 270

11. Federer, Ibid., page 655

12. Allen, Ibid., page 244

13. Ibid., page 451

14. Ibid., page 537

15. Ibid., page 544

16. Ibid., page 445

17. Ibid., page 463

18. Ibid., page 510

19. Ibid.

20. Ibid., pages 456-457

21. Hickey, W., *The Constitution*, (Philadelphia: T. K. & P. G. Collins, 1853),page 212

22. Allen, Ibid., page 457

23. Ibid., page 521

24. Ibid.

25. Hickey, page 212

26. Federer, Ibid., pages 273-274

27. Allen, Ibid., page 383
28. Ibid.
29. Ibid., page 521
30. Ibid., pages 403-404
31. Ibid., page 515
32. Ibid., page 532-533
33. Ibid., page 521
34. Ibid., page 256
35. Ibid., page 532

Chapter 10
Politics and the First President

1. Allen, W. B. *George Washington*, (Indianapolis, IN: Liberty Fund, Inc., 1988), page 537
2. Ibid., page 417
3. Federer, William, J., *America's God and Country*, (Coppell, TX: Fame Publishing, Inc., 1994), pages 643-644
4. Allen, Ibid., page 243
5. Ibid., page 448
6. Ibid., page 518
7. Ibid., page 373
8. Ibid., page 538
9. Ibid., page 542
10. Ibid., pages 520-521
11. Ibid., page 521
12. Ibid., page 126
13. Ibid., page 520
14. Ibid.
15. Ibid.
16. Ibid., pages 519-520
17. Ibid., page 517
18. Ibid., page 520
19. Ibid., pages 518-519
20. Ibid., page 119
21. Ibid., page 259
22. Ibid.
23. Ibid., page 211
24. Ibid., page 279
25. Ibid.
26. Ibid., page 286
27. Ibid., page 393

Chapter 11
Hope for a Happy Nation

1. Allen, W. B. *George Washington*, (Indianapolis, IN: Liberty Fund, Inc., 1988), page 370

2. Ibid., page 322
3. Ibid., page 319
4. Ibid., page 80
5. Ibid., page 314
6. Ibid., page 522
7. Ibid., page 183
8. Ibid., page 386
9. Ibid., page 485
10. Ibid., pages 522
11. Ibid., page 490
12. Ibid., page 498
13. Ibid., page 325
14. Ibid., pages 524-525
15. Ibid., page 522
16. Ibid., page 301
17. Ibid., page 400
18. Ibid., page 394
19. Ibid., page 468
20. Ibid., page 488
21. Ibid., page 524
22. Ibid.
23. Ibid., page 620
24. Ibid., page 525
25. Ibid., page 320
26. Ibid., page 306
27. Ibid., pages 323-324
28. Ibid., page 499
29. Ibid., page 249
30. Hickey, W., *The Constitution*, (Philadelphia: T. K. & P. G. Collins, 1853), p. 240
31 Ibid., pages 247-257
32. Federer, William, J., A*merica's God and Country*, (Coppell, TX: Fame Publishing, Inc., 1994), page 664
33. Hickey, Ibid., page 243
34. Ibid., page 264-265
35. Ibid., page 266-267
36. Federer, Ibid., 327-328

Chapter 12
Masters of Deceit

1. Kurtz, Paul, Editor, *Humanist Manifestos I and II*, (Buffalo, NY: Prometheus Books). Copyright 1984 by Paul Kurtz, (Used by permission of the publisher.), page 3
2. Cappon, Lester J., Editor, The Adams-Jefferson Let*ters*, (Chapel Hill, NC: University of North Carolina Press, 1959), page 375
3. Kurtz, Ibid., page 8
4. Ibid.
5. Federer, William, J., *America's God and Country*, (Coppell, TX: Fame Publishing, Inc., 1994), page 199

6. Ibid.
7. Ibid.
8. Kurtz, Ibid., page 8
9. Ibid.
10. Ibid.
11. Ibid.
12. Ibid., page 3
13. Ibid.
14. Ibid., page 10
15. Ibid.
16. Ibid.

Chapter 13
The Subversion Reaffirmed

1. Kurtz, Paul, Editor, Humanist Manifestos I and II, (Buffalo, NY: Prometheus Books). Copyright 1984 by Paul Kurtz, (Used by permission of the publisher.), pages 24-31
2. Ibid., page 15
3. Garraty, John A., *Encyclopedia of American Biography*, (New York, NY: Harper and Row, Publishers, 1974), page 275
4. Kurtz, Ibid., page 8
5. Ibid., page 17
6. Ibid., page 18
7. Ibid.
8. Ibid., page 22
9. Ibid., page 19
10. Ibid., page 13
11. Ibid., page 15
12. Ibid., page 14
13. Ibid., page 13
14. Ibid., page 16
15. Ibid., page 15
16. Ibid., page 21
17. Ibid.
18. Ibid., page 22
19. Ibid., page 21
20. Ibid.
21. Ibid., page 15
22. Ibid., page 21

Chapter 14
Ministers of Another Sort

1. Kurtz, Paul, Editor, *Humanist Manifestos I and II*, (Buffalo, NY: Prometheus Books). Copyright 1984 by Paul Kurtz, (Used by permission of the publisher.), page 9
2 Ibid.
3. William A. Donohue, *Twilight of Liberty*, (New Brunswick, NJ: Transaction Publishers, 1994), page 85

4. Medved, Michael, *Hollywood vs. America*, (New York: Harper Collins Publishers, 1992), pages 313-319

5. Fort Worth Star Telegram, August 27, 1995, page C8

6 Medved, Ibid., page 38

7. Kurtz, Ibid., pages 9-10

8. Ibid., page 15

9. Dannemeyer, William, *Shadow in the Land, Homosexuality in America*, (San Francisco: Ignatius Press, 1989), pages 106-107

10. Oursler, Will, *Protestant Power and the Coming Revolution*, (Garden City, NY: Doubleday & Co., Inc., 1971), pages 1-60

11. Ibid., pages 61-91

12. Barton, David, *The Myth of Separation*, (Aledo, TX: Wallbuilder Press, 1992), page 207

13. Donohue, William A., *The Politics of the American Civil Liberties* Union, (New Brunswick, NJ: Transaction Publishers, 1985), page 13

14 Ibid., page 51

15. Donohue, *Twilight of Liberty*, page 87

Chapter 15
Countdown to Global Bondage

1. Kurtz, Paul, Editor, *Humanist Manifestos I and II*, (Buffalo, NY: Prometheus Books). Copyright 1984 by Paul Kurtz, (Used by permission of the publisher.), page 19

2. Ibid., page 16

3. Ibid.

4. Botkin,Geoffrey, *Certain Failure, Part I*, (Chantilly, VA: The American Policy Center, 1994), page 12

5, Schafly, Phyllis, *The Nationalist Times*, February, 1998, p. 14.

6. Kurtz, Ibid., page 17

Chapter 16
From Plowshares to Swords

1. Madison, James, *Notes of Debates in the Federal Convention of 1787*, (New York: W.W. Norton & Co., 1987), pages 209-210

Chapter 17
A New Birth of Freedom

1. Allen, W. B. *George Washington*, (Indianapolis, IN: Liberty Fund, Inc., 1988), page 118

BIBLIOGRAPHY

The Bible, May be purchased in any Christian bookstore and most other bookstores. The King James Version (KJV) was in general use at the time of the nation's founders. Its literary style and language is the most compatible with theirs. The New International Version (NIV), a translation in modern English, is sometimes quoted in this book. The New American Bible is a Catholic version in modern English.

1. Eidsmoe, John, *Christianity and the Constitution* (Grand Rapids, MI: Baker Book House, 1987)

2. Barton, David, *The Bulletproof George Washington,* (Aledo, TX: Wallbuilders Press, 1990)

3. Marshall, Peter, and Manuel, David, *The Light and the Glory,* (Grand Rapids, MI: Baker Book House, 1977)

4. Bancroft, George, *History of the United States,* (Boston: Little Brown, and Company, 1858) Volume VII.

5. Adams, John, *Diary and Autobiography of John Adams,* (Cambridge, MA: The Belknap Press, 1961)

6. Federer, William, J., *America's God and Country,* (Coppell, TX: Fame Publishing, Inc., 1994)

7. Madison, James, *Notes of Debates in the Federal Convention of 1787,* (New York: W.W. Norton & Co., 1987)

8. Barton, David, *The Myth of Separation*, (Aledo, TX: Wallbuilder Press, 1992)

9. Cappon, Lester J., Editor, *The Adams-Jefferson Letters*, (Chapel Hill, NC: University of North Carolina Press, 1959)

10. Mayo, Bernard, *Jefferson Himself*, (Charlottesville, VA: The University Press of Virginia, 1970)

11. Millard, Catherine, *Rewriting America's History*, (Camp Hill, PA: Horizon House Publishers, 1991)

12. Hickey, W., *The Constitution*, (Philadelphia: T. K. & P. G. Collins, 1853)

13. Musto, David F., *George Washington and the Temptations of Political Life*, (Washington, DC 1982) An address delivered at the Smithsonian Institute on the 250th anniversary of the birth of George Washinton.

14. Washington, George, *Rules of Civility and Decent Behaviour in Company and Conversation*, (Mount Vernon, VA: The Mount Vernon Ladies Association, 1989)

15. Allen, W. B. *George Washington*, (Indianapolis, IN: Liberty Fund, Inc., 1988)

16. Botkin,Geoffrey, *Certain Failure, Part I*, (Chantilly, VA: The American Policy Center, 1994)

17. Halley, Henry, H., *Bible Handbook*, (Grand Rapids, MI: Zondervan Publishing House, 1965)

18. DeMar, Gary, *The Untold Story*, (Atlanta, GA: American Vision Publishers, Inc., 1993)

19. Kurtz, Paul, Editor, *Humanist Manifestos I and II*, (Buffalo, NY: Prometheus Books). Copyright 1984 by Paul Kurtz. Used by permission of the publisher.

20. Cheney, Lynne V., *Hijacking America's History*, Reader's Digest, January, 1995,.Reprints available from Reader's Digest.

21. Chavez, Linda, *One Nation, One Common Language*, Reader's Digest, August, 1995, page 87.

22. Garraty, John A., *Encyclopedia of American Biography*, (New York, NY: Harper and Row, Publishers, 1974)

23. William A. Donohue, *Twilight of Liberty*, (New Brunswick, NJ: Transaction Publishers, 1994)

24. Medved, Michael, *Hollywood vs. America*, (New York: Harper Collins Publishers, 1992)

25. Fort Worth Star Telegram, August 27, 1995

26. Dannemeyer, William, *Shadow in the Land, Homosexuality in America*, (San Francisco: Ignatius Press, 1989)

27. Oursler, Will, *Protestant Power and the Coming Revolution*, (Garden City, NY: Doubleday & Co., Inc., 1971)

28. Donohue, William A., *The Politics of the American Civil Liberties* Union, (New Brunswick, NJ: Transaction Publishers, 1985)

29. Churchill, Winston S., *A History of the English Speaking Peoples*, (New York: Barnes and Noble, 1956) Volume III, The Age of Revolution.

30. Amos, Gary T., *Defending the Declaration*, (Brentwood, TN: Wolgemoth and Hyatt Publishers, Inc., 1989)

31 Kirk, Russell, *America's British Culture*, (New Brunswick, NJ: Transaction Publishers, 1993)

32 Wright, Esmond, *Fabric of Freedom* 1763-1800, (New York: Hill and Wang, 1961)

33 Wright, Esmond, *Causes and Consequences of the American Revolution*, (New York: Quadrangle Books, 1966)

34. Ferris, Robert G., and Morris, Richard E., *The Signers of the Declaration of Independence*, (Flagstaff, AZ: Interpretive Press, 1982)

35. The People Shall Judge, *Readings in the Formation of American Policy*, (Chicago: University of Chicago Press, 1949) Selected and edited by the Staff, Social Sciences 1, The College of the University of Chicago.

36. Paine, Thomas, *Common Sense*, 1776, (Printed in the People Shall Judge)

37. Bonomi, Patricia U., *Under the Cope of Heaven*, (New York: Oxford University Press, 1986)

38. Bradford, M. E. *Founding Fathers*, (Lawrence, KS: University Press of Kansas, 1982)

39. Bradford, M. E., *Original Intentions*, (Athens, GA: The University of Georgia Press, 1993)

40. Eastland, Terry, *Religious Liberty in the Supreme Court,* (Lanham, MD: National Book Network, 1993)

41. Marshall, Peter, and Manuel, David, *From Sea to Shining Sea*, (Grand Rapids, MI: Baker Book House, 1986)

42. *The Constitutions of the Sixteen States which compose the Confederated Republic of America*, (Boston: Manning and Loring, 1797)

43. Jensen, Merrill, *The Articles of Confederation*, (Madison, WI: The University of Wisconsin Press, 1940)

44. Hitchcock, James, *What is Secular Humanism*, (Harrison, NY: RC Books, 1982)

45. Johnson, Phillip E., *Darwin on Trial,* (Washington, DC: Regnery Gateway, 1991)

46. Chandler, Russell, *Understanding the New Age*, (Grand Rapids, MI: Zondervan Publishing House, 1991)

47. Ball, William Bentley, Editor, *In Search of National Morality*, (Grand Rapids, MI: Baker Book House, 1992)

48. Felton, Eric *Ruling Class: Inside the Imperial Congress*, (Washington, DC: Regnery Gateway, 1993)

49. Gross, Martin L., *A Call to Revolution*, (New York: Ballantine Books, 1993)

50. Smith, Hedrick, *The Power Game*, (New York: Random House, 1988)

51. Brallier, Jess M., *Lawyers and other Reptiles*, (Chicago: Contemporary Books, 1992)

52. Stachey, William, Editor, *Lawes Divine, Morall, and Martiall*, (Charlottesville, VA: The University Press of Virginia, 1969)

53. Thomas, Andrew Peyton, *Crime and the Sacking of America*, (Washington, DC: Brasseys, 1994)

54. Foner, Philip S., Editor, *Basic Writings of Thomas Jefferson*, (New York: Wiley Book Company, 1944)

55. Olasky, Marvin, *The Tragedy of Compassion*, (Wash., DC: Regnery Gateway, 1992)

56. Gross, Martin L., *Washington Waste from A to Z*, (NY: Bantam Books, 1992)

57. Olasky, Marvin, *Abortion Rites*, (Washington, DC: Regnery Gateway, 1992)

58. Vickery, Donald M., and Fries, James F., *Take Care of Yourself,* (New York: Addison-Wesley Publishing Co., 1986)

59. Gross, Martin L., The Tax Racket: *Government Extortion from A to Z*, (New York: Ballantine Books, 1995)

60. Daniel, James, *Illegal Immigration: An Unfolding Crisis*, (New York: University Press)

61. Weinfield, Irving, *HUD Scandals*, (New Brunswick, NJ: Transaction Publishers, 1992)
62. Annis, Edward R., *Code Blue: Health Care in Crisis*, (Washington, DC: Regnery Gateway, 1993)
63. Nelson, Frank C., *Public Schools: An Evangelical Appraisal*, (Old Tappan, NJ: Fleming H. Revell Co., 1987)
64. Duffy, Cathy, *Government Nannies, The Cradle-to-Grave Agenda of Goals 2000 and Outcome Based Education*, (Gresham, OR: Noble Publishing Associates, 1995)
65. Eakman, B. K., *Educating for the New World Order*, (Portland, OR: Halycon House, 1991)
66. Kincaid, Cliff, *Global Bondage: The U.N. Plan to Rule the World*, (LaFayette, LA: Huntinghouse Publishers, 1995)
67. Smyth, Albert Henry, Editor, *The Writings of Benjamin Franklin*, (New York: Haskell House Publishers, Ltd., 1970)
68. Franklin, Benjamin, *The Autobiography of Benjamin Franklin* (Reading, PA: The Spencer Press, 1936)